NAKED AMBITION

A MALE STRIPPER'S TRUE ACCOUNT OF MAKING GIRLS BEHAVE BADLY

THE LAST TEMPTATION EDITION

STEFAN DIAMANTE

Naked Ambition

A Male Stripper's True Account of Making Girls Behave Badly

Written, Photographed, Designed, and Published by Stefan Diamante

Second Edition, 2021

First Edition, 2019

Paperback ISBN: 978-1-7340268-7-0

Text & Illustrations Copyright © 2019 Stefan Diamante

Photographs Copyright © 2004, 2009, 2013, 2025 Stefan Diamante

All rights reserved. No part of this book may be used or reproduced in any manner whatsoever, including internet usage, without written permission from copyright holder. Publications are exempt in the case of brief quotations in critical reviews or articles.

The names of certain individuals – chiefly entertainers as well as women with whom the author engaged in sexual conduct – have been changed to protect their identities. Additionally, some details of events such as date and location involving these individuals have been altered for the same purpose.

stefandiamante.com

This book is dedicated to every woman who enthusiastically indulged my antics as a professional exotic entertainer, showed me the kindness and respect I showed her, and gifted me with as many cherished memories as I provided her. I literally couldn't have done it without you. The names of some of you may escape me after all these years, but the feeling of us playing off one another in the heat of the night shall never fade away. There will forever be a special place in my heart for each of you sexy ass motherfuckers.

EMILY STRIPPED BARE   3

ALL TOMORROW'S PARTIES (2004 – 2006)

CHAPTER 1	13
CHAPTER 2	21
CHAPTER 3	28
CHAPTER 4	35
CHAPTER 5	41
CHAPTER 6	48
CHAPTER 7	56
CHAPTER 8	63
CHAPTER 9	69
CHAPTER 10	77
CHAPTER 11	84
CHAPTER 12	92
CHAPTER 13	99
CHAPTER 14	105
CHAPTER 15	111
CHAPTER 16	118
CHAPTER 17	124
CHAPTER 18	131

DON'T DREAM IT'S OVER (2007 – 2012)

CHAPTER 19	139
CHAPTER 20	145
CHAPTER 21	151
CHAPTER 22	158
CHAPTER 23	164
CHAPTER 24	170
CHAPTER 25	176
CHAPTER 26	183
CHAPTER 27	192
CHAPTER 28	198
CHAPTER 29	204
CHAPTER 30	211
CHAPTER 31	217
CHAPTER 32	223
CHAPTER 33	230

MORE THAN THIS (2013 – 2018)

CHAPTER 34	239
CHAPTER 35	245
CHAPTER 36	251
CHAPTER 37	258
CHAPTER 38	271
CHAPTER 39	282
CHAPTER 40	288
CHAPTER 41	295
CHAPTER 42	302
CHAPTER 43	314
CHAPTER 44	320
CHAPTER 45	327
CHAPTER 46	334
CHAPTER 47	340
CHAPTER 48	347
AMARILLO BY MORNING	355
MAGNUM STRIPPED BARE	367

You are in violation of penal code 6969.

Dancer: **Magnum** Date Received: **4/12/2018**
Contact Name: **Becky** ▬▬▬ Phone Number: **501-**▬▬▬
Date: **4/21/2018** Time: **7:00 pm** Location: **Sherwood, AR**
Rate: **$150⁰⁰** Guests: **25-40** Costume: **Cop**
Occasion: **Birthday Party** Guest Of Honor: **Emily**
Advertising Reference: **Google Search**
Notes: ~~▬▬▬▬▬▬~~

~~Venters~~ Client requested pool service costume. Just do cop instead.

EMILY STRIPPED BARE

I'm totally hot for Emily, drama and all, but it goes deeper than that…

The phone rang as I showed my body no mercy. Heart racing. Breathing heavy. The sound of metal on metal surrounded me like some avant-garde industrial symphony. My chest and back muscles were pumped and throbbing from the brutal workloads inflicted upon them. Shoulders were next. I moved to train them as if I just had sex and was immediately gunning for another round.

I wondered if Becky thought she interrupted me having sex. Others have asked that when calling me during a workout. This happened more often in the past. My exotic entertainment agency, Hardbodies Entertainment of Arkansas, had once been something of a mini business empire. By April 2018, however, it limped along as I contemplated new entrepreneurial possibilities while attempting to complete my B.A. sometime in this century.

"Are you available for a birthday party a week from this Saturday in Sherwood?"

While I certainly needed the money, I played it cool as always. Enthusiasm is an excellent deal maker, but desperation is a surefire deal breaker one way or another.

"Yeah, I can still get you in for that date."

As I headed for the locker room to retrieve my scheduling binder, I swaggered past hopeless souls churning out poorly executed deadlifts and curls simply because they could. Becky filled me in on the details. By the sound of her voice, I had her pegged as a fifty-something woman and no stranger to flavor country. She asked me a variety of questions about what my performance entails and mentioned how pretty the birthday girl is. That last point stuck out to me as it's something clients never mention because it shouldn't matter. I wasn't interested in fucking the birthday girl. Not yet, at least.

As for Becky and the rest of her friends…

"We're a bunch of horny old broads."

…followed by nervous laughter. Not the sort of women I'd talk into making out with one another for my amusement, as I'm wont to do at times.

As I sat in an empty corner of the gym and jotted down pertinent details into my black binder of professional debauchery, I couldn't help but cringe at that statement. Although nominally made in jest, I instantly recognized and felt bad that she was selling herself short. If only she knew the extent of unrelentingly harsh self-criticism to which I had subjected myself all these years, but it wouldn't have made a difference.

With no obvious red flags present, I booked the party and had all the information I needed including time, number of women present, and the name of the birthday girl. Emily. I'd get online later and put faces to names, as I do with clients, bachelorettes, and birthday girls. In the meantime, I returned to that cast iron jungle lined with mirrors and resumed my physical catharsis.

***

A special perk for strippers is entertaining people they find attractive. So, when a guy returns from getting a lap dance and gushes about how the stripper genuinely liked him, his buddies shouldn't be too quick to laugh at and dismiss his claims. There's a legitimate chance she may have the hots for him and was extra flirty as a result. She's still human after all.

The same holds for male strippers. While I take excellent care of all my bachelorettes, birthday girls, and their girlfriends, I admit that it's exciting to encounter a woman who makes me think, "Yeah, I'd do her." Not only is this a personally satisfying development when it occurs, but it's something I can use as an entertainer to further turn up the heat of the moment by making things extra scandalous.

With my workout completed, I arrived home and cooked dinner. Sitting down at my computer to eat, as I do with nearly every meal, I jumped on Facebook to learn about Becky and Emily. My online snooping should come as no surprise to anyone, given what I'm about to do in a strange place full of strange women.

Becky was pretty much what I expected. From there, I scoured her friends for a pretty girl named Emily, and there she was.

Those eyes. That smile. She's beautiful. So embarrassing beautiful, apparently, that I can only describe her in sentence fragments. "Yeah, I'd do her," doesn't begin to scratch the surface in describing my immediate intentions towards Emily. I don't believe in things like angels, yet not only was there now one right before my eyes but one who is sexy as all fuck. It was truly lust at first sight, damn her.

It was like the exact moment when I knew I had entered puberty. I was sitting in class a few days before summer vacation when I happened to casually glance in the direction of the cute girl who sat a couple of desks away from me. Without warning, a strange new feeling swept over me. The specifics were vague, but I immediately recognized it as a sexual attraction. Ultimately, it went no further than me throwing rocks at her later.

My desire to throw rocks at Emily was even more intense. As a stripper, you can bet her sexy ass that she was getting extra-special attention. And, as a man, I had every intention of making a move on her. Emily made a strong impression on my Machiavellian sensibilities. It's not every day I encounter a girl who's even more beautiful than me.

Beyond the erotic sensations, however, the sight of Emily made me reflect upon living a life akin to the immortal words of the great David Lee Roth:

"I found the simple life ain't so simple

When I jumped out on that road

I got no love, no love you'd call real

Ain't got nobody waiting at home"

There's a want for that special girl in my life. It's something I think about at this late stage of my stripping career. One who possesses the vanity to match mine along with the sassiness to compliment my swagger. A girl who rocks heavy black eyeliner, shares my affinity for leopard print, and owns a smile that could talk me into killing for her. I have no intention of giving up my decadent ways. If anything, they've been restricted all these years without the ideal partner in crime present to equally share in the delicious fun night after night. Is Emily that girl? I have no fucking clue, but I'd love to find out just how alive we can make each other feel.

***

As much as I wanted to meet Emily, I questioned hitting on her before an audience of horny old broads and how they would react. I pondered one strategy after another while figuring out a way to take her home with me. The problem solved itself when Becky texted four days later to renegotiate the booking fee by $30. It's not that she didn't have the money. Rather, she wanted to run my show. Fuck that. Emily or not, no booking is worth the drama of a troublemaking client. So, I canceled.

Not surprisingly, Becky went for the jugular in retaliation:

"It's your loss."

I immediately wanted to punch her in the face. By my loss, she wasn't talking about money. She was talking about Emily. It was now clear that Becky always intended for the brief pleasure of Emily's company to serve as part of my compensation. I was offered a one-hour chaperoned date with a hot girl, after which I would be expected to exit her life forever due to possibly the harshest cockblocking in history. Fuck Becky.

Still, my intuition told me it wasn't over. I kept waiting for another phone call. It came late on the eve of the party. Although I missed it, the caller left a voicemail.

You might think that anyone attempting to get me back on board would make a conscious show of respect and humility. Nope. Instead, I was introduced to a woman named Charolette via possibly the most passive-aggressive and blatantly insulting voicemail in history. She decided to take the, "He's a stripper, so he must be a fucking idiot," approach and acted like she wanted to book me for an entirely different party in Sherwood, Arkansas on the same date that also had a "really pretty" birthday girl for me to entertain. I didn't bother returning Charolette's call.

I received a strange phone call from yet another woman on the day of the party who hung up when I informed her it wasn't happening. For me, that night was spent losing myself in alcohol and music. I attempted to reconcile the mistreatment I had received with the frustration of not being pressed up tight against Emily before carrying her off into the sunset. As I sat in the dark with Rick James and Jack Daniels keeping me company, I attempted to take solace in the disappointment that my new enemies were also feeling that night by their own fault. But it didn't help.

The drama didn't end for either side on that muggy late-April night, as I received the occasional strange phone call or text over the succeeding months. While this was nothing new for me, there was a different vibe about these calls and texts. Take the following text exchange for one example:

"Is this Magnum?"

"Yes. What can I do for you?"

And nothing more. I Googled the number and learned it belonged to a makeup artist, which is notable. Does that prove anything? Of course not. But it's strangely coincidental and not an isolated incident.

In the meantime, I struggled with articulating the entire incident to others beyond the simple explanation that I had booked a party and canceled it a few days later over money. The people who received this watered-down explanation knew I wasn't telling them the entire story. I took multiple stabs at writing about it, but the results were half-baked at best despite my desire to lay it all out for myself and others.

I needed to confess my hunger for a hot piece of Emmie Pie to someone in the know, and that someone was Charolette. Why Charolette? Because she afforded me the efficiency of killing two birds with one stone. I could cure my writer's block by admitting my attraction to Emily and deliver payback for that awful voicemail she'd left me. So, I packaged my confession within a bullshit apology about how everything was my fault and blah, blah, blah... I still managed to brag about having dated other hot girls, because I couldn't help myself. And because fuck Charolette.

This was no easy task as I would write a couple of sentences, lie down and stare at the ceiling, write a couple of sentences, do some laundry, write a couple of sentences, admire myself in the mirror, write a couple of sentences, go to Walmart, write a couple of sentences, and then dance like no one was watching. Because no one was.

Finally, my "apology" was complete. It was glorious in its manipulative, vindictive, and discomforting rhetoric. As soon as I hit send, I felt the weight of the world lifted from my shoulders at

Charolette's expense. Bless her heart. She never responded, nor did I expect her to. Because that wasn't the point. My objective was achieved as I immediately sat down afterward and began writing the first draft of this prologue.

I could now express in words what had been going through my mind for so long. Not only could I write about it, but I began sharing the story with others to a positive response. This includes telling it at bachelorette parties – complete with voice impressions of Becky and Charolette – to women gathered around me as I stand there in a g-string and sip whatever cocktail they fixed me. The twentysomethings in particular, who always ask for stories, are so taken with my desire that they run through every girl named Emily they know in the slim chance they can introduce us.

***

So, how would things have played out had I performed at Emily's birthday party? I imagine something like this:

With total authority, I enter through a gate into a middle-class backyard dressed as a cop (Becky requested some pool maintenance guy thing but that's stupid) who is here to break up the party due to noise complaints from the neighbors. I take note of the recently constructed swimming pool, as Becky has money for pools but not strippers.

Upon being greeted to the excited squeals of horny old broads and the stench of lingering cigarette smoke, I demand to speak with Emily. The broads point in unison towards my thoroughly embarrassed birthday girl, seated in the middle of my audience like an unbelievably gorgeous flower rising from a compost heap, and I demand she explain to me what's going on here tonight. After giving me some silly non-answer, I make her stand, bend over, and assume the position. I frisk her by running my hands up between her legs, then tell her I know she's been in this position before as I enthusiastically thrust and grind my pelvis against her firm, round butt. Once the hysterical laughs subside, I make her take a seat, place her in handcuffs, and inform her that she's in violation of penal code 6969.

I press play on my phone. The "Bad Boys" theme from *COPS* blasts from my portable speaker as I straddle Emily, looking into her amazing brown eyes and physically expressing a combination of playfulness and sexual dominance. The music quickly changes to "Salt Shaker" by the Ying Yang Twins. A song perfectly suited for bump-and-grind movements as I dance on my birthday girl. She accepts this hot stranger suddenly all over her. I tear off my shirt and place her hands on my rock-hard pecs, then slowly guide them down my abs. When the belt comes off, I have her stand and assume the position once more for a light birthday spanking. She sits down. I have her grab the waistband of my tear-away pants as I step backward out of them to the delight of my audience. I fall forward and catch the edge of Emily's chair. Placing my face in her thighs before moving slowly up her legs and along her torso. Stopping to rub my face in her ample breasts, until we finally end up face to face. I know I'm giving her the bedroom eyes and voice. I can't help myself.

Then comes my signature move when I straddle Emily facing away and fall forward to land on my hands. Simultaneously kicking my legs back and squeeze her thighs as we're crotch to crotch. The music changes to "Hold On, We're Going Home" by Drake. This is where the performance takes an interesting and unique turn. The slower song gives me an excuse to take things into more sensual territory. I gently run my fingers through Emily's long, dark hair and stroke her cheek as I lower myself face to face with her. My chest pressed tightly against her tits. I lose myself in her eyes. Her smile is killing me. I slowly lean in and press my lips against hers.

Pandemonium breaks loose amongst the horny old broads as I literally sweep Emily off her feet and carry her away. To do every naughty thing we've already done countless times in my imagination. Her friends threaten to call the cops, but they forget that I'm the law around here. And my ridiculously stunning birthday girl is in dire need of an all-night strip search. The party is dead, but I've never felt so alive.

Happy birthday, Emily.

ALL TOMORROW'S PARTIES

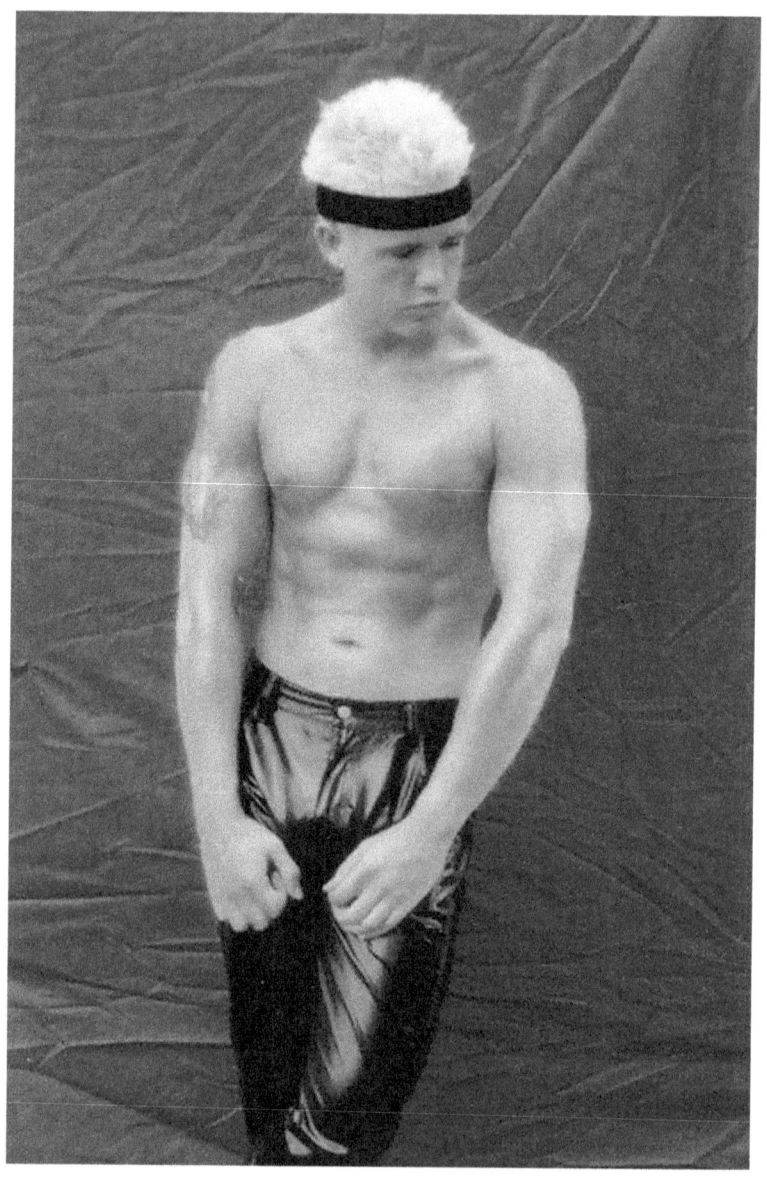

2004 – 2006

CHAPTER 1

Emily isn't my only stripping related tie to Sherwood, Arkansas. In fact, that's where this wild and crazy odyssey began on a Saturday night in April 2004. The spacious retail showroom by day made for an outstanding after-hours discothèque by invitation. Its gray tile floor commandeered by dancers with dirty moves. Others took advantage of the display pools and spas. Alcohol flowed as stereo speakers blasted the likes of OutKast, Nelly, and the unholy alliance of Usher, Ludacris, and Lil Jon. Yeah.

Not once did I feel guilty for earning extra money this way. If anything, my employer was in the wrong for totally fucking up what should've been a successful pool and spa dealership targeting an upscale clientele. There was always something special about this location, and the magic was undeniable on that night. The full moon projecting silvery rays through a glass façade. Outlining silhouettes relentless in their miming of carnal desires.

I knew I could not keep that job a moment longer than necessary. That night, I had proved to myself all I was capable of conceiving and executing as a born agent provocateur. This moment of clarity enhanced by a party girl who put her arms around my neck and kissed me. She took my hand, pressed a penny into my palm, and gave slurred instructions for me to toss it into the pool before us and make a wish. With the taste of too much lipstick and Smirnoff Ice in my mouth, I went for it. Upon flipping the coin into the air, the crowd vanished as I stood alone before my future incarnated as an aboveground swimming pool. All was silent except for the sound of the penny breaking the water's surface. Like glass shattered. The ripples continuing into infinity…

Hardbodies Entertainment of Arkansas came to be.

***

Hardbodies, as inherently nicknamed, was years in the making. Originally slated to be based in Denver under a never determined name. That's where I began my stripping career. Quickly moving into private parties by virtue of my willingness to be a road warrior. Traveling to bachelorette and birthday parties throughout parts of Colorado, Wyoming, Nebraska, and Kansas. Where other eagles refused to dare. Over time I began securing bookings for a handful of like-minded male and female strippers in the Denver area. Strippers who shared my displeasure with the local agencies already in existence. We wanted to do something different with an agency that served our individual niches as exotic entertainers.

It was within my grasp until circumstances beyond my control reduced me to the entrepreneurial equivalent of chasing the dragon. A great economic recession hit Colorado around this time as people began losing jobs left and right. People had less money to spend on strippers. We all took a giant financial hit. I accepted a pay cut to remain at my day job. A few months later, my employer could no longer afford my services at any price. I wasn't alone in this. Everyone else within my motley crew of Denver associates experienced the same struggle. Many of us dispersed throughout the nation in search of pastures less brown. For better or worse, my only viable option was Central Arkansas.

Little Rock is nothing like Denver, to state the obvious. Assuming I would catch on with a local exotic entertainment agency only to learn that none existed. The act of bringing together some guys for a weekly ladies' night at a cozy nightclub, something which occurred almost effortlessly in Denver, would never happen in Little Rock. Too foreign a concept for the locals to fathom.

Despite now living in an area void of direct competition, I didn't immediately jump to launch my own agency. Instead picking up occasional bachelorette and birthday parties from agencies based in other states while I enjoyed a steady paycheck. I sold a few pools and many spas to customers in the northern half of the state. A region vital to the eventual success of Hardbodies. All of this allowed me to commence my ongoing exploration of Arkansas as I traveled all over the state.

Now, one year to the month after leaving the Mile High City, I was cleaning up a pool and spa showroom in a town I'd never heard of until I moved to Arkansas. Picking up empty bottles and shocking the fuck out of pools and spas. One of my pet peeves is people who are afraid to properly shock their swimming pools. Fucking pussies.

I was both the assistant manager and a salesperson at Splash Pools, Spas & More. The factory outlet store for Splash Superpools. An Arkansas based manufacturer of excellent aboveground pools as well as shitty portable hot tubs that break down if you look at them wrong. The store also carried the amazing Coast Spas line of acrylic hot tubs, which accounted for most of my sales to the chagrin of upper management. My process for selling hot tubs to couples was simple. Flirt with the wife to get her on board, then close the husband by throwing in $200 worth of accessories that cost the store maybe twenty bucks. The product sold itself. All I did was sell myself.

We should've been rockin' like Dokken, but corporate did nothing to advertise us or the products. Resulting in little customer traffic. By this time, the staff was down to me along with the manager. A useless dumb fuck named Peter who possessed the sort of tall and dumpy physique I refer to as "Arkansas beefcake." He embodied every classic negative stereotype of a car salesman, and I've always believed he was directly involved in the theft of a $10,000 Coast Spa from the store. He spent most days losing money at online Texas hold 'em in the face of mounting financial woes and a crumbling marriage. It was like having Shelley "The Machine" Levene as my boss.

While waiting for hot tub customers and tuning out Peter's constant nuggets of life wisdom rooted in nothing, I spent my days plotting and planning in the first of several black binders I would carry with me to this day. No way in hell was I going down with this store or that lowlife piece of shit. The idea of launching an upscale exotic dance agency in Arkansas wasn't merely daunting. It was fucking crazy. To the point that I got chills thinking about it. All the more reason I had to do it.

Peter was now throwing me under the bus to save his job. Not even a week after my big showroom party, he accused me of something I didn't do as I left for the day. When I returned the following gorgeous spring morning, he was ready and waiting to throw down.

"Well, did you think about what I said yesterday?" he asked in a tone that smacked more of compensating than authority.

"I think you're full of shit," I responded as only I can.

Whatever nonsense he spewed after that went ignored as I strutted out that door for the last time and into an exciting new world. Neither Peter nor the store would last another twelve months. By the end of the day and $400 later, I was a shiny new entrepreneur. My life was about to get all sorts of crazy.

***

My typical performance is not the free for all orgy imagined by many. While undoubtedly sexual, risqué, and often involving the licking of Reddi-wip from body parts (tits, mostly), it's a casual affair of girls cutting loose in the company of a hot guy with a dangerous amount of self-confidence. My role is that of agent provocateur. Rooted in my belief that men can and should be their own gatekeepers of sex like women. I'm no one's boy toy. The girls in the audience are my toys for the night.

That being said…

"Oh yeah, baby. You work his big cock," cooed the client as she videoed the bachelorette giving me a hand job.

A week after walking out of the pool and spa dealership, I was performing at the inaugural Hardbodies Entertainment of Arkansas booking in the unincorporated community of Hattieville. My excitement ran high during the hour drive there. The final minutes especially magical as I traveled AR 213 shaded from the late afternoon sun by endless rows of majestic trees. Arkansas has many flaws, but it's fucking gorgeous.

I was a cowboy that evening. Rocking tear-away jeans and repeatedly cracking my bullwhip to the sound of Kid Rock. The festivities got off to a shaky start as the groom's mother quickly became upset with my presence and left. Not sure why she was there in the first place, but whatever. It was still better than my first ever stripping performance at a male revue in Denver. One for which I earned $14 in tips and was flashed by a woman with crooked titties and no front teeth.

With monster-in-law gone, I immediately gelled with my audience and delivered an enthusiastic performance. Inspired by excitement for my new entrepreneurial journey. My bachelorette paid me the compliment I would receive at nearly every performance:

"Mmmm… You smell good."

Along with my impeccable hygiene, I've always been a cologne enthusiast. Mainly rotating between Preferred Stock, Eternity, and

Bottega Veneta. Being told I smell good is one of the highest compliments I can receive from a woman.

The bachelorette wasn't the only one to cut loose. I allowed another girl to eat food off my bare ass. Mini quiches, tiny chicken salad sandwiches, and other standard bachelorette party foods of the era. I would go on to eat a lot of these myself over the years but not off anyone's bare ass. Not usually, anyway.

***

Without knowing how this whole Hardbodies thing would turn out, I applied for jobs during this time but to no avail. While I focused on shamelessly self-promoting my mad skills, interviewers were only interested in knowing if I had kids and/or how long I would promise to stay. The dubious legalities of such questions notwithstanding, nothing about these interviews instilled me with any confidence regarding job security or potential advancement. So, I said, "Fuck 'em all."

My financial situation was adequate as I racked up parties while collecting unemployment. My living expenses were minimal. Allowing me to embrace my inner bohemian during the early months of Hardbodies. An average day found me waking up around noon, working out, and plotting my world domination. On many nights, whether I had parties or not, I'd hit the clubs in Little Rock during an era before they all became pretentious, boring, and rude. I loved getting out no matter where it was.

I looked great. Of course, I had to. But I was content with where I was at that time. My weight hovered around 180 lbs. Although longing for increased muscularity, my even six-foot frame was undoubtedly a lean, mean stripping machine. My head was held high everywhere I went as I rocked platinum blonde hair and an athletic physique in the tightest jeans I could squeeze into. People noticed as I received equal amounts of cheers and jeers everywhere I went. These were halcyon days indeed.

Young, hot, and self-employed. I was truly living the dream.

In launching Hardbodies, I hit the ground running. My expectations were sky high and nothing could kill my buzz. I was the only entertainer at first but kept busy. Being a true professional male stripper with an eagerness to travel anywhere made me an instant hit. A far cry from the fly-by-night wannabe who may or may not show up. And whose audience will be better off if the latter scenario occurs. Savvy Arkansas party girls proved appreciative of a local agency they could trust to deliver high-quality exotic entertainment to their homes.

My naked ambition ran rampant as I regularly scoured every place from mall boutiques to secondhand stores for potential costume items. I replaced my Denver-era costumes with ones that truly represented what I wanted to express as an entertainer. A single pair of tear-away pants took eight hours to sew by hand. And began a Sunday tradition of camping out on the sofa for a movie marathon as I stitched away while stabbing my fingertips with straight pins.

I took many self-portraits during this time for both personal satisfaction and promoting my new business. Hardbodies didn't have a website in the beginning, so I utilized online directories like PartyPOP at a time when they were influential. While the other agencies listed for Arkansas showcased stolen professional photos of fitness models, the amateurish quality of my images worked to my advantage as discriminating clients knew they'd get exactly whom they were seeing.

Save for performing, there was nothing more exciting than when the phone rang. My initial startup investment included a cell phone strictly for business use and was glued to me at all times. Not unlike those Coast Spas, my excitement for what I was selling led me to close many prospective clients who were simply calling for prices. I'd beat myself up over those I didn't close even if most were an issue of money. Or lack thereof.

Stripping was my niche. A domain in which I could own and operate a business how I saw fit. No longer did I have to endure the failings of incompetent employers. Or the excuses of backstabbing coworkers. Now, when I received praise from clients, it didn't paint a target on my back. I could give VIP treatment to my wonderful and respectful clients while rejecting the overtures of would-be clients who were clearly nothing but trouble. Things were finally the way they ought to be.

CHAPTER 2

It didn't take long for Hardbodies to score its first booking gone bad in the form of a bachelorette party in Batesville. The first of many parties in that town, my swag was cranked to eleven as I drove ninety minutes northeast of Little Rock. Once U.S. 167 split from U.S. 67, I took in the fresh air as the late afternoon sun highlighted a lush, green landscape punctuated with rock faces. I leaned back as best I could in the driver's seat as Terror Squad blasted from my stereo on that summer day. Nothing could bring me down, or so I thought.

The client expressed disdain for my cop uniform and the fact that it didn't have sleeves. Let's be honest... No one is going to mistake me for a real cop. And fuck sleeves. This was clearly the sort of person who believes that a film adaptation of a book is obligated to be a carbon copy of its source material, and that's just stupid. The entire audience was so devoid of excitement and curiosity that I couldn't help but wonder why I was there. If I got too close to any of the married girls, she'd immediately thrust her wedding band in my face like a self-styled Van Helsing of virtue signaling under the guise of faithfulness.

I may have played a cop, but they were totally the fun police. As I prepared to wrap up this sad affair early due to a lack of hospitality and gratuity, the party shut down on its own when the bachelor arrived. I never saw him, but he was apparently in the backyard crying like a total fuckwad. If he thought I might seduce his bride-to-be, he had no reason to worry as rudeness is a turnoff for me. They were on their way to a happy and successful marriage for sure.

Upon walking outside, I noticed the neighbors across the street. Waving me towards them. With time to kill, I headed over and met this friendly young couple who'd been observing the drama from their front porch. Over a beer, they filled me in on the crying bachelor scandal from their vantage point. And the fact they didn't care for those neighbors. While disappointed that the party was a dud, even if by no fault of mine, I still managed to make a few bucks and meet some nice people. This wouldn't be the last instance of me spending more time chatting with the neighbors than entertaining a horrible audience.

In a fitting epilogue to this tale, the client had the nerve to call two days later and complain about my performance. I informed her that the only person with any right to complain was me. The phone went dead.

***

That drama aside, the Summer of Stefan raced ahead at a breakneck pace both professionally and personally. Take the hot and humid July night when I performed at a joint bachelorette-birthday party in El Dorado. I regularly booked parties in the southern half of Arkansas before it completely died economically by the late-2000s. While every town down had its unique charms, El Dorado was the crown jewel with its small yet action-packed downtown area with drinking and dancing options. There's also the charming Union Square Guest Quarters hotel, which was the setting for this night's performance.

The sun was setting as I met the client on Main Street in front of a hotel comprised of an 1875 house and 1925 mansion. She led me around the corner and through a green metal gate as we entered through the rear. Upon reaching room number five, my sexy firefighter persona was greeting by ten sweet and enthusiastic young women who instantly made me feel right at home. Audiences have an obligation to help put entertainers at ease and receive the best performance possible. Not every audience gets this, so it means everything to me when one does.

If I was present to put out their fires, then I failed miserably by engaging them in lap dances. And sixty-nine position moves as I laid them down and hovered oh so dangerously close over them. This wasn't an especially wild group of girls, and that's perfectly fine. They were kind, generous, respectful, and lots of fun. I can't ask for more than that. After an hour, they were properly amped up to hit the town as I made my exit a few hundred dollars richer. Totally pumped for my rendezvous with Megan.

My love life was barely existent during my first year in Arkansas as I adapted to this new cultural geography. I went on a few dates that ranged from banal to "I can't get away from her fast enough." The latter scenario involved a girl named Katie. She showed up for our date with two friends in tow. Including a shabby looking dude obviously carrying a torch for her. Although I found Katie to be an odious individual, I nevertheless made out with her for the sole purpose of antagonizing her male admirer for being there.

Jump forward to the summer of 2004. I'd posted one of my stripping photos on Hot or Not. While basking in the fact that my score never dipped lower than 9.6 out of ten, I came across the photo of a petite brunette with a great smile. Great smiles being important to me because I wish I had one. I saw that she lived in Southern Arkansas and made my move. She reciprocated, and we began getting to know each other through a series of late-night phone calls.

I was impressed with Megan's adventurous and shameless attitude towards sex. Especially since she was only eighteen and fresh out of high school. I prided myself on making progress with a younger woman. Mistakenly assuming I'd shed all my naivety by age 25. She'd grown tired of her apprehensive high school sweetheart. The final straw coming when he refused to finger her ass. She enjoyed masturbating in the shower and regaling me with tales of rubbing and fingering her pussy until she squirted all over the place.

But it wasn't all sex talk, which is good because I require intellectual substance in a girl. Born and raised in Arkansas, she proved an excellent consultant in helping me better understand my surroundings and the people within. We also had a shared interest in fitness as well as nude sunbathing as we discussed these topics ad nauseam. She professed a fascination with my bitchin' California English dialect, while I found her mix of Arkansas twang with a soft and somewhat raspy voice downright sexy. A voice that gave me more chills than the air conditioner on those hot summer nights.

Still, I was cautiously optimistic as I drove through El Dorado that night from one hotel to another. Where Megan waited for me. Despite how much we'd shared between us over the phone, it would be an entirely different story in the flesh. I knew there was a chance we'd have no spark and immediately drive home in separate directions. If that was the case, then so be it. But I had to know. Rejection doesn't hurt. Never knowing hurts.

Megan was already checked in by the time I arrived at the Comfort Inn or whatever chain it was. She was waiting by the door when I got to the room. All smiles as she looked ready to jump into my arms yet clearly anxious herself about how I'd react. I immediately set down my bags, took her in my arms, and kissed her as we simultaneously sighed in relief. I broke out my boombox and contributed to the delinquency of a minor by handing her a beer. We danced and drank as she asked about my party and talked about her day. As innocuous as it seems, there was a special intimacy about this exchange that I hadn't felt in a long time.

She wanted me to strip for her, but she had no money. I suggested we take a tit for tat approach. Her eyes lit up as she giggled.

"I think you want to see me naked," she eked between giggles.

"Can you blame me?" I asked while trying to sound smooth.

With no suitable chair for a lap dance, she sat on the edge of the king-size bed. I bumped and grinded against her as "In Da Club" by 50 Cent blasted forth. She placed her hands on my rocking hips. Never breaking our gaze into each other's eyes. Until I took off my t-shirt.

"Aren't you supposed to tear it off?" she asked with a sassy tone.

"Maybe I should tear yours off," I responded after shaking my head at her smartass question.

Before she could laugh at that, I was removing her tank top. Her faux shock so adorable as she'd instantly raised her arms when she saw what I was doing. I slipped my right hand behind her back and unclasped her bra with my thumb and index finger in one fluid motion. My touch was perfect that time. When it's not, I unclasp all but the bottom hook. The key is to grip it hard and do it fast. That's what she said.

Megan did a little dance of her own as she removed her bra and dropped it to the floor. I was greeted by a pair of perky, round B-cup tits sufficiently ample for her tiny frame. My hands immediately found my way to them as she placed hers on my bare chest. I broke out the second can of Reddi-wip I'd brought that night and applied a small amount to each of her nipples. We looked into each other's eyes as I licked her nipples clean and sucked each one long after the whipped cream was gone. Then she did the same to me as I unbuttoned her shorts and let them slide down her legs.

I wasn't the only one who wore a g-string that night. Much to my surprised delight, I didn't get a chance to remove hers as she did it herself and ran to the window.

"Watch this!" she exclaimed as if on a sugar high. Between the beer and Reddi-wip, she probably was.

She stood on the heater, opened the curtains, and pressed her bare butt against the window for the world to see. I was taken in by such a crazy act so risqué and envelope-pushing yet rooted in a playful innocence and lust for life. The perfect metaphor for my life at that time and how I'd once again like it to be.

Once Megan finished shaking her booty for an audience of parked cars, she jumped on me as I caught her hot, naked body in my arms. Neither of us could get my jeans off fast enough. I once again assumed a sixty-nine position with a girl that night but for real this time as my tongue did its own dance on her clit. Then it was my turn to be on top of her as we fucked. Talking dirty using Arkansas word pronunciations and colloquialisms, because of course we did.

***

Despite all my driving and physical exertion that night, I barely slept. I've always had trouble sleeping in strange places. Not even my comfort level with Megan could save me this time. At 5:00am I gave up and decided to take a shower. As I closed my eyes and let the hot water hit my face, I could sense Megan slipping into the bathroom. As she stepped into the tub at the other end, I turned around and took her in my arms.

It was only for a minute, but it felt like an eternity. Not a word was said. Each of us knew that the other was thinking the same thing. She was the first person with whom I'd shared any trace of emotional connection since moving to Arkansas. While I was willing to see where things between us would lead, I had no expectations. My intuition told me not to get my hopes up. But we were soulmates at that moment in time and seized that moment to its fullest.

As Megan lifted her head from my chest to look at me, I leaned in and kissed her. Once we finally came up for breath, I took the soap and washed her body. An act of sexual dominance that felt more protective than controlling. After shutting off the water, I wrapped her in a bath towel and led her by hand out of the shower. We maintained our romantic silent treatment as if fearing a single word could instantly break our spell.

It wasn't long before we cut the melodramatic nonsense and returned to our talkative and humorous rapport while preparing to leave. She had to be at work by 10:00am, while I needed to get home for a few hours of sleep before my next party that night. I sipped black coffee and soaked up another beautiful summer drive up U.S. 167 as the stereo blared forth an eighties station I happened to find. There's a lot I could say about how I felt at that moment with everything in my life, but Love and Rockets said it best that morning:

"I'm alive. So alive."

CHAPTER 3

Unlike that Batesville bachelorette party with the crybaby bachelor, there is the occasional party gone wrong due to obtusity rather than maliciousness. Such clients and audiences don't believe they're being disrespectful. While inexcusable if for no other reason than there being no excuse for ignorance, it's a touchy situation. Any dissent I voice will seemingly come from nowhere. In that sense, a blatantly rude audience is the lesser of two evils. Because it's no surprise when I reach my breaking point and shut down the party.

Take this booking on a Friday night in early August 2004 as an example of the greater of those two evils. I drove two hours northeast to the farming community of Wynne for a 67th birthday party. Being a little too eager to please in the early days of Hardbodies, I agreed to pick up the client's cousin at a Shell station on the edge of town and give him a ride to the party. I can't remember his name, so let's call him Eddie. Cousin Eddie was an odd duck who refused to converse beyond telling me where to turn. I don't think it had anything to do with me being a stripper. Dude was just fucking weird. And he was in my truck.

It took us about five minutes to reach the party. Which, in stereotypical backwoods Arkansas fashion, was hosted in a single-wide mobile home. It wasn't much of a party. Along with Cousin Eddie, there was my birthday girl, her daughter (my client), and a couple related to them somehow. I arrived as a construction worker. A new costume I would abandon by 2005 because it was fucking boring compared to cop or firefighter, but I digress.

The ladies were beside themselves when I entered the trailer. So much that they climaxed way too soon. Ready for a cigarette before the first song was finished. After making the birthday girl's night in less than a minute, she and her daughter went outside to smoke with Cousin Eddie. I spent the next twenty minutes slow dancing with the third woman as her husband observed from the kitchen while drinking Busch Light. The look in her eyes suggested she wanted to take me home, and the expression on his face indicated he'd like to watch.

Fuck that. After twenty minutes and a bountiful $13 in tips, it was time to leave. And because I'm apparently a glutton for punishment, I agreed to give Cousin Eddie a ride to his car. Why the hell didn't he have his car in the first place? It wasn't broken down, so I don't get it. And why was he even at the party? All he did was sit outside and smoke. Not that I wanted him watching me, but still. Ultimately, it was my fault for being too nice.

***

A common complaint amongst male strippers is having their junk constantly grabbed by women. If you're a male stripper with this problem, you have only yourself to blame. This is not something I've encountered. Because I own every single performance as any stripper, male or female, should. Whether a private party or male revue, I always make my entrance in an authoritative manner that instructs the audience, "This is my show, and we're doing it my way." Not only does this protect me from unwanted groping, but it's exactly the alpha male presence that gets every woman's motor running. Women with money to spend want their male strippers to dominate them.

Having said that, there was a party at which physical boundaries were overstepped in a big way. It occurred the night after the Wynne party and couldn't have been any more different from my encounter with Cousin Eddie and the gang. This is the one party I was reluctant to write about as I still wrestle with what happened, but I'd be intellectually dishonest to hold it back. Plus, it's not without juicy drama too good to ignore.

This bachelorette party is notable from the start because it changed location twice. Originally located 25 miles west of Wynne in McCrory, it briefly moved to the unfortunately named Bald Knob before settling in a large home on a golf course in Searcy. The two clients can be aptly described as Young Becky and Young Charolette. This is not to say they crossed personal boundaries right out of the gate. That would come later. While detecting a bit of smarminess on their part, I chalked it up to girls being nervous around a male stripper. That's not uncommon.

Initially, the party was a motherfucking smash with approximately twenty girls present. All in that wonderful 18-25 age range. The bachelorette was shy yet game to play along as I performed to her comfort level. The other girls weren't shy at all as they couldn't get enough Reddi-wip and lap dances as well as generous both in gratuity and pouring me shots. More than making up for the night before.

One girl was having a total blast and couldn't stop giggling. She repeatedly laid on the floor so I could get on top in various positions. I practically titty fucked her as I rubbed my cock (still in my g-string) between her breasts (still in her top). Why did I do that? Because she asked me to, and I felt comfortable enough with her and the rest of my audience to do it. A huge aspect of establishing dominance over my audience is the mutual respect that comes with it. I go as far as they're comfortable with and vice versa.

The bachelorette became less shy as her alcohol consumption increased. While not my type personally, she was sweet, and I liked her. Even as she rocked the most obvious – and, therefore, most hideous – bra inserts I've ever seen. These hard, plastic discs. They looked like fucking frisbees underneath her tight blouse. If you're flat-chested as this girl was, why wear inserts that are also flat? That odd fashion faux pas aside, it was great to see her let loose and demand my attention for herself.

And that's when shit got weird as Young Becky and Young Charlolette pulled me into the nearest bedroom. My first thought was that they wanted to complain. About what I hadn't the faintest clue as they were partaking in the fun as much as everyone else. Once in the bedroom, Young Becky dropped a bombshell.

"How much would it cost for you to fuck the bachelorette?" she asked in a dead-serious tone.

I'm not sure what it is, but the offer of taking money in exchange for having sex with a woman has always made me uncomfortable. I never know how to respond, and this time was no exception as I stared at her blankly. She doubled down on her sales pitch.

"Come on. She's a cute girl, and she clearly likes you. How much would it take? $200? $300?" kept pressing Young Becky.

As I searched for a reply, Young Charolette offered forth a concurrence worthy of her passive-aggressive namesake.

"Here's the thing. She's a sweet girl, but the guy she's marrying isn't right for her. We just want to give her the best bachelorette party possible to show her what she'll be missing out on if she goes through with it," she oozed forth in a sickeningly saccharine voice.

Now I really didn't know what to say as things quickly went from awkward to full-on duplicitous. Here were two women throwing their friend one hell of a bachelorette party for the sole purpose of destroying her relationship with her soon-to-be husband. And with me as a pawn in their insidious plan. After a few seconds, I responded as best I could:

"Let me think about it."

Sensing that they'd made me uncomfortable, *Becky and Charolette: The College Years* quickly tempered their expectations and agreed to this. On that note, we returned to the festivities at hand.

There's no shortage of guys who will read this and say, "Dude, I would've totally been all over that shit." Perhaps they could've, but I couldn't. And no one knows for sure how they'd react until they're in that situation. The motivation behind this proposition made it worse than if the bachelorette had been single and insecure. For all I know, this guy could totally be her perfect match. Maybe her friends are the ones wrong for her. That seems more likely. My own history of being cockblocked is long and frustrating, so perhaps I felt a pang of sympathy for this mystery groom. In any instance, I didn't rename these girls after Becky and Charolette simply for laughs.

I should've wrapped things up then and gotten the hell out of dodge. Instead, I returned to the living room to find all the girls up and dancing. I couldn't resist placing myself right in the middle. They loved this as we danced and drank our way through song after song.

The house didn't belong to either of the clients. Our hostess was a girl who, in all honesty, was the least attractive of the group in my opinion. And intoxication had brought forth her obnoxious side. Not horribly bad, but not becoming of her.

As I danced within this mob of wild and crazy young women practically on top of me, I felt something warm and wet on my cock. I looked down to find that the hostess had pulled down my g-string and was giving me a blowjob. The other girls saw this and dispersed in unison as I stood there frozen. Since boys are never taught a proper response to being offered unwanted head from obnoxious women (that's not a joke), I had no idea what to do. To their credit, Young

Becky and Young Charolette pulled her off me and apologized profusely.

Now it really was time to call it a night as I walked to my boombox and turned down the volume. Without warning, the hostess was on me again. This time rushing up from behind, dropping to her knees, and giving me an unsolicited rim job. Once again, I froze like a deer in headlights as the other girls pulled her off me and apologized some more. Two girls had the foresight to take her out back as I wrapped up inside.

After packing everything and returning from the bathroom fully dressed, I could see the hostess sitting on the porch swing as another girl comforted her. She realized what she'd done and felt guilty about it for multiple reasons. And yet, despite the other girls remaining apologetic to me until I left, I felt guilty too. I did nothing wrong. But, owing to my self-critical nature, I couldn't help but wonder if I had.

As I walked towards the front door, in strolled the man of the house. A friendly and soft-spoken guy who introduced himself and shook my hand. This made me feel worse. Even though, by any objective standard, I was the victim here.

That's where things get sticky for me personally. Contrary to what some may believe, forced oral copulation upon a man by a woman is sexual assault. And me being a stripper did not justify or excuse her actions. By my personal standards, to which I am fully entitled like anyone else, I would never consent to any form of legitimate sexual engagement with this woman. I gave her a lap dance earlier, but that was in the context of professional entertainment. Going no further than light teasing.

I do accept some degree of responsibility for what happened. I should've left after my clients propositioned me for sex with the bachelorette. Instead, I lost myself in the moment with all those attractive women dancing in the living room. This was the only time in my career that I relinquished control of a party. Consequently, it's also the only time I received unwanted sexual contact without warning. For better or worse, I learned my lesson moving forward.

I harbor no anger towards the hostess. There are plenty of people who've figuratively screwed me far worse over the years. The only punishment I want is for her to be forever embarrassed by the memory of her actions and never repeat them with anyone else. I don't feel like a victim, but I wish it hadn't happened.

What didn't kill me made me stronger as I looked towards my next stripping victory. 2004 still had oodles of action in store for me. Including an encounter with the one and only Maury Povich.

CHAPTER 4

I introduced myself to the *Maury* production staff by making the most painfully obvious joke imaginable. One they've heard ad nauseam:

"I don't have to take a paternity test, do I?"

And began the telling of my transformation from geeky teen to sexy stripper. Ostensibly.

This appearance was scored through a fellow exotic entertainment agency owner out of Seattle named Stan. One of the few talent agent contemporaries I liked. A guy who was probably too nice for this business much in the way that Jimmy Carter was too nice to be president. I lost touch with him once he bowed out of the industry a few years later. Sadly, he passed away in 2015 due to complications from both leukemia and brain cancer.

Upon arriving in NYC on a Sunday afternoon in late August 2004, I hit the studio to lay down voiceover for the reenactment segment of my adolescent low lights. I hung out in a dressing room where I was brought dinner while responding to voicemails. As I booked a birthday party for the following Saturday night, I heard kids yelling something I hadn't heard in years. Eventually realizing they were reenacting my junior high days. After that wrapped, I entered the studio to record an opening narration I wrote with a producer along with some ad-libbing.

Once completed, I was taken to Southgate Towers (Stewart Hotel in 2019) across the street from Madison Square Gardens and Penn Station. I entered my suite as night fell and enveloped the city that never sleeps. After setting down my bags, I looked out the window to observe steam rising from the back alley. Like I'd seen in countless films and television shows set here. This simple visual made me grasp the implications of my current situation.

The *Maury* producers expected me to get a good night's sleep and be fully rested for shooting the next day. Fuck that. I was in New York City. Manhattan. I did the most sensible thing in my mind and enjoyed an all-night drinking binge before the show. Exhaustion notwithstanding, I knew I'd be more relaxed for taping if I stayed up and partied instead of turning in like someone's grandmother. And there was no way I'd fall asleep. I was in fucking New York City. To not hit the town would have been a crime against all that is right in the universe. Since I wouldn't meet any of the other strippers until tomorrow, I took to the streets alone.

New York City totally fucking rocks. A few things I've always heard about it are true. Most notably, that traffic is an absolute clusterfuck. But it's much friendlier than I'd ever imagined. The people are intense and unapologetically direct. And that's what I like about them. A complete absence of Southern passive aggression. I met friendly people and received some of the best customer service of my life everywhere I went. Unlike in Arkansas, where a convenience store clerk had recently told me to go fuck myself after asking him why he suddenly insisted that I, a regular customer, prepay for fuel. New York is one hell of a city, although I'd never encountered such expensive alcohol in my life. Six bucks for a Corona at the hotel bar was eye-popping in 2004.

I left Southgate Towers and headed down 7th Avenue towards Times Square. Intending to see firsthand all the famous New York City landmarks I could. I walked the entire length of that Disneyfied cesspool along 7th and then Broadway, which I followed to Central Park before taking 59th Street to 5th Avenue and passing the Trump Tower. I headed back toward Broadway, spotting the Museum of Modern Art and the former location of Studio 54, before ending up on Columbus and in front of Lincoln Center.

I stopped in various bars along the way. Drinking Corona as well as Jack and Coke. I would pop in for a drink and tell the bartender or whoever would listen about why I was in this amazing city to their amusement. My adventure also allowed me to visit a nice gentlemen's establishment with attractive ladies. Standing in stark contrast to Arkansas, where every strip club is a drug-infested shithole.

I talked to a couple of girls about my impending television appearance. They told me not to worry about, as I clearly knew my shit. One insisted that I give her a lap dance, which I did briefly as mafioso dudes looked on. They were cool as shit. Some guy from Arizona who'd won a bunch of money at an Indian casino upstate bought my drinks as I regaled him with tales of my three years in the industry to that point.

I caught a cab and arrived back at the hotel around 4:00am. I loved how someone could drink all night and always have an instant and affordable ride home. Once in my room, I turned on HBO and watched the Jeff "Lawnmower Man" Fahey vehicle *Body Parts*. Although set in New York City, it was obviously filmed in Toronto. Following those ninety minutes of my life I'll never get back, I jumped in the shower, shaved my entire body, and got ready to check out and head over to the studio.

I checked out at 7:30am and sat in the lobby. Waiting for the limo to arrive. The other strippers appeared one by one. We congregated immediately since each of us contrasted greatly from the average guest. Piling into the limo at 8:00am and heading to the studio, where we were herded into a green room that was blue. Breakfast was delivered as we filled out various contracts and release forms. We hung out there for six hours while the first episode of the day was shot before ours.

The first was one of those "who's my baby daddy?" segments for which the show is most infamous. I don't know what went down, but I overheard the audience boo the holy fuck out of one dude in particular. He must've been a lot of babies' daddy. I asked a production assistant where they find these guys to take paternity tests and come on the show. He told me they average four to five guys per day who call and ask to do it. What is it about nasty people and their desire to be on television?

The other strippers were groovy as fuck. We all got along well and shared stories about our respective experiences like a stripper version of *The Breakfast Club* as we spent the day in green room detention. Aside from me, there were four girls, along with a guy who went by Chocolate. Because most black strippers feel compelled to have racially self-referential monikers. He informed us that he got stoned in his suite the night before. Proving that I wasn't imagining things when I smelled the foul stench of Mary Jane coming from the hallway vents on my floor. It was a good group. We all clicked as each of us prepared to appear on television for the first time.

Rehearsal began at 2:00pm and consisted of each stripper running through his or her entrance and moves. As for Chocolate and me, we would strip and give quick lap dances to a few female audience members. We also taped introductions that had each of us, through the magic of video editing, bursting out of an old photo of ourselves before we came on stage. I nailed my rehearsal on the first take. Because I'm just that good. The combination of intoxication and sleep deprivation had me feeling totally relaxed. I was cocked, locked, and ready to rock by showtime.

Taping immediately followed rehearsal with my segment filmed last. As I stood backstage, I watched the reenactment of my adolescence. It was surreal to see myself portrayed by a professional actor. And yet it remains possibly the most absurd piece of video I'd ever seen. While there's truth to the fact that I was a homely and unpopular teenager, things were blown out of proportion. When the audience laughed at certain parts, I laughed too because they were so ridiculous. The entire point of presenting my past so negatively made me appear even more impressive. It's all in the framing.

Maury announced me, and I made my entrance. The word I received beforehand was that my transformation was the most drastic of everyone. I called bullshit, but the audience was blown away when they saw the new me. It was like *The Swan* without cosmetic surgery. After doing my stripping and lap dance thing, I walked over to Maury. He greeted me with a ghetto handshake. We did a quick interview as he read from his prompter questions that I'd mostly written. After answering my own questions, I headed offstage while they brought on some girl named Angie who remembered me from junior high.

As I waited to make my reentry, Maury talked to her about how she knew me and whatnot. Then I returned to show her that I'm a stripper now and rattle off some bullshit about how she shouldn't have been so quick to write me off back in the day. I probably should've been more animated and melodramatic, but I was starting to drag. And I still for the life of me don't remember that girl from junior high, although she remembered things about me. The experience constituted an unholy alliance of sorts between us. I got to appear on television and promote myself on an all-expenses-paid trip to New York City. She and two of her girlfriends also received an all-expenses-paid trip to New York City. That's all there ever was between us.

Things got hectic after the show as we were rushed out of the studio and into black sedans. My flight was out of Newark. Giving me the bonus of (along with spending a few minutes in Canadian airspace) seeing nothing but shipping containers before flying back to Little Rock via Chicago. As I sat on the plane while takeoff was delayed for an hour (because fucking New Jersey, I guess), I reflected upon my decision to appear on *Maury*. The reenactment was god-awful, and my confrontation with Angie couldn't have been more anticlimactic. But I did get a free trip to New York City, a $200 check to cover my drinking spree, and my first television writing gig so to speak. I cringe at my appearance in hindsight. But I think most people have a habit of downplaying certain things they did before knowing what they know now.

On the flight home, I decided that I was moving to Manhattan if this Hardbodies thing didn't work out. In hindsight, I probably should've forgone Hardbodies altogether and just moved to New York City. I knew talent agents who could've gotten me bachelorette parties throughout the region along with male revue appearances. But I was hell-bent on building a successful business. Even if it was in Arkansas. I don't regret my decision. It was far from a foregone conclusion that I'd thrive in the Big Apple. I probably would have, but the high cost of living would've made the overall decline of this industry in later years even more painful.

As my flight descended upon Little Rock, I looked out my window and sank into depression. Partly because Little Rock pales in comparison to the glitz and glamour of New York City. But also, I knew my magical mystery summer was now over. Not that my crazy adventures wouldn't continue into the fall and winter. But it was time to make some seasonal changes if I was to get serious about building my agency into a force with which to be reckoned.

CHAPTER 5

As the summer of 2004 ended, so did my brief and sexually charged relationship with Megan. She returned to her high school sweetheart after he asked her to move with him to Alabama. Because what girl could say no to that? I was disappointed but not heartbroken. We enjoyed a few wild nights together. And that was it. It's not like I wanted to settle down. I was married to Hardbodies. And there would be other girls.

It was time to get serious about building Hardbodies into a real agency. And that meant finding other strippers. Surely, I would have no trouble finding enough attractive and dependable guys and girls eager to earn good money. Right?

***

My first booking after returning from New York City was a 56th birthday party on the outskirts of Pine Bluff, approximately one hour south of Little Rock. One of countless parties I've had for which the client was the birthday girl's husband and the audience was mostly couples. A nice thing about these gigs is they usually don't take long, and the gratuity is generous. When it works out that way, they make for nice "warm-up bookings" before bachelorette parties. But I stayed for a while this time

This was a party with some rural folks but a far cry from the birthday party in Wynne with Cousin Eddie. Over the course of my stripping career, I've met numerous people who are educated, cultured, and world traveled yet call rural Arkansas home. Conversely, there's no shortage of urban, self-congratulatory, cultural elitists who've never even heard of Federico Fellini. Don't judge a book by its cover.

At 56-years-young, my birthday girl looked terrific. Age was nothing but a number to her. She was as lively and energetic as the most hyper of twentysomethings. Flirting with her was fun. She ate up the fact that a hot, younger guy was providing her with so much attention. I kept teasing her by rubbing my cock between her tits, then turning around and pulling down my g-string in the rear. The experience made her feel even sexier on her birthday, and I considered that mission accomplished.

I spent an hour entertaining my birthday girl and the other wives. The husbands appreciated that I was handling the night's foreplay for each of them. These girls particularly enjoyed me removing dollar bills from their cleavage with my teeth. It's a longtime staple of my performances at odds with my quasi-germophobic nature. But that's the price of delivering top-notch entertainment. The Reddi-wip was also popular, and I allowed one girl to lick some off my butt crack.

After the show, I hung out for a while and had a beer or several as I chatted with my audience. My birthday girl stayed close and asked many questions about my profession. So too did one young man who wasn't much older than me. He was fascinated with the whole thing as if he wanted to get into it. Then again, as a married man, perhaps he was merely seeing role-playing possibilities.

People feel comfortable opening up to me about their sexual interests and activities. I'm generally flattered by this because my main objective as a stripper is to make people feel relaxed and free of judgment. The young man told me all about his wife's bisexuality and the fun they have with it. Perhaps he was bragging to some degree, but I didn't blame him. She was attractive, sweet, and full of life in the brief time I knew her. Most of all, however, I think he just wanted to have a normal conversation with someone about it. I understood because I'd had my own experiences with girls who like girls. And there were more to come.

***

September 2004 brought with it not only autumn but the first Hardbodies Entertainment of Arkansas stripper not named Stefan. Err... Magnum. Whatever.

The first stripper I represented professionally was a young woman we'll call Amber. A fit, 21-year-old bleached blonde with perky C-cup breasts to go with a friendly demeanor. She had private party experience through a couple of fly-by-night agencies that briefly existed before Hardbodies, so she hit the ground running. Not only was she prepared, reliable, and drug-free, but she had a steady day job to boot. Her shit was together for the most part, and I did well in finding her as my first recruit.

And this is where I felt like I was looking a gift horse in the mouth. While Amber was a perfectly adequate private party stripper, that's just it. There was nothing wrong with her as an entertainer, but there was nothing great either. Conventionally attractive, but not especially sexy. Outgoing, but not overly endearing. Performance-wise, she was the ultimate paint-by-numbers stripper. She did all the right things but never anything unique or memorable. Her sole talent was being superior to those god-awful Arkansas club dancers, and that's a mighty low bar to clear.

While Amber was light years ahead of the pregnant teens and meth addicts who comprised most of my female applicants at the time, she wasn't without her shortcomings. Not only did she not have a cell phone, but her parents (with whom she lived) didn't even have a landline. I had to call a neighbor and leave messages for her. After a couple of parties, I took Amber to Best Buy and made her purchase a Virgin Mobile phone. There was also an incident in which a bachelor party client called to tell me that she'd brought her brother as security.

Still, I was grateful to have Amber. She settled into a niche as the old reliable of Hardbodies. I'd get calls for bachelor and birthday parties. And she'd do them. Clients were happy enough with her, and she stopped taking her brother to parties after I told her not to anymore. It worked at the time.

Good male strippers were, and forever remained, an absolute bitch to find. The issue with male strippers is they need male revue experience before attempting private parties. It's always been my contention that the bachelorette party is the most challenging and difficult performance in the entire stripping universe. Which is why there are so few male strippers who do it successfully. Becoming a male stripper is a sink or swim proposition. If a guy can't stay above water with several other guys there to carry some of the weight, how the fuck will he survive a solo performance? What's he going to do when the client waits until showtime to inform him that the bachelorette has postpartum depression and he should avoid getting close to her? This is a real scenario I found myself in while writing "Emily Stripped Bare". I still made the party a success due entirely to experience, because experience counts.

There's also the matter of startup investment and overhead. It costs money to get started as a stripper and to keep stripping. Parties are nothing without costumes, props, sound systems, and everything else a good male stripper needs to bring down the house every time. Depending on what he already owns, he can expect to spend $300 to $500 getting started. This is why I found it irksome when some jackass called to tell me that he'd been laid off (fired, probably) and wanted to start stripping that night. On a fucking Wednesday, no less.

My first male recruit was a guy in Fayetteville who had both male revue and private party experience in other parts of the country. I thought, "Great. He can handle bachelorette and birthday parties in Northwest Arkansas as well as in neighboring areas of Oklahoma and Missouri." Nope. He only wanted parties in Southern Arkansas, which made no sense as I was closer and therefore did them for less. I didn't know what sort of drama he had going on up there, nor did I want to. I thanked him for his time and moved on.

That brings us to Freaky Tales. I'm already breaking my rule about stripper names, but this one is too fucking stupid not to share. Yes, he called himself Freaky Tales. It's one thing if he included that Too $hort song in his performances, but it doesn't mean he needed to use it as his stripper name. Of course, I have myself to blame for not putting my foot down on that. I simply chalked it up to being a black thing. He had legitimate experience, and I was a little too anxious to fill my roster. So, against my better judgment:

"Welcome aboard, Freaky Tales."

***

I attended a lot of concerts during my first few years in Arkansas. Mostly of the eighties hard rock variety. One week after moving here, I saw Night Ranger at the unfortunately named Toad Suck Daze in Conway. I also saw the likes of Mötley Crüe (and Vince Neil solo), Def Leppard, Poison, and David Lee Roth. There was the time I saw Faster Pussycat with Enuff Z'Nuff and Pretty Boy Floyd opening. During the Enuff Z'Nuff set I glanced towards my right, and Poison guitarist C.C. DeVille was standing next to me. Glam rock has always been a huge influence on my personal style, fashion sense, and over the top nature of my stripping performances.

I took off a Saturday night in October to see Slaughter, Firehouse, and L.A. Guns at the Riverfest Amphitheater in Little Rock. I was still making money as Amber had a bachelor party. Freaky Tales had his first Hardbodies gig that night, and I was excited to know how it went. I felt great because I had other people out making money for me while I did something fun. It's the entrepreneur's dream.

After L.A. Guns and Firehouse, I pulled some strings to go backstage and watch Slaughter from the sidelines with members of the first two bands. Following the show, I briefly chatted with Mark Slaughter before I wound up in L.A. Guns' dressing room. Drinking beer with drummer Steve Riley. He and I were pretty buzzed. Talking about the music we were each into at the time. It was a surreal moment as I've been a fan of his work since childhood. Not only was he in L.A. Guns but W.A.S.P. too. Fuck yeah.

As I chilled with a glam metal icon, my phone rang. It was the client from Freaky Tales' bachelorette party, and she was furious. After calling her to say he was getting a haircut (on a Saturday night?!), he arrived ninety minutes late. Upon opening the front door to greet him, she noticed that his cock was exposed as he walked towards her. My guess being he used a penis pump (a common practice among black male strippers) in the car, although that doesn't explain why it was out. He also wasn't in costume. She immediately shut the door in his face and locked it.

With my night now ruined, I bid farewell to my rock star company and headed for wherever the fuck I was parked. As I walked, I called Freaky Tales to inform him that he owed me $75. I didn't care that the client never paid him. I'd held up my end of the deal and wanted what was mine. Not surprisingly, he let my call go to voicemail and never returned it. He still owes me that money. I'm never going to see it, am I?

It feels like I've devoted a good chunk of my stripping career to damage control because of guys like that asshole. Granted, too many clients have themselves to blame for not exercising due diligence when booking a male stripper. But this doesn't excuse the lowlifes who take advantage of them. I've interviewed many candidates whose idea of stripping at bachelorette parties is the live performance equivalent of sending dick pics to girls. I've pushed the envelope on numerous occasions but always within the context of professional entertainment. It's the difference between seducing my audience for entertainment's sake versus forcing something upon them out of personal desperation.

2004 was quickly winding down but wasn't over yet. There was more excitement to come as I looked towards the coming year.

CHAPTER 6

It was a crisp November night as I filled my gas tank on the edge of town. I'd just completed a bachelorette party in Bono, Arkansas after driving two hours northeast of Little Rock to get there. As I took in the cool air along with the sight and sound of a passing freight train across the road, I thought about the long night ahead. Rather than drive home, I would make the nearly three-hour trek to Hot Springs for a second bachelorette party. It was 9:30pm, and I was due by 1:00am. Piece of cake.

To stay busy as a private party stripper, being a road warrior is a must. This truth was always one of many obstacles I had with recruiting strippers. Most didn't want to travel outside their hometown. Even in prosperous times, there aren't enough bookings in the Little

Rock or Fayetteville areas to stay busy without traversing the state constantly. And if I received two booking requests for the same night, I did everything in my power to handle both no matter how far apart they were.

I love every minute of my road trip parties and this night was no exception. My spirits were high as I left the convenience store and headed west on AR 230 through acres of farmland. As on the drive there, I cranked the stereo and switched between radio stations. Often winding back on *Retro Pop Reunion with Joe Cortez*. Because eighties music. I should've been exhausted by the time I rolled into Hot Springs at 12:30am, yet I was cocked, locked, and ready to rock. And rock is exactly what I did before going home and crashing at 3:00am.

Those night drives remain one of my favorite aspects of being a private party stripper, and I'll have to find an excuse to keep making them after I retire. As enjoyable as they are alone, having the right girl by my side would totally amplify the magic.

***

There was no road trip when I wrapped up 2004 with a December bachelorette party in Little Rock. It was the sort of audience for which both experience and self-confidence counts in spades. These girls were my counterpart in the sense they were collectively self-aware of how excellent an audience they were and had equally great expectations for me in return. Young, attractive, and fun-loving with enough disposable income to make it worth my while. A lesser male stripper would've been skinned alive by these chicks and rightfully so. It was the sort of audience I would grow to love over the years as we kept each other on our toes from start to finish. Challenge accepted every time.

Superficially speaking, it was the bachelorette party of which every would-be male stripper fantasizes. A bevy of hot girls with cheerleading and beauty pageant backgrounds throwing around gobs of cash and feeding me alcohol like the rapture was upon us. My performance was a tour de force of lap dances, body shots, and Reddit-wip licked off one another. I continually pushed the envelope, only for them to challenge me to push it a little further. I'd respond by pushing it even further than that. They asked me to flash them. I insisted on tit for tat, pun intended.

One girl by the name of Renée was conspicuously restrained the entire time, but not because she harbored any aversion to the proceedings. She egged on her girlfriends throughout the party as we clicked and conversed. Incredibly sweet and the most beautiful girl in a room full of aesthetically pleasing women. A real-life beauty queen, but I didn't care about that. She was hot, and I enjoyed talking to her. I could tell she was holding back her own desire to get wild.

After two hours of unbridled raciness, my audience was ready to call it a night. I passed out business cards to everyone and packed my stuff. Most of the girls, including Renée, left with me as we dispersed into the night. I was satisfied with the fun and profitable time I had. The drive home felt stifling. It was late, yet I was all kinds of fired up. I'm used to leaving my audiences hungry for more, but these girls made my immediate appetite for fun insatiable. What the hell was I going to do with this excitement? I didn't have anyone to call, and that's when the phone rang.

"Is this Stefan?" asked Renée as she correctly pronounced my name. I was all ears as she took a deep breath to push out what she wanted to say next.

"Hey... Uhhh... Do you want to come over to my place? I mean... I understand if you don't want to... I know it's getting late and all," she stammered forth with a vulnerability in her voice that hit me like a punch to the stomach.

"I'd like that," I wasted no time in responding. This was no time to act cool.

It was a few years before smartphones and GPS became de rigueur, so I pulled into the next parking lot to write down her address and directions. I acted reflexively as the implications of what was happening hadn't yet absorbed into my mind. But I was totally game.

My beauty queen, however, was already concerned about me having second thoughts.

"So, you're sure you're coming over?" She asked in a way that made me want to kiss her right then and there.

"Definitely. I'm on my way right now," as I turned around and floored it in the opposite direction.

I know people think I'm constantly hooking up with women because they bring it up all the time. Speaking for myself, and only myself, the hookups are few and far between. First, I must encounter a girl I want to sleep with, and I'm seeking specific qualities inside and out. Second, there's the cockblocking aspect that alone has resulted in countless missed opportunities for me. I shake my head at all the guys who fear rejection. Little do they know it's the least of their problems should they get past it.

And, for the record, I hadn't been with a woman since my final rendezvous with Megan a few months prior. So there.

As I raced towards my destination, I began to think about what I was doing. It's not that I saw Renée as being out of my league. It was that she comes from a different world. A world I didn't want to be a part of and would never accept me if I were to date a girl like Renée. I wasn't trying to get ahead of myself, but I couldn't help but wonder what to do if we wanted to see each other a second time. Or third. Or forth. Or… You get the idea. Still, she was sexy. And it had been a while for me.

I parked on the street a couple of lots down when I arrived at her cozy three-bedroom home in a new housing tract. There was a man in her life, so I tried to be clandestine where the neighbors were concerned. Yes, I knew about him and didn't give a fuck. I still don't, in all honesty. Stealthily I grabbed my duffle bag of stripping gear and briskly walked to her front door. Clearly sharing my train of thought, she was waiting at the door and quickly ushered me inside.

Renée had made it home only a few minutes before I arrived and rushed around the living room to set the mood. She asked me to put on some music as she lit candles, fixed cocktails, and turned out the lights. We gazed at each other while sipping vodka cranberries and listening to my stripping mix CD I put in her stereo. After a moment of this adolescent nonsense, I grabbed a chair from her dinner table and set it in the middle of the living room. Taking her drink, I maneuvered her into taking a seat and gave her the lap dance she rejected earlier.

Afterward, I took her hand and led her up from the chair. Putting my hands on her hips, I spun us around as our eyes remained locked. Then I sat.

"Show me what you've learned," I demanded.

She took a drink as I skipped tracks until reaching "Lovers and Friends" by Lil Jon. Not only did this slower jam agree with our increasing intoxication, but it fit the mood of the moment. Renée slipped off her moccasin boots, removed her sweater, and dropped to her knees as she put her face in my lap and slowly made her way up my torso until we were face to face. She sat in my lap and grinded with her tits pressed against my chest. Her arms around my neck as she looked at me with bedroom eyes. She stood up, turned around, and dropped forward onto her hands while kicking her legs backward. Or came close to doing it as it's harder than it looks. We laughed as I helped her into position. Her sexy ass in black leggings bouncing up and down in my lap.

After finally losing her balance and falling over, I helped her up. She immediately pushed me back and sat in my lap. I put my hands on her ass and pulled her tight against me. She placed her hands on my face as I looked up at her. Then she lowered her face to mine as we locked lips for what felt like an eternity. Our tongues slow dancing together. She lifted her arms as I removed her tank top. I almost got her bra off with my thumb and forefinger, but that bottom hook thwarted me this time. I'll blame that on the alcohol. She trembled while pushing her breasts against my face. Letting out a long sigh as I kissed and sucked them while pulling down her leggings in the rear and squeezing her bare butt.

Next thing I knew, Renée and I were naked on her bed in a passionate embrace. Making out intensely as outside light subtly illuminated the bedroom in uniform lines through Venetian blinds. I kissed her neck while moving my hand down her body and between her legs. Rubbing her clit with my middle finger before sliding it inside her soaking wet pussy and massaging her g-spot. Holding onto me tighter, she shook while moaning as loud as she would allow herself to. Barely above a whisper.

These reactions continued when I licked my way down her stomach to her pussy. Drawing circles on her clit with the tip of my tongue, sucking her delicate lips, and licking her deeply. I couldn't believe how incredible she tasted. She held my hand all the while. Whenever she squeezed it, I squeezed back a little tighter. When my tongue needed a break, she pushed me over and returned the favor. Sucking and stroking my cock. We continued holding hands. Squeezing ever tighter as she hit every nerve ending with her tongue.

Renée rose to her knees and straddled me before lowering her throbbing pussy onto my rock-hard cock. She was so tight that it took a minute to penetrate her completely. From there, she rode my cock with long, slow thrusts. I assisted by grabbing her hips and lifting her up and down. The feel of her curves and soft skin. The smell of Tommy Girl. The sensation of fucking her. It was so much sensory overload that every muscle fiber in my body contracted tighter and tighter until finally releasing in an orgasmic tidal wave multiple times.

But the sensations were more than physical. Although we'd just met, there was emotional chemistry between us. One that enveloped us in an aura of melancholy as we both knew this would be our only encounter. Even in near darkness, I could see tears building in Renée's eyes. I could feel them despite being nowhere near her face as she towered above me. This dreamy moodiness turned into hormonally driven frustration as we fucked harder and harder. She laid on top of me, and I grabbed her ass tightly. Thrusting furiously against each other. Kissing with reckless abandon before climaxing together in an epic sexplosion.

We held onto each other in silence for the longest time. There was no point in saying anything. It would've made us feel more crestfallen. I could feel the tears once again building in her eyes as she repeatedly switched between burying her face in my neck and softly kissing my cheek. I continuously kissed her cheek and shoulder while stroking her long, voluminous hair. It smelled amazing like the rest of her. Neither one of us wanted that moment to end, but it would have to soon.

Renée lifted her head and stroked my face while gazing into my eyes.

"You can stay tonight if you want," she offered with a combination of heartache and sass.

"I'd better go," was all I could say. I didn't want to hurt her feelings, but I knew neither of us could take any more heartache that night. Much less in the morning

She nodded in reluctant agreement as she rolled off me. I stood and headed for the bathroom while she laid in bed. Upon my return, she watched almost lovingly as I dressed. I touched her face and leaned over her naked body to share a goodbye kiss that came dangerously close to making us go for another round. Looking at her one last time before turning to leave.

"Don't worry about getting up. I'll lock the front door behind me," I said as I turned and walked out of her bedroom forever.

"Stefan?"

I looked back as she continued in a soft and breathy voice:

"Thank you."

All I could do was nod my head and leave.

The drive home took forever as I sought to process so many conflicting thoughts and feelings. I had no regrets about my sexual encounter with Renée. That itself was a pleasurable experience. She was amazing in every way, and I'm all about quality of quantity. Any dude can bang a ton of chicks, but some will inevitably be garbage for any number of reasons. Renée was that girl who occasionally comes along and catches my eye in multiple ways. That alone was worth it.

On the other hand, I was devastated because I did want to see her again. Not only did I want to wake up next to her, but I wanted to take her out to breakfast in the morning and call her later in the day. I wanted her as my girlfriend. And as much as she may have liked that idea too, it could never work. Everyone else in her life would've mobilized to sabotage any semblance of a relationship between us. It wasn't simply a matter of me being a stripper. I could've been a successful entrepreneur in any industry. I'm an outsider, and that's all that matters.

Some might suggest that I should've reinvented myself to fit in, and that's the catch-22. The one thing above all else that attracted her to me was Stefan being Stefan. She already had a man in her life who fit in, and she stepped out on him with me because I wasn't one of them. That's why I made her feel alive that night. It's what she thanked me for when I left. The sex we had wasn't the kinkiest or most outrageous, but it was probably the only honest sex she's ever had. If my choices are sex by numbers or no sex at all, I'll gladly choose the latter. It's not a matter of just being with someone. It's about two people making each other feel alive together.

For one moment in time, Renée and I achieved that. And I was left with the lyrics of her namesake song:

"Your name and mine inside a heart upon a wall.

Still finds a way to haunt me, though they're so small"

So, in the days leading up to both 2005 and my 26th birthday, I gave up on love. Not as a cry for sympathy (because I never told anyone this story until now), but because it seemed like a pragmatic decision. Besides, I was married to Hardbodies Entertainment of Arkansas. And a girl who would inject excitement into both Hardbodies and my life was just around the corner…

CHAPTER 7

I entered 2005 kissing Marilyn Monroe. That's to say I kissed a girl who found me on Myspace. She'd shared with me photos of herself as a respectable Marilyn on Halloween and mentioned not having plans for New Year's Eve. Once again proving that Myspace at its peak is the greatest social network ever.

We rang in the new year at the Electric Cowboy in Little Rock. One in a chain of shithole faux roadhouse nightclubs throughout the Mid-South. I took part in male revues at multiple locations over the years. Each venue and staff sucked. That aside, I had a fun time with Marilyn. She was a good conversationalist and dancer with excellent kissing skills. Still, I didn't feel anything with her beyond hanging out and making out. After the midnight hoopla, I walked her to her car and kissed her goodnight. I think we spoke on the phone a few days later, but that was all she wrote

***

It was time to get serious about building Hardbodies Entertainment of Arkansas into a full-fledged exotic entertainment agency. Amber remained in tow, but I needed more entertainers. Including other male strippers, so I didn't have to handle every bachelorette party myself, I wanted to seek club bookings for male revues. Where female strippers were concerned, I was keen on offering two girl shows. This was something Amber was not down with herself, so I was starting from scratch there. I planned to add lean mass to my frame while further distinguishing myself as a professional entertainer. I began 2005 with a lot on my plate for sure.

So, naturally, I agreed to co-produce and star in a feature-length film being directed by an acquaintance I met through LiveJournal. It was a ridiculous proposition for me to even consider, but I couldn't help myself. I've been seriously interested in filmmaking since first seeing *Eraserhead* as a teenager. It blew my mind that not only could such a brilliantly absurd film be made, but that it could be done with little money and no studio support. For better or worse, I signed up to be one-quarter of a four-headed monster production team that also included my co-star. A girl named Rebecca.

I also began the trend of pursuing additional moneymaking opportunities during the week. These were independent contractor gigs that ranged over the years from retail merchandising to building decks to technical writing. They allowed me to work alone, set my own schedule, and answer incoming calls for strippers. Even during periods when I didn't need the extra money, these projects got me out of the house and kept me from getting bored while waiting for the phone to ring.

As my filmmaking cohorts and I set to work casting our movie, I concurrently began holding my own casting sessions for Hardbodies. Fortunately or unfortunately, depending on how you look at it, most applicants didn't make it past the initial email or phone call. It should surprise no one that oodles of scummy people applied with us over the years. Many were so bad in every way imaginable that I didn't bother to respond, and they couldn't have seriously thought they stood a chance in hell. Right?

When I made my first serious push to find strippers, the most common demographic by far to apply was black females. A trend that continued throughout our existence. Black females were also the least requested strippers throughout our history by about a million miles. Hardbodies wouldn't even receive its first request for a black female stripper until 2013. The shame was that I had a few such applicants over the years who were beautiful, charming, and on their game. I would've snagged them in an instant if I'd had a clientele for them.

Most white female applicants were either built like ten-year-old boys or significantly overweight. Pregnant chicks were frighteningly common in the early days for some reason. A few being as far along as six months. I know there are dudes with a pregnant chick fetish, but I never wanted their business. I'd get calls from girls who I could tell were experiencing drug withdrawals by the agony in their voices. Desperate to pay for a fix any way they could. Recreational drug use is mostly a female stripper thing and (save for marijuana) uncommon in male strippers. Us guys are more partial to a different realm of illegal drugs.

I also compiled a waiting list of guys who wanted to be security escorts for our female strippers. A do-nothing job, as bachelor party audiences are self-policing. If a guy gets out of line, several of his buddies will immediately pull him aside. Still, I had to weed out the candidates who were either looking to hook up with my girls and/or wanting to start fights with party guests.

Although we ideally needed male strippers with professional experience, I was willing to consider guys with no experience given our market. Overall, male applicants were more obnoxious than females in making ridiculous demands and other diva-like behavior even with no experience. Most looked like complete shit, and many sent dick pics. As for the few who were physically attractive, they refused to assemble tear-away costumes or remove body hair. One dumbass had the nerve to tell me, "I ain't stripping for no fat bitches." It's not like he had to fuck anyone, so who cares?

Speaking of body hair on men… Women generally don't care for it but have resigned themselves to tolerating it. "You should stop shaving your body," said no woman to me ever. Food for thought, dudes.

The early search returns weren't inspiring. Would I find anyone on the level of the best male and female strippers I knew in Denver? Was Amber as good as it gets in Arkansas? Hardbodies wasn't even one year old yet had already lasted longer than numerous would-be competitors to come. Unlike them, I brought a definite knowledge and acumen for this business to the table but still had much to work out on the fly.

***

At least I could always depend on myself as an entertainer, and I kicked off the new year with two bachelorette parties on a Saturday night. There was no road trip this time as these parties were thirty minutes apart in the Little Rock area. Both clients requested a cowboy, so plenty of girls got their butts spanked with my bullwhip that night. These were my first two parties since the one with Renée, and I was relieved to start putting distance between me and that gig. I couldn't wait to get 2005 off to a kick-ass start.

My first party was in North Little Rock for a group of dolled-up twentysomethings. The client took to me immediately. A petite brunette in a red party dress, she kept lifting her skirt for some bullwhip action. I obliged each time, gently smacking her black silk panties. She and the equally cute bachelorette tag teamed on licking Reddi-wip off my nipples several times. So often, it's the simplest things that make my audience's night one they'll never forget.

I was on such a total fucking high that I didn't even notice the drive to my second party in Benton. Next thing I knew, I was cracking my whip for a group of women ranging from twenties to fifties. It was a different crowd from the first party, but the fun had by all was the same. Such is the magic of stripping. I spent most of my time one on one with the bachelorette. She moaned and arched her back incessantly, and I wasn't even doing anything beyond the norm. What can I say? I'm just that good.

I hung out for another hour. Conversing and drinking with my audience. A few of us stood in the kitchen talking as I rocked nothing but a g-string and cowboy boots. I had pulled down my g-string in the rear earlier and left it there. A form of light antagonism on my part as they snuck glances behind me. They debated my hair color, which was my most polarizing feature in those days. There were always women hell-bent on having a dark-haired stripper. After going black years later, I was swamped for months with requests for a blonde guy. Go figure.

I stopped at Wendy's on the way home because fuck you, I was starving. As I scarfed down value menu burgers, I took a drive through Nellyville via the underrated "American Dream" from *Sweat*:

"I should be put on display for the display I displayin'."

My entire life in a nutshell.

***

There was a film production meeting the following Monday afternoon. Most of these meetings were held at a Little Rock coffeehouse named Sufficient Grounds. Located in an old, gray, two-story building on a side street, it was a gathering hub for various creative types. I even utilized it for Hardbodies related business at times. Something about the atmosphere reminded me of my old haunts in downtown Denver for which I still pined at the time. They also brewed excellent beer onsite.

Being the one producer without an actual day job, I was usually the first to arrive. I'd head upstairs and snag the two sofas facing each other. As I drank beer and waited for my cohorts, I alternated between making notes on the screenplay and jotting down ideas and plans for Hardbodies. This rainy January day was no exception. I stared out the window and watched from the warm comfort of my upstairs sofa as cold rain fell. Surrounded by art as eighties new wave filled the air, while water streaked across the foggy window. I contemplated the search for additional entertainers and overall expansion of my business when my phone rang.

"Hey, are you looking for strippers? I have experience," proclaimed an enthusiastic male voice.

And that's when Slade came into the fold. He'd done private parties and male revues consistently through the late-nineties and wanted to get back into performing on a steady basis. His experience checked out, which brings me to another one of my pet peeves. Applicants lying about having experience when they have none. After talking to them for thirty seconds, I know if they're telling the truth. There's a specific way that experienced strippers of either gender speak when talking shop. It's in the tiny details of performances and audiences. Things only experienced strippers would know because they're shared experiences. My experiences as a career private party stripper aren't at all uncommon amongst my peers.

Slade met the aesthetic requirements as per the photos he'd email later. He also had a friend who occasionally did parties and convinced me to bring him on board as well. In one fell swoop, Hardbodies went from one male stripper to three. Having Slade and Dylan on the roster left me to all sorts of new devices moving forward. Not only could I push for more bookings than I could cover by myself, but I could commence working on a male revue. I threw caution to the wind and thought big.

I could barely contain my excitement during the production meeting. It wasn't just the new talent that had me jacked. It was everything. Stripping, my own business, and making a film. I would even start composing music in anticipation of using it in the movie. All this combined would inevitably be a mixed bag, but I'd nevertheless make great strides through this new year. And when it came to stripping talent, things were only getting started. The best was truly yet to come, and it wouldn't be long.

CHAPTER 8

Seemingly five minutes after Slade and Dylan showed up on Hardbodies' doorstep, I received an email from Leah. She impressed me with her bachelor party experience, professional demeanor, and an assortment of topless and fully nude images. As a rule, I don't like receiving nude photos from applicants. Not only could an applicant be underage (thankfully a problem I've never endured), but such photos are mostly cringe. Both guys and girls have sent me snapshots of their genitals as if I wanted or needed to see that.

But Leah was an exception. Not only was she clearly over eighteen, and I mean that in the best way possible, but her photos were classy and professionally shot. And she was hot as hell. Leah was Hardbodies' first A squad female stripper. Fitting to a T the female stripper archetype I wanted for my agency. She was glamorous, athletically built, and had fake tits along with bleached blonde hair. Amber had bleached blonde hair too, but Leah's was obviously cut and colored by a professional stylist and not some relative or neighbor. And she received extra points for her love of leopard and zebra print.

   She also had an attractive girlfriend named Rachel whom she brought in for duo performances. That was huge, as guys requested this constantly. When it came to those, the booking fee merely guaranteed the presence of two female strippers at a party. Watching them go down on each other or ride a double-ended dildo were add-ons negotiable with the entertainers. And these didn't come cheap. I never took a cut of this money or any tips my entertainers made. My take was always half the booking fee.

   Beyond aesthetics, Leah was confident, gregarious, and educated. More than capable of charming men with her intellect and hot body all at once. Like me, she fully understood the importance of owning her shows and immediately establishing dominance over her audiences. I went along to one of her parties as security and was blown away at how she had men eating out of her hand. She was not only the most accomplished bachelor party entertainer Hardbodies ever had but the best I've ever seen.

   Along with having a steady day job, Leah was married. They were into some lifestyle stuff, and he was totally cool with her stripping at bachelor parties. I got the impression he was playing with Rachel too so that probably helped. He was never an issue, and that's all that mattered.

***

With Valentine's Day 2005 upon us, I spent everyone's favorite greeting card holiday entertaining a houseful of single ladies in Little Rock. It's a novel experience when I score a party that doesn't center around someone getting married or having a birthday. This event took place in a fifties ranch style home located within a cozy neighborhood west of Park Plaza Mall. I remember arriving to encounter an unusual cul-de-sac consisting of a narrow roadway wrapped around a sizeable patch of grass, trees, and rocks. Even after dark, it caught my notice.

Given that one of Arkansas' unofficial state mottos is "anyone is better than no one," I remain surprised all these years later that my client pulled together a dozen or so women with nothing else to do on Valentine's Day. It was a somewhat reserved audience, so nothing crazy happened. That's not to say they didn't have fun as we enjoyed lap dances and Reddi-wip all around. At one point, I changed into a black fishnet thong that I sometimes rocked with a g-string, but this time without. I suppose out of curiosity to see how wild they could be.

Not experiencing a spark with any of these ladies, I drove home to sleep alone. And that was perfectly fine. Things could've been worse as I contend there's no greater loneliness than being in a lousy relationship. It was a Monday night. I kept thinking it was Saturday. I was all out of whack. Right as I am about relationships for the sake of relationships being an awful idea, I was anxious to do something. And I preferred someone's company doing it. Whatever it may have been.

My entertainers and I weren't friends. I was the boss. Some guys were keen to visualize me surrounded by a harem of beautiful, naked women. But nothing could've been further from the truth. I only spoke to Amber when I had a party for her. Leah and I were only ever in the same place two or three times. And I never spoke to Rachel. I didn't consider her a Hardbodies entertainer. More a prop for Leah. This was fine with me. Not only did I represent entertainers strictly for the money, but I cringed at the idea of getting personal with them. That's what I'd hated about "real" jobs. Coworkers and bosses getting wrapped up in one another's personal bullshit. It brings nothing but trouble.

It was around this time that I began dating Rebecca. Chalk it up to my excitement over making a film combined with occasional boredom. We'd go out for dinner, drinks, and/or a movie. I'd also watch her perform in various community theatre productions. This was in addition to time spent working on our scenes together, which probably had something to with it. I imagine these dates provided her some degree of method acting motivation as our respective characters lived together.

Still, Rebecca was a "what the fuck was I thinking?" moment for me. We had little in common beyond a shared interest in both filmmaking and the unfairly maligned Richard Marx. Other guys found her attractive, but I'm not seeing it now. She wasn't particularly sexual and once admitted to having a thing for Jeff Goldblum. For a thirty-year-old woman, she was naïve about men. I don't want to sound mean, but for fuck's sake. At least she didn't go by Becky.

This was the genesis of the girlfriend by committee approach my personal life would take for years to come.

***

I spent the first quarter of 2005 getting accustomed to all these shiny new advancements. The carefree days of sleeping until noon were over and not a moment too soon. In less than a year, my agency had gone from one entertainer to five. And it wouldn't stop there. I utilized online advertising and Myspace to drum up bookings for all of us. And I launched the official Hardbodies Entertainment of Arkansas website. Version 1.0 rocking a flames-on-black aesthetic that screamed web design circa mid-2000s.

Applicants continued pouring in and being quickly rejected for all sorts of reasons. There was one criterion that stood above all others in evaluating would-be strippers. I'd ask myself, "Would I feel comfortable allowing this person into my home?" If the answer was no, and it most often was, there was no way my conscience would allow me to send that person to someone else's home. Regardless, most applicants disqualified themselves by demanding big money while offering nothing of value.

Not only was Harbdodies landing its own bookings, but we handled entertainer requests from out of state agencies that offered nationwide service. With some of these outfits scoring better search results yet having nowhere else to turn for entertainers, such arrangements helped me to build the Hardbodies brand at their expense. The downside was that these agencies weren't particularly honest and never shied away from lying to both us and clients. I would terminate all such working agreements before the end of the year after learning that every one of these agencies was slandering us to prospective clients while coming to me for help.

My own bookings kept coming. There was a bachelorette party thirty minutes northeast of Little Rock in Cabot. I don't know how to explain it, but there's the occasional party that embodies a dreamlike quality. The drive itself was tranquil. More so once I turned onto a street of older homes. There was one with several vehicles parked in front as colored lights flashing through the living room window. I was greeted by a group of buzzed twentysomethings full of life. In my cop persona, I made my way inside to bust my bachelorette named (ugh) Becky.

We did all the standard-issue fun including lap dances and Reddi-wip. They danced around me. Bright colors relentlessly bounced off white walls as we bumped and grinded to one hip hop groove after another. We sipped Bacardi Silver as midnight grew closer. I was loose and relaxed in a way I hadn't been in a few months. It felt so surreal. I didn't want the feeling to end and kept it going for as long as I could before girls started getting sleepy. The spell continued as I drove home and went to bed myself.

Perhaps I was worried that my performances were becoming formulaic regarding my personal sense of accomplishment. That stripping was turning into work and nothing more. I feared there eventually would be no magic for me at parties. The work aspect certainly didn't scare me. I founded Hardbodies for me to work constantly and ensure my efforts were better rewarded than they'd been by "real" employers. But I was addicted to that labor of love feeling. I never wanted it to end. Was I already getting tired of it all, or was it simply a lull? Would this be the price of growing my business? Only time would tell.

I soldiered forward with enthusiasm for the big picture. After all, I was working for myself and had others working for me. That alone meant I was living the dream. And I never took it for granted. The film project also kept me busy with its constant barrage of production meetings and rehearsals located throughout Central Arkansas. The combined inexperience of everyone involved became increasingly obvious as time went on, but I didn't care. There was no rest for the wicked, and I preferred it that way.

***

Hardbodies picked up two more entertainers before the end of March. The first was a dude named Viper. He rolled into town from the Washington D.C. area where he'd racked up private party and male revue experience. He also had a day job that would not tolerate him fucking up in any way, which was to my benefit. As meticulous as my screening process was, there was always the lingering threat of an entertainer dragging me into the middle of a civil or criminal mess. It would take only a single thoughtless act to bring everything crashing down upon me.

Viper only stuck around for a few weeks before deciding he didn't want to risk losing his job due to stripping on the side. I gave my well wishes and promptly forgot about him.

The second entertainer who came on board was a beautiful, statuesque nineteen-year-old brunette whose athletic physique was punctuated by a terrific ass and a pair of the most expertly sculpted breast implants I've ever seen. Along with her physical attributes, I was impressed with her maturity as well as a sense of professionalism, lack of sentimentality, and naked ambitiousness that reminded me of mine. She believed herself too good for the local gentlemen's clubs and was goddamn right.

My lull ended, and Hardbodies changed forever when Kyra arrived on the scene.

CHAPTER 9

"Who does she remind me of?" I asked Kyra.

"*Desperately Seeking Susan*-era Madonna?" she offered on point.

"Thank you," I replied.

Kyra and I were instantly on the same frequency. She hit the ground running as Hardbodies exploded into Spring 2005. I felt rejuvenated and ready to take my game to new and even more provocative heights. And I now had a roster of entertainers to help get me there. I wondered how I'd keep them busy with at least two bookings per month each, but that concern worked itself out easily enough. Aside from Viper bailing almost immediately, Dylan proved fucking useless. Whining about every booking I sent his way. His typical response being one of my biggest pet peeves regarding subordinates:

"Why don't you ask Slade to do it?"

"Because I'm asking you to do it," I'd retort in unflinching boss mode.

I finally stopped calling him altogether as I wouldn't beg someone to make money while being doted on by a roomful of women. Slade and I were soon joined by one of my Denver cohorts named Brandon. He'd moved to Dallas and subsequently helped Hardbodies expand into Northeastern Texas. I still took the lion's share of male stripper bookings, but I had the most availability. More importantly, I had no qualms about spending my Friday and Saturday nights tearing up bachelorette and birthday parties throughout the region. And my reputation as a great entertainer was starting to precede me. Also, it was my agency. Let any of them start their own and feel my pain.

As much as I appreciated Leah's talent and Amber's… um… availability, Kyra quickly became my favorite once I saw her perform. It was her first Hardbodies gig. A poolside birthday party in Sherwood, because of course it was. I saw why her talents were wasted in the local strip clubs, and it wasn't only for her stunning looks. The girl was an unequivocal force of nature. Brilliantly owning her audience from start to finish. Though she lacked Leah's polish, it worked to her advantage. She was so confident and in control of her sexuality for a woman of any age. Much less one who was nineteen.

Kyra's birthday boy was a man old enough to be her father, yet she had him willfully and happily at her mercy. When he touched her anywhere, it was because she made him. Her lap dance balanced tease and sleaze in an effortless manner that wowed every man and woman in attendance. Seamlessly moving from chatting with him to smothering his face with her ample titties. And then back to chatting as she slowly slid off his lap to her knees and stared seductively at him from between his legs. I was jaded about receiving lap dances by this point, yet I couldn't wait for the inevitable moment when she'd give me one.

With our client thoroughly convinced that the birthday boy would dick her extra deep that night, Kyra and I split for a bachelorette party I had in downtown Little Rock. Not only was it convenient to bring her along, but she was excited about seeing me in action. She wanted to learn from watching me and apply that to her performances. This was not an isolated thing. Multiple female strippers over the years expressed the same sentiment. Would-be male strippers typically weren't interested in learning shit. It's the biggest reason why I enjoyed working with girls far more than guys during my career.

We arrived in the River Market and strutted to the hotel. The party was in a suite packed with approximately twenty girls. Most of whom were sufficiently buzzed by this time. With Kyra in tow as my personal assistant, I made my entrance as a cop and interrogated the bachelorette before giving her a lap dance. It was quite the luxury to have someone keep an eye on my stuff as I performed. While the bachelorette was friendly and polite, she was shy and a little uncomfortable no matter how easy I went. Her friends and Kyra offered encouragement to no avail.

The other girls were also shy, except for one. She'd met us with the client in the lobby beforehand, where Kyra and I had our exchange about who she looked like. There are occasions when the saving grace is one girl who clicks with me, and the party is suddenly brought to life. I focused my attention on Madonna as she sat in a recliner and followed my lead with every move I made. The other girls immediately split into two camps. One worried that things were going too far. The other desperately seeking a wild show.

Between Kyra and Madonna, I was incredibly turned on by this point. I bumped and grinded my hard, g-string clad cock between Madonna's tits and positioned myself on the recliner with my crotch in her face. Grabbing her hair and thrusting my pelvis in her face. That's when Kyra chimed in and nearly made me fall off the chair.

"You should totally suck his cock," she offered as if no big deal.

Madonna responded by removing my cock from its g-string prison cell and sucking it. Half the girls instantly fled the suite. The other half exploded with delight. And no one was more delighted than the bachelorette as she put her face close to the action. Kyra and the client teamed up to encourage us. The other girls giggled incessantly and talked about how unbelievably hot this was. I was excited to find something the bachelorette loved. And the blowjob was pretty bitchin' too.

Madonna had legit technique as I would expect from a woman who sort of looked and dressed like a young Material Girl. With the recliner arms starting to kill my knees, we moved to the king-size bed. Everyone else piled around us. Kyra and the bachelorette remained up close and personal, with the latter opining about her love of voyeurism. This constituted the remainder of my performance.

The girls prepared to hit the bars. Madonna provided play by play as I dressed. She was into me, and I was down for returning the favor and then some. Only Kyra noticed when Madonna stealthily wrote down and slipped me her phone and room numbers for later. It was our little secret. Lest any of her friends immediately descend into full cockblocking mode. I said goodnight and left with Kyra. Before taking her home, she agreed to stop for dinner since we were starving.

We drove to the nearest IHOP. The only restaurant still open at that hour not named Waffle House. As I refueled for my impending rendezvous with Madonna, Kyra and I conversed about the night and what we had in mind moving forward. It amazed me how much we had in common. Perhaps too much. It felt like I was talking to myself at times. She seemed like a female version of me in certain regards. Not only as a stripper but as a person. And while she'd prove herself prone to melodramatic outbursts at times, I'd chalk that up to her being a woman of twentyish.

She also wasn't one to beat around the bush as she asked, "So, are you going to hook up with that girl?"

"Yeah," I responded nonchalantly as if asked about the weather.

Her next words were like a two-by-four across the face:

"Can I come, too?"

When I launched Hardbodies, I swore that I'd never fool around with my girls. And that was a stupid pledge to make. It wasn't an issue of utilizing casting couch tactics or demanding sexual favors in exchange for work. That's something I would never do in a million years if for no other reason than I never wanted to get laid on any basis other than the merits of my attractiveness to a given woman. If one of my girls and I were to click on a personal level, one that didn't negatively affect the agency or other entertainers, then what was the big deal? Self-denial is not mutually inclusive with professionalism. But I didn't always see that. I would've made a great Calvinist.

But my subconscious was clearly clear on this matter as I responded, "Yeah, if she's cool with it."

"Oh, trust me. She will be," laughed Kyra without a hint of nervousness.

We resumed our conversation about stripping as we finished eating before leaving for what was now our late-night rendezvous with Madonna. This wouldn't be my first experience with two girls at once but may as well have been. Excitement and anticipation hung thick in the air between Kyra and me. Bright lights and shadows fell upon us relentlessly while "Disco Inferno" by 50 Cent blasted from the speakers. The mutual physical attraction between us was one thing. And I already knew she liked girls. But nothing could have prepared me for this. I imagine it was the same for her.

I called Madonna to let her know I was on my way.

"I'm waiting for you," she cooed.

I dropped the bombshell, "Kyra is coming with me."

"Ooh. Even better," she responded enthusiastically.

"You were right," I said to Kyra as I hung up.

"Yeah," Kyra responded with sassy authority.

Upon returning to the hotel, we each made a pit stop in our respective restroom to primp before heading up to see Madonna. Kyra and I were on a mission as we rode the elevator in silence. Nothing could break our focus. I wasn't sure if we were on our way to seduce this girl or assassinate her. Either way, we were taking no prisoners.

Madonna invited us into her room. Illuminated only by city lights invading through its window. Music played on her laptop as she handed Kyra and I each a watermelon flavored Bacardi Silver. I was already feeling a buzz from the sheer magnitude of the situation at hand. As we danced together, I leaned in to kiss Madonna. Our tongues danced with all the intensity of two people hell-bent on finishing what they'd started earlier. Then it was Kyra's turn to lock lips with Madonna. In what would prove to be true Kyra fashion, her competitive streak drove her to demonstrate she could hold her own against me with any girl.

Upon breaking their oral embrace, we all stood in silence as Madonna stared at Kyra and me to say it was our turn. As attracted as I was to Kyra, I'd yet to allow myself one concrete sexual thought about her. Partly due to my promise and because I still didn't know what to make of her. But since we were all living in the moment together, I grabbed Kyra by the back of her head and pulled her lips onto mine.

This kiss was even better than the one I shared with Madonna because there was something special about it. No, it wasn't love. Besides the obvious thrill of Kyra and me finally indulging in our mutual attraction, there was an undeniable feeling of comfort. It told me everything I could expect from her over the next two years. Like me, she had her flaws and much to learn about life, but she would always be true to our shared cause. Never attempting to placate me or blow smoke up my ass. Challenging me every step of the way with great expectations. Making her the perfect foil to me as an entertainer and entrepreneur.

Enough with the kissing. It was time to have some fun with Madonna. Kyra and I undressed her, laid her on the bed, and took turns licking and fingering her pussy. It was a contest between Kyra and me, and Madonna was the biggest winner of all. Kyra sat on Madonna's face as I fucked her. Kyra and I laughed and egged on each other as we each got off watching what the other was doing. As Madonna experienced a vicious orgasm, Kyra leaned in and kissed me before giving me one of the sexiest looks ever.

"Save some of that for me," she demanded.

Madonna sat spread eagle against the headboard, and Kyra got on all fours. As she ate Madonna's pussy, I got behind my partner and grabbed onto her firm, round ass, Sliding my cock deep inside her pussy. With that arbitrary point of no return in my rearview mirror, I fucked her with all the reckless abandon my heart desired. I was living the dream. Fucking one hot girl as she ate out another hot girl. I would've been an asshole not to seize this opportunity by the throat. I've made some idiotic decisions in my life, but this was not one of them.

Once playtime was finished, Kyra and I said a final farewell to Madonna and made our exit into the early Sunday morning hours. The drive to Kyra's was made mostly in silence. She was getting sleepy. I was totally fucking wired. While figuratively in the mood to jerk-off over my accomplishments that night, I nevertheless began to question whether I had committed an unforgivable sin against my internalized definition of consummate professionalism. Kyra was experiencing the same crisis of conscience.

"Are you going to keep sending me parties?" she asked with the first twinge of nervousness I'd witnessed from her.

"Of course," I replied without hesitation.

We resumed our silence. It was truly the dead of night with hardly any other vehicles on the road as I drove across Little Rock. After dropping off Kyra and watching to make sure she got inside her apartment safely, I headed for home and my own empty bed waiting for me. There was nothing else to do except compartmentalize the thoughts racing through my head. My promise was broken. Yet I felt so alive.

CHAPTER 10

From my wild night with Kyra and Madonna emerged PussyQuest 2005. My name for a 48-hour stretch in April 2005 during which I had sex with four different women. None of whom were Kyra or, thank God, Rebecca. I'd decided that I would seduce as many hot girls as I could. And that's what I did over the most decadent three-day weekend of my life. I didn't know from where this raging promiscuity came. Maybe I wanted to know how sexually desirable to women I truly was. Whatever the reason, I gladly freefell into this carnal abyss.

PussyQuest 2005 commenced on a Thursday night with two events. The first was a going-away party in Little Rock I did as a favor to an agency in Dallas. It was a white trash audience that didn't tip and acted too good for me. This is probably why they never contacted

Hardbodies and went straight for an agency that made promises it could never keep. And no, none of these women participated in PussyQuest 2005.

It was at the second event, a bachelorette party also in Little Rock, that I kicked off PussyQuest 2005 with a bang. A great crowd with solid energy. I had a blast entertaining them. This party was much more fun and profitable than its predecessor. The girls were classier for sure. A pair of hot blondes matched my energy in lockstep throughout the show as the other girls began to fatigue during the back half. By the end, I had my dynamic duo side by side on a loveseat as we did shots together. I talked them into flashing their tits and making out with one another as the other girls giggled and feigned shock.

"What happens at the bachelorette party stays at the bachelorette party," I reminded everyone.

What happened at this bachelorette party continued at another venue. This night I wasn't driving home after the party. I was on my way to keep celebrating with Heather and Candice at the former's home. Still feeling cocky about my threesome two weeks prior, I was all over the possibility of instigating another so quickly. Anticipation be damned. I knew to play it cool. Even a sexual encounter as momentous as this requires an "I can take it or leave it" attitude. No one likes a desperate person. Least of all me.

It was a small home on the west side of town. The seventies architecture extended from outside to indoors. Complete with shag carpeting and paneled boxed beams. Dated yet stylish without being campy. There was also a lava lamp, but this was clearly nineties vintage. Probably a dorm room souvenir. Which would be fitting since these two had been best friends and roommates in college. With Candice now living on the East Coast, they had precious little time to relive the good old days. Every moment counted. I sat on the sofa and sipped Grey Goose and cranberry juice as they fulfilled the 42nd Street grindhouse stereotype of college girls before my eyes.

With coffee table pushed to the side, Heather and Candice danced and made out as "Hypnotize" by Notorious B.I.G. played. "This was our college jam!" they exclaimed. As they exclaimed for every song that played. But was I complaining? Fuck no.

They continued dancing as they stripped each other. Now topless, Heather went for her purse to retrieve the can of Reddi-wip leftover from my performance. Ever the gentleman, I provided encouragement as they licked and sucked whipped cream off each other's nipples. Then it was my turn as they each straddled one of my legs and leaned in close. I'd already had my fill of Reddi-wip that night, but I couldn't say no to four perky tits right in my face.

Heather laid a blanket on the carpet. She and Candice finished stripping each other until they were completely naked. They kissed and giggled while play arguing over who would go down on whom first.

"Why don't you go down on each other at the same time?" I suggested as if directing my own personal girl on girl porn.

They laughed hysterically at this and assumed the position. With alcohol working its magic on all three of us, I continued offering encouragement as I got on the floor and up close to the action.

Heather ran off to the bedroom and returned with a blindfold. Each of us taking a turn wearing it as we played a game called Guess Who's Going Down on You. I fucked Candice as Heather cheered us on. Then they switched places. I left Heather's place late that night lugging my enormous cock in both hands after scoring two threesomes so close together. And I still had Friday and Saturday night ahead of me.

***

Although the Hardbodies male revue was still a work in progress, I was taking part in club performances by groups passing through the region. This allowed me to pass out business cards and make a few bucks to boot. These outfits would either license (or steal) well-known names like Chippendales and Men of Playgirl. Or create a fancy-sounding moniker like Hollywood Male Stripshow or something similarly contrived. It was always a bunch of guys who had never performed for the Chippendales Las Vegas show or posed for *Playgirl*. Not that they were missing out on much from not doing either.

The second night of PussyQuest 2005 took me all the way to Fort Smith, Arkansas for a male revue with Men of Playgirl this time. I think. It was hard to tell. None of these guys seemed to agree on what they were called. I still use the Men of Playgirl credit on my stripping resume to this day. I should mention that I spoke with *Playgirl* the previous summer about appearing in a photo spread. My idea was to work with a photographer acquaintance out of Detroit as I liked her portraiture work and felt comfortable with her. I also wanted to shoot on a rundown farm near Texarkana. The magazine said no to all of that. In hindsight, I'm glad it fell through.

Anyway, the Men of Insert Generic Male Revue Name Here gifted the ladies of Fort Smith with a run of the mill male revue on a warm April night. The manager of this crew was a smarmy motherfucker with a Napoleon complex. I didn't like him or this other dude who'd taken on a self-styled house mom role. That was fucking weird and unprecedented for a group of male strippers as house moms are strictly a gentlemen's club thing. Seriously, he was trying to sell me condoms and shit. Of course, I had my own condoms. Magnums. This was PussyQuest 2005 after all.

I got along best with the third member of the crew. He was less experienced but more gregarious and enjoyable to watch than either of his cohorts who had fallen into the trap of being too polished and refined for their own good. Solid entertainers who earned every dollar. But they'd lost (or never possessed) the ability to make a legit human connection with their audience. A trap I would fall into one day. But for now, I ran on the naked ambition that had been sustaining me over the past twelve months. And it showed as I took to the stage. A firefighting beast who stalked his vast audience of overstimulated ladies for gratuity like a man on a suicide mission.

I hung out by the bar afterward and surveyed my surroundings while downing Coronas. Getting a laugh out of watching General Tom Thumb fail to find a single buyer for his autographed 8x10s. I noticed several guys lined up in chairs at the back of the club slipping money to a pretty, petite, and sassy brunette as she strutted the line back and forth. She had these sexy eighties dance moves and knew how to work an audience. Motivated by my personal intrigue and concern that someone may rat her out, I walked over and introduced myself to Destiny.

She was excited to meet me. Excited enough that she didn't mind when I dismissed her clients with a dirty look. Once they straggled off, I asked for a lap dance of my own. I can't even remember the song as I was transfixed on her performance. Raw enthusiasm and sexual energy carried her from start to finish. I asked her where she worked, and she named some strip joint to the north in Fayetteville. She'd attended the male revue to observe the operation and see if she could learn anything. This fascinated me as I would go see female strippers in Denver when I started for the same reason. It's how I learned much of what I know about working individual audience members.

As we drank at the bar, I asked Destiny what she'd learned tonight. She remarked about my "obvious and genuine" enthusiasm for performing. That it made her want to focus on her own passion for entertaining others. We then shared an uncomfortable silence while looking at each other. Taking this as a green light, I asked her if she'd accompany me to my motel room across the street. She accepted, and we made our exit. As we walked through the parking lot, we passed dude still trying in vain to sell his stupid photos that no one wanted. He looked further dejected as we strolled past and bid him goodnight.

What happened next was perhaps the most Arkansas one-night stand ever. Upon entering my room, Destiny turned on the radio and found a country station. She slipped off her sandals, stood on the bed, and stripped naked to "Amarillo by Morning" by George Fucking Strait in quasi-Lynchian glory. When the song ended, she jumped into my arms and kissed me. We then banged to the sound of classic country, although I tuned it out since I'm not a country fan. And I was too preoccupied with her to care fuck all about what was on the radio.

It was around 3:00am when we finished. I had to leave in three hours to do some film shooting. Destiny and I took turns drifting in and out of slumber as we laid facing each other. She was slipping into angel of the morning territory. That concerned me. After showering, I shaved my face as she held me from behind. I gave her a goodbye kiss and sent her on her way before hitting the road myself. We stayed in touch via email for a brief period afterward. Although I liked her, she lived too far away, and we had nothing in common besides stripping. And even then, she wasn't interested in doing private parties.

***

Now feeling the fatigue of all this stripping and fucking along with filming and various daily errands, I was running on pure adrenaline by Saturday night. I don't even remember much about the bachelorette party I had in Hot Springs. Most of my time was spent with the bachelorette as the other girls hid in the kitchen. That irks me to no end. Be a fucking adult and let yourself enjoy the performance if for no other reason than to show politeness towards your entertainer. The client took a few lap dances of her own. Single-mindedly obsessing over my g-string. She wanted it as a souvenir. I asked her what she would give me in return.

The other girls left after the show. I watched them as I sat in my truck and waited. Once the coast was clear, the client called and invited me back inside. She was an attractive blonde, but I was strictly padding my stats by this point. And she just wanted to fuck a stripper for her own personal satisfaction. The sex wasn't bad, but it wasn't exceptional either. Quick and dirty. Thank God because I was ready to pass out from exhaustion. I kept up my end of the deal and gifted her my blue g-string. As I drove home, I began to worry that this arrangement made me a john. And so ended PussyQuest 2005.

After a few hours of sleep, it was back to shooting bright and early on a beautiful Sunday morning. Since my character was an insomniac, I was able to explain away my obvious sleep deprivation as method acting. Not that I was fooling anyone. I'd been sharing the details of my sexual exploits online. The film's director passed them onto Rebecca. She didn't disapprove of my activities so much as she frowned upon people engaging in and documenting sexual activity in general. I didn't give a fuck what she or anyone else thought. This was what my life had become, and I fucking went with it.

CHAPTER 11

   With PussyQuest 2005 and a taste of the Gene Simmons lifestyle behind me, I got seriously cranking on business. And just in time. If April showers bring May flowers, then Hardbodies was in full fucking bloom by May 2005. Balls to the wall as my entertainers and I repeatedly crisscrossed Arkansas and beyond night after night. I also began adding muscle to my frame and brought myself up to an even 200 lbs. This caused issues with my filmmaking cohorts. Although shooting was to have wrapped by now, it was nowhere near finished. With no apologies for having a business to run, I stuck with my plan to bulk.

  Perhaps the biggest myth about exotic entertainment agencies is that you can choose your entertainer. This is rarely an option anywhere as good private party strippers are few and far between. And by good, I don't mean just looks. A good stripper must show up and deliver a solid performance every time. It's akin to asking for the moon and why I was always tough with clients who insisted on nitpicking and complaining about my entertainers for the sake of being difficult. Especially in a market like Arkansas.

There's also the matter of specialization. It was fascinating to watch my female strippers carve out distinct niches. Leah was the bachelor party specialist both on her own and working in tandem with Rachel. In either scenario, she knew how to push the envelope and dominate a roomful of men. Amber had an all-purpose quality, and it wasn't necessarily bad. Her solid yet unspectacular performance style made her ideal for clients not wanting something too racy.

Although she shared Leah's headstrong tendencies and penchant for delivering overtly provocative performances, Kyra wasn't clicking with bachelor party audiences. I didn't click with these guys either. They were the clients with whom I had the hardest time dealing. The notion of a guys' night or weekend doesn't exist in my world. Compounding the matter was Kyra's insistence that I accompany her to every booking. She felt more comfortable with me present. While flattered, I had more important things to do than run security at bachelor parties. And I mingled with those guys about as well as she did.

The guys were an issue. I overheard more than a few disparaging remarks about her. Typically, regarding her height or preference for rocking black fishnet tops. It was extremely petty as she was gorgeous with a sexy sense of style. Her failure to connect with these assholes was not for lack of effort. She even had a cute blonde girlfriend named Jessy for hot girl on girl action. At one bachelor party, I held Jessy's legs open as Kyra ate her pussy. We ensured the bachelor had an up-close view of the action, and yet the client still bitched and complained about Kyra. Nevertheless, he referred us to someone for another bachelor party. Whatever.

Kyra did exceptionally well with coed audiences such as those at birthday parties. It also wasn't a stretch for me to sell these clients on booking us as a duo. I was able to do the same thing with bachelorette party clients looking to splurge on something extra sexy and unique. Kyra and I became professional partners in crime to smashing effect. We also continued our sexual involvement in secrecy, which was ridiculous. It's not like us strippers all hung out together. Clients picked up on our involvement right away. It was plain as day when we pushed the envelope with each other to achieve ultra-provocative performances. Like the birthday party where she sucked my cock before giving the birthday boy a special treat by eating out his wife.

I had plenty of solo bookings as well in May 2005. Such as the night I had two bachelorette parties in Northeast Arkansas. The first was at a community event space outside Pocahontas where I was greeted by a mob of attractive and glamorous young women. Many of whom, when not getting personal with me, rode a giant inflatable dick several at a time. It was always amazing to enter the sticks and encounter the sort of party girls you'd expect to find in, say, Miami. They were a fucking blast to boot.

As were the ladies at the second party thirty minutes away in Paragould. These girls and I danced on tables in the banquet room of the local country club. Afterward, I drove three miles east. Entering Missouri just to say I'd been there. Then making the long yet magical drive home down U.S. 49 through Jonesboro and various small farming communities. Reveling in the rural ambiance with music blasting until catching I-40 at Forrest City.

Speaking of Forrest City, I did a bachelorette party there as well that month. One of those, "Why the fuck did you even call me in the first place?" bookings that I get every so often. This is when I enter a room full of resting bitch faces seated with arms folded who preemptively dislike me. As I've always ensured my clients know exactly what they're getting in an entertainer, there's no excuse for this. I was out of there after ten minutes.

The following night more than made up for that disappointment with two great parties. Unlike the Pocahontas/Paragould bachelorette party extravaganza, these two were nearly three hours apart but so fucking worth it. I drove eighty minutes west to Russellville for a going away party. This went down at 6:00pm and only lasted about fifteen minutes. It was quick and dirty, but that's all they wanted. The client not only tipped me $100 upfront but fixed a plate of mini quiches and tiny chicken salad sandwiches for my nearly three-hour drive to Hope.

I arrived in Hope, birthplace of Bill Clinton, around 9:15pm for a bachelorette celebration with attractive twentysomethings in cute and sexy party dresses. A sweet and fun-loving group who expressed appreciation for my long journey that night. It meant a lot to me as there are audiences who take for granted all that I do for them. Gratitude makes it easier for me to cut loose and have even naughtier fun with my audiences. In this instance, and without remembering how it came about, I wound up titty fucking some of the girls. For all involved, it seemed like the thing to do.

***

Federico Fellini's *La Dolce Vita* is one of my favorite films. Its narrative framework being perhaps the single biggest influence on my writing style. And it's the closest thing to an accurate cinematic portrayal of male strippers ever produced. Change Marcello Rubini's profession from tabloid journalist to stripper and the film still works. I know *8 1/2* is generally considered the piece de resistance of Fellini's oeuvre, and I greatly enjoy it as well. For my subjective money, however, *La Dolce Vita* is his finest moment.

It's a film I watched repeatedly during the summer of 2005. Or, more accurately, played while working on stripping related business. Other cinematic favorites around this time were Andrei Tarkovsky's *Stalker* and Wim Winders' *Wings of Desire*, but *La Dolce Vita* was my go-to celluloid gem. Not only did I spot parallels between Marcello and me regarding our respective chick issues, but the supporting characters reminded me so much of the people I encountered night after night. That was Fellini's greatest strength as a director. An uncanny ability to provoke the most realistic human behavior from actors I've ever seen on film.

Brief lulls aside, Hardbodies held steady through the summer. I continued knocking out party after party, either solo or in tandem with Kyra, while also keeping my other strippers reasonably busy. The film project dragged on. Though getting tired of the whole thing, I enjoyed engaging with people far more colorful than the film's characters.

Like an actor named Daniel. Something of a paradox in that he owned multiple cars equipped with powerful V8 engines yet was afraid to drive on the Interstate. I had to back one such vehicle, a decommissioned Crown Victoria pursuit special with a 460 ci power plant, out of a long driveway for him because he couldn't do it. I was also charged with teaching him how to dress formally for one scene. Showing what he'd learned by arriving in a navy suit with white socks, brown loafers, and a black belt.

Rebecca and I continued going on dates that typically consisted of dinner and a movie. Kyra would remark about how cute that was. Whether she was antagonizing me for reasons right or wrong still escapes me, but maybe she was onto something. As much as I want to slag on Rebecca, she provided me with a sort of simple, no-frills companionship that I probably needed. Kyra and I did little more together than work and fuck. When we did go out, it was always somehow tied to business. Between Rebecca and Kyra, the girlfriend by committee was in full swing.

Being consumed by Hardbodies, the film project, the girlfriend by committee, and more was probably why I never noticed Beth. Okay, I noticed her. But I didn't notice that she was making a concentrated effort to get my attention. And I didn't realize what she was doing until I began researching my history for this memoir. I'm not even sure her name is Beth, but I want to say it is. I'm embarrassed by how dense I was about the whole thing for all these years.

I made Beth's acquaintance via Myspace. Like Rebecca, she was a stage actress in local community theatre productions. She didn't know about Rebecca or Kyra since I never made mention of them on the platform. Rebecca wasn't even on Myspace, and Kyra was rarely active. Beth and I became social media friends. She'd regularly comment on my posts and vice versa. Petite and attractive with reddish-brown hair, she had an overall sense of class and style about her. I enjoyed our online exchanges but didn't give her much thought beyond that.

This was around the time I kissed a bachelorette one night in Little Rock. I know how sleazy that sounds on the surface, but the context makes it one of the most poignant moments of my career.

It was another successful performance on my part. But a strange tension between the bride-to-be and her friends hung in the air from start to finish. As I walked back to my truck afterward, she caught up with me and asked if I had a few minutes to chat. We sat on the tailgate and drank Raspberry Bacardi Silver while she opened up about her impending nuptials. She was tying the knot with a man she didn't love. Whom she felt pressured by family and friends to marry. She thanked me for making her bachelorette party the best part of this entire experience. And for making her feel comfortable enough to confess this secret to me.

We then simultaneously leaned into each other for a kiss. It may have been inappropriate, but it felt natural. There wasn't any tongue action. Just our lips softly pressed together for a moment as we sought emotional refuge within each other's warmth. She was surrounded by other people yet was so alone. I knew that feeling all too well. Our kiss goodnight was a show of mutual understanding and a brief grasp at comfort for both of us. We were two ships passing in the night as per the great Ian Hunter. I still get chills thinking about it all these years later.

***

One of the most popular misconceptions about my industry is that stripping sells itself. Nothing could be further from the truth with scores of indirect competition options available for parties. My success as an agent was built on being a hard closer with prospective clients. Even when I received calls from people who immediately told me, "Shut up and take my money!" I still impressed upon them every single way that doing business with me would make their party the absolute best. It's easy for clients to get wary about how much they're spending on a party and start cutting amenities. I had to ensure that my clients remained fired up about their stripper from start to finish. It's why so few agencies last. If you can't close sales, then you can't keep the doors open.

Remember Viper? The male stripper who was briefly with Hardbodies in early 2005? He and his wife resurfaced in August with their own agency named Hog Wild Dancers.

The University of Arkansas Razorback football program is a huge fucking deal throughout Arkansas, save for the Jonesboro area and its ASU Red Wolves. It's common for businesses to capitalize on this phenomenon by having names that evoke visions of Razorback football. But you don't use the word "hog" in the name of a business that ostensibly specializes in selling attractive people. Granted, their entertainers weren't all that attractive, but that's beside the point.

I reached out to Viper and his wife for the sake of being a friendly competitor. It's something rarely seen in this industry. And I already had enough would-be competitors slandering Hardbodies left and right. I also felt compelled to warn them about Freaky Tales, whom they'd picked up as an entertainer. They had male and female strippers. Mostly Hardbodies rejects. The Hog Wild Dancers logo was an illustration of three anthropomorphic pigs dancing over the agency name, which was in some god-awful font straight off the cover of a children's book. This was a stillborn business venture if I ever saw one, and I've seen many.

When Viper's wife called me one day in tears because they weren't scoring any bookings, I didn't know what to say. I asked her how she was closing her clients, and she had no idea what that meant. The only advice I could offer her was to not let prospective clients off the phone without telling them how great their entertainers are. Of course, that wasn't true. Everything about Hog Wild Dancers was shit and everyone knew it. They couldn't hold a candle to Hardbodies. Amber was my weakest female stripper yet superior to all three Hog Wild girls combined. On a personal level, I liked Viper and his wife. I liked them enough to cut them off so this abomination of a talent agency could die a quick death. Allowing them to move on with their lives.

That agency may have sucked, but I'd take 1,000 Hog Wild Dancers every day over future competitors who had no qualms about slandering Hardbodies or stealing my intellectual property. This industry is filled with people seeking easy money. Wasting no time resorting to desperate measures when they fail to become wealthy overnight. I never expected Hardbodies to be smooth sailing. Yet even I wasn't fully prepared for how extremely fucking difficult it is to run a successful business in this industry. Although I have no regrets, I have one word of advice for anyone thinking of starting an exotic entertainment agency: Don't.

CHAPTER 12

As summer segued into fall, I found myself knee-deep in the hoopla of preparing for the first Hardbodies male revue. I was no longer the leading man in the film project. My character had been continually rewritten so extensively that I no longer recognized him. As better actors also failed to grasp the character, he was scrapped and yet another draft of the screenplay was written. I remained on board as a producer but continued losing interest. My attention to Hardbodies became increasingly undivided as it should've been in the first place.

The show was booked at a nightclub in Hot Springs. I canvassed the area with flyers and hit up female-centric businesses such as boutiques and beauty salons. So naked was my ambition that I covered nearby towns like Arkadelphia, Benton, Glenwood, and Mount Ida. I visited

Malvern one sunny weekday afternoon. Upon entering a tanning salon to drop off some flyers, I noticed a vaguely familiar face looking at me curiously. Being so wrapped up in my own world at the time, I paid no mind and left. As I began walking down the street to the next business, I heard a soft voice behind me:

"Are you Stefan Diamante?"

I turned around to see the smiling face of the girl from the tanning salon, whom I finally recognized as Beth. We chatted for a moment about things I don't remember beyond her saying she planned to attend the show. I said, in strictly business mode, that I looked forward to seeing her there and went about my way like the obtuse jerk I was in that moment.

It was around this time when Chantelle entered the Hardbodies universe. A veteran performer in upscale East Coast gentlemen's clubs. Family circumstances brought her to Arkansas. A thirtysomething blonde with a killer body and exquisite breast implants. I didn't blame her for being proud of her tits. She sent me several topless photos to share with prospective clients, and I'm looking at one as I write this. With every booking, she'd ask, "You showed them my tits, right?" Chantelle was Amber on steroids. Not the wild child that Kyra and Leah were, but a sweet and fun entertainer perfect for more conservative (so to speak) bachelor and birthday parties. We enjoyed regular phone conversations on a variety of topics. She was the closest I came to a friend without benefits amongst my entertainers.

It was November. In less than a year, Hardbodies had grown from one female stripper to four. And I had one other male stripper in Slade to handle parties when needed. Brandon in Dallas having quit weeks earlier after finding Jesus or something. Enough personnel to handle nearly every request. But not enough to satisfy my naked ambition. Wanting more entertainers and a fuckload more bookings, I invested in a full-color yellow pages ad in multiple editions for 2006. Next year couldn't get here fast enough as I raged hard to blow up this entire region.

***

November brought the first Hardbodies Entertainment of Arkansas male revue at the now-defunct Club 2720 in Hot Springs. Going head to head that night with the annual "cheapest group of four guys we could find" male revue at the Electric Cowboy in Little Rock. I'm not joking. That's exactly what the Cowboy general manager, some nasty old bag named Phyllis, told me when I inquired. Our show was in a great location next to Lake Hamilton in beautiful Hot Springs as opposed to the crack infested ghetto that is Southwest Little Rock. Our show was fucking superior as well with fire, motorcycles, and live rock and roll. I lost money, but my objective was to use the show as a loss leader for scoring private parties.

Along with yours truly, the lineup consisted of Slade, Dylan, and Dylan's younger brother Chase. I scraped the bottom of the barrel with Chase, but he was the best option available to fill that fourth slot. The sort of young, scrawny, and boyish stripper that horny old broads in 2018 totally lose their shit over. But standards were different (read: better) in 2005. There was also the issue of this vogueing garbage he did as if trapped in 1990. I did what I could to get him prepared, stuck him in the final slot to take advantage of the audience at its most intoxicated, and hoped for the best.

Kyra was slated to be present as my personal assistant and part of my stage performance, but I scored her a birthday party in Little Rock that night. Chantelle offered to replace her. I had her stick to the original plan of attending the Electric Cowboy male revue and reporting back to me (she said it sucked). It was always my dream to incorporate female strippers into male revues and present audiences with erotic scenarios akin to a Jackie Collins novel come to life. I don't get why male revues must be a fucking sausage fest, but I digress.

With so much on my plate, I still needed an assistant, if nothing else. So, I pressed Rebecca into service. She did an excellent job despite being in, what was for her, Sodom and Gomorrah, as she'd never been anywhere near a male revue before that night. Along with serving as my liaison with club management, she spotted Dylan placing his own business cards on every table before the show and picked up each one before the crowd arrived. Perhaps I wouldn't have minded Dylan pulling that stunt had he not done fuck all to promote the show.

We performed to a packed house. Along with my roles of entertainer and manager, I served as the emcee with my nonstop banter and calls to action for tipping. Slade got us started by hitting the stage as a cowboy to the theme from *The Good, The Bad, and the Ugly* before immediately jumping into the crowd and stripping among screaming women. I totally dug it as it was way cooler than dancing alone on stage like a jackass. Or, even worse, dancing in synchronization with other dudes.

Dylan was next as he rode his crotch rocket through the audience to the stage. His set peaked there as he spent the next few minutes twirling glowsticks on strings. He wasn't supposed to do that, and I was just as annoyed as the audience. I picked up my banter on the mic as best I could while prepping to perform next and win back the crowd.

Speaking of the "male strippers as boy band" analogy… The entire reason I got into stripping, besides money, was to live out my rock and roll fantasies. I'd been active in the Denver music scene before stripping. Playing my own brand of glam rock with original songs that largely resembled the disco-rock hybrid of "I Was Made for Loving You". This came from growing up in the eighties. Listening to artists who wrote and sang of banging hot chicks. By the turn of the century, however, whining about not getting laid had become the de rigueur of rock music. Sharing bills with such bands truly cramped my style.

Because my ego won't allow me to do anything simple, I hit the stage with one of the most overblown male revue performances ever. Candelabras and fire columns awaited as I solemnly marched onstage covered by a brown hooded cloak to the opening of "Black Sabbath" by – wait for it – Black Sabbath. Without warning, I tossed off the cloak to face my audience in studded black leather and tear away black vinyl pants. An electric guitar slung over my shoulder as I channeled my inner Billy Idol with a rousing rendition of "Dancing with Myself". I sang and played guitar to a bass and drum track on CD. Leaping into the audience and straddled women in chairs as I continued riffing and soloing.

This went over much better than glowsticks on strings as the audience was now back in the game. I'm not so sure they were impressed with the performance itself or the sheer audacity of a male stripper doing such a thing. Probably more the latter, which makes sense as my stripping career and success is largely based on my audacity to do wild and crazy things. That was the beauty of my career in those days. I never worried about the status quo. If I wanted to do something, I fucking did it. Fuck that Vegas corporate male revue bullshit.

I traded my guitar to Rebecca for the mic and resumed my regular music programming. I'd remixed "Hypnotize" by The Notorious B.I.G. with a generous helping of reverb. It thundered throughout the club as I tore off my pants and collected tips. Working a couple of hundred women as fast as I could. Rebecca trailed behind to hold my money as I repeatedly cleared my g-string to make room for more. All while verbally engaged my audience with every manner of risqué conversation I could conceive. It didn't matter how raunchy any woman was towards me. I had no problem upping the ante to show her who was boss.

It was all down to Chase. And the less said about his performance, the better. Bless his heart. A handful of girls, through a combination of sympathy and drunkenness, led him through his set by dancing around him. Slade and I worked the rest of the crowd for additional tips while also drawing attention away from Chase. We posed for Polaroids with girls for ten bucks a pop and called it a night. The club and the audience were happy, as were my cohorts. I needed time to see if this gamble paid off with additional parties. Ultimately, I broke even.

I took a few minutes after the show to visit with Beth. She complimented and congratulated me, and I thanked her for coming. I still wasn't putting two and two together. Rebecca, who was already whining about wanting to go home, came up and introduced herself to Beth. An aura of cattiness immediately filled the air around us. Indeed, Rebecca talked shit about her as we drove back to Little Rock in the rain. Even now, with the whole Beth thing finally through my thick skull, I don't understand what Rebecca's problem was. Did she fear losing what we had? We didn't have much between us besides dinners and movies. As fun and helpful as Rebecca could be, she was fucking weird.

Beth and I chatted on Myspace a few days later. Still not seeing the forest for the trees, I made a horrible crack about her being just another girl chasing after me. She immediately took offense, responded with denial, and unfriended me. We never spoke again, and I forgot all about her until now. It was okay if I didn't want to go out with her, but I have no excuse for not handling the matter in a kind and respectful fashion. She showed guts by placing herself in a vulnerable position to get my attention, and I responded by being a total dick. I know it's ancient history. That she's long forgotten all about me. But I still have to beat myself up over this.

***

I wrapped up 2005 as an entertainer with two parties in Sherwood on the same December night. What are the odds? After completing a thirtieth birthday party, I grabbed dinner with two hours to kill before my upcoming bachelorette party. Sitting alone in a booth amongst the dark wood interior of Casa Mexicana while eating carne asada tacos and drinking Corona, I reflected upon my experiences over the previous two years. It had all begun in Sherwood, where I made plans while suffering through a dead-end job. And I was now on my way to building a business doing something that I was crazy enough to enjoy on an emotional level. I wasn't rich. But Lord, I was free.

And just like that, the cover band in the lounge area began its set with, of all things, "Amarillo by Morning". This wasn't the first time I'd heard it during stripping related activities, and it wouldn't be the last. It's kind of an eerie thing.

I didn't see it at the time, but the first two years of Hardbodies packed a certain innocence. Those were my formative years as an entrepreneur, and I had fun putting things together. The fun would intensify in 2006, but so would the stakes. There would be no limits as to how far I would push myself and my entertainers as I sought to go above and beyond in entertaining the good people of Arkansas. I wouldn't care how many miles I drove night after night. Or what I injected into my body. I was willing to pay any price. Hardbodies Entertainment of Arkansas was about to reach its pinnacle.

CHAPTER 13

For the first three years of Hardbodies' existence, I drove a 1981 Ford F150 Lariat. Scored for $800 shortly after moving to Arkansas and becoming my daily driver when my Eclipse bit the dust. What had once been a nice and luxurious truck was now a ragged eyesore with its banged-up two-tone copper body and shredded bench seat. The interior door panels were falling apart, and I eventually removed them. There was no stereo. I listened to CDs and the radio on a boombox seated next to me. The power windows didn't work. Neither did the air conditioning. There were wing windows and a sliding back glass to generate cool airflow that, provided everything was positioned correctly, didn't pound me in the face.

My truck performed well enough that it was something of a sleeper on the road. I did a lot of work on the 400ci V8 engine including the removal of all emissions components. The original exhaust and catalytic converter were tossed in favor of dual pipes and glasspack mufflers. I ran 93-octane unleaded as it closely mimicked the richness of the leaded fuel for which the engine was best suited. This was a little pricy as the truck got horrible gas mileage, which I calculated at eight miles in the city and ten on the highway. The carburetor was touchy, and I was constantly adjusting it. Still, once I let the truck warm up in the morning – one minute in the summer, two during winter – it was good to go all day.

For a full-size, four-wheel-drive pickup, it was quick and light enough to outpace all the Escalade and H2 drivers foolish enough to judge a book by its cover. The engine was so loud that any conversation inside the cab was a shouting match by default. If someone called me, I had to pull over to hear them and vice versa. Rebecca tolerated riding in it. Kyra hated it. I'd grown up around Ford and Chevy trucks of this vintage and was comfortable with owning, driving, and working on them. I had no qualms about driving it all over the state and as far away as Dallas and Oklahoma City. I put approximately 70,000 miles on that truck over the three and a half years I owned it.

I've always had a knack for getting so much from so little.

***

The Year of Hardbodies started a tad sluggish for me, although the girls held steady. I had high hopes for our yellow pages ad. It was a matter of waiting for all the 2006 phone books to be delivered with the anticipation of Navin Johnson.

My first booking of the year was a bachelorette party in Mountain Home, Arkansas. Which I prepared for by injuring my lower back two days prior. I was rearranging my garage/gym and got a little cavalier about moving a plate tree holding 300 lbs. of weight. There was a sharp pain in my lower back. I knew I'd torn something. Being the play through pain person I am, I continued with my project.

Mountain Home is approximately three hours north of Little Rock. Due to icy roads, the drive that night was closer to four. Most of the journey on U.S. 65 is treacherous enough at night as the highway continuously twists and turns through the southern edge of the Ozark Mountains. The scenery is absolutely stunning during the day. At night, however, you're simply trying to reach your destination in one piece. It's an exhausting drive after dark. More so when there's just enough ice on the road to demand extra caution.

Only minutes from my destination, I was pulled over by the Flippin police. The same police department featured in that famous internet meme. I had a taillight out and was let go with a warning. The Flippin police officers were friendly and provided more detailed directions to where I was headed. I haven't had much interaction with law enforcement while taking care of business, and I'm not complaining. What I have experienced has generally been positive.

I drove a few miles west of Flippin and turned north to drive along the White River. Even at night, it was easy to see why the Whitewater Development Corporation began with such lofty aspirations. A unique aura enveloped me along with the fog that rolled off the river. So sinister that it made the rustic Fisherman's Lodge appear gothic on that cold winter night. I could feel the energy of forty hyped up women before I reached the parking lot. It was going to be a legendary night, and nothing would stop me.

Not even the excruciating pain in my lower back as I got out of my truck. It was so intense that I nearly fell to the ground. Fuck that. I had a party to do, and my stubborn resolve wasn't about to let me fail my audience. I spent an hour going balls out, not literally. Entertaining my audience and projecting a normal appearance of erotic mischief. Every move I made felt like someone stabbing me in the back and twisting the blade as I held in countless screams. I had to make my bachelorette's night special. My physical suffering would have to wait.

Try as I did to hide it, the bachelorette picked up on my affliction near the end as we danced together on a small wooden dancefloor. I confessed my predicament when asked what was wrong, and so taken by my unwavering dedication that she responded most amazingly.

"Maybe these will help you feel better," she said while lifting her top and flashing her tits in my face.

Not only was she attractive and her breasts round and perky, but it was a sweet gesture on her part. She probably saw it as an opportunity to show off the goods, and I don't blame her. It made me feel appreciated for all I'd gone through for she and her friends. Showing her to be a kind and caring person. This simple yet sexy act made that long and painful night worth it for me. Along with the money, of course.

After saying goodnight, I began the long drive back to Little Rock. I was starving yet would have to wait three hours to find a restaurant open that late.

It was an excruciating drive out of the Ozarks as I once again navigated a winding and icy mountain road. But this time with intense lower back pain. Upon reaching Conway, I couldn't stand straight and walked into Denny's at a ninety-degree angle. When asked if I wanted smoking or nonsmoking, I requested the nearest booth in either section. As I drank coffee and ate my Grand Slam breakfast, I listened to the early morning regulars converse about God knows what. They brought me into the conversation at some point, but I can't remember what we discussed.

Upon making it home at 3:00am, I located a third full bottle of cough syrup with codeine, chugged that motherfucker, and passed out for twelve hours. I spent the following three days in bed. It hurt to lie down but hurt even worse to sit or stand. There was something vaguely decadent about conducting business while watching movies in bed. My back would heal but not quite right. Leading to occasional spells of pain that continue to this day. The things I do for you women.

***

The film project spilled over into 2006. Perpetually spinning its wheels through rewrite after rewrite. Since losing the starring role, I'd continually lost interest in the project to the point where I simply didn't give a fuck anymore. Yet I felt compelled to stay since I'd already invested so much time into it. The classic scenario of being reluctant to cut one's losses at the right time. I attended all shoots and production meetings but don't remember a damn thing about them.

I escorted Kyra to the Little Rock home of a well-to-do middle-aged couple. It was his birthday, and the wife had booked Kyra to entertain him before a small gathering. The classic one song birthday performance that Hardbodies booked time after time. All the clients wanted was one lap dance for the birthday boy or girl. And they'd often tip handsomely for it. I once made $400 for giving a birthday girl a single lap dance. Driving one hour each way but still.

Kyra was Kyra as she rocked the birthday boy's world. Practically smothering him with her big, luscious titties. After the song ended, the client asked if she could give him a second lap dance in private. She was down for it. Since these were the kind of people who couldn't afford to get in trouble, I gave the okay. The three of them absconded to a nearby bedroom as I kept the guests occupied with conversation. Five minutes later, Kyra strutted confidently from the bedroom followed by the wide-eyed birthday boy and his giggly wife. Kyra and I said our goodbyes and left.

As soon as we were in the truck, I looked at Kyra.

"What happened in there?" I asked.

"I let her eat my pussy," she responded matter-of-factly.

She wasn't getting off that easy as I followed up with, "How was she?"

Kyra shook her head and said, "Definitely her first time. Like she was trying to sip coffee that was too hot."

I had a birthday party of my own a week later. It was in the same neighborhood, in a similar home, owned by a similar couple. To complete the bizarro world effect, Kyra accompanied me as my personal assistant. I gave my birthday girl a tremendous lap dance to rave reviews. And, in an unusual turn for me, the husband/client asked if I could give his wife a second dance in private. I agreed since I felt safe about leaving Kyra on her own with the guests. And because the money was right.

Nothing crazy happened. I did the same performance as in the living room. But this time, my birthday girl relaxed and enjoyed the experience even more. Allowing herself to orgasm as she ran her fingers along my back and thighs. I must admit that her touch was excellent. It's hard to explain what happened between us. She and I bonded over a sensual encounter. There was an ego stroke she was feeling from me being all over her. Although a little old for my personal tastes, I was nevertheless flattered. She was an attractive woman and incredibly nice.

Upon completing my foreplay for hire, Kyra and I made our exit. Once in the truck, she turned to look at me in a reversal of the previous week.

"What happened?" her inquiring mind wanted to know.

"I let her suck my cock," I replied as if on cue.

"Really? How was she?" asked a dumbfounded Kyra.

"Outstanding," I said without a hint of bullshitting.

Kyra sighed and shook her head as we hit the road, ridin' dirty to the sound of Chamillionaire. Lights and shadows passed through the cab as they did every night. Whether in the city or country, I love night driving. As 2006 progressed, I would find myself driving for hours night after night to my heart's and bank account's content.

CHAPTER 14

I watched Rebecca act in a few local productions including *You're a Good Man, Charlie Brown*, the surprisingly amusing *Love Letters*, and the excruciatingly boring *Our Town*. I'd take her out for dinner and drinks afterward. She always gave 100%, and it was important to me that I show her my appreciation. Live performance was the biggest thing we shared as we both live for entertaining others. We also enjoyed ripping other people to shreds.

In March 2006, I took Rebecca to see a production written and directed by a local playwright. It contained a character written specifically for her, but she passed because the role required nudity. Shortly into the show, a morbidly obese woman appeared on stage.

"Is that the character written for you?" I whispered into Rebecca's ear as I feared the worst.

"Yeah," she sighed.

The nude scene was brief but more than enough. An uncomfortable silence filled the theatre when the actress, in the role of an artist's model, turned away from the audience and dropped her robe. No one's body is perfect, and I know what it's like to have people go over my physique with a fine-tooth comb, but that girl was fucking gross. Big as she was, she didn't have much ass and was mostly thighs and love handles wracked with serious hail damage. It was like the play suddenly turned into a burlesque show. She was also a shitty actress with a chip on her shoulder. Clearly in the role because she was willing to get naked on stage. I blame the writer/director for not cutting the nude scene, so Rebecca would've taken the role and delivered a superior performance.

The play was now ruined. Rebecca and I spent the remainder of the show whispering insults back and forth about the fat girl. As did every couple around us. I don't remember the play's title, but it may as well have been *Naked Fat Chick*. I remember nothing else about it and guarantee no one else does either. As I chastised Rebecca for not taking the role with nude scene intact and doing the audience a favor, the fat actress returned on stage. Someone behind me muttered, "I hope the fat girl doesn't get naked again." Thank fuck she didn't.

***

It was March when Hardbodies' year truly got in gear. The new phone book was out, and I received calls left and right. Many were from looky-loos and lonely guys, but bookings were on the rise. And that's when Slade called it a day. Despite my best efforts, I would be the only male stripper I represented until the end. I never found anyone who came close to matching my dedication and professionalism or had appropriate experience. This also put an end to my male revue aspirations. But I was already on the fence about that after breaking even from the Hot Springs show. Private parties had become my specialty, and I was more than happy to focus exclusively on them.

Amber also bowed out as Chantelle became my go-to entertainer for their ideal bookings. So overshadowed was Amber at this point by the other girls that I forgot all about her until going over my books in preparation for tax season the following year. While I appreciate Amber's contributions to the early days of Hardbodies, she had every opportunity to step up her game and never did. I don't feel bad that I stopped sending her work. That she never asked why she wasn't getting any parties tells me she no longer gave a fuck anyway. C'est la vie.

I always knew that Amber and Slade would quit one day. As I knew that Kyra, Chantelle, and Leah would all quit eventually. It's the nature of the business. Should I get two solid years of quality performances from an entertainer, then I had no reason to complain. I remained vigilant in my perpetual talent search. Interviewing and working with new female entertainers with the expectation that today's Amber would grow into tomorrow's Kyra. All I could do was hammer away and keep my fingers crossed.

In the meantime, my trio of phenomenal female strippers and I formed our own ultra-sexy version of *Charlie's Angels* (sans Bosley) and took the region by storm.

***

One thing most people don't know about being a career male stripper is how ragtag the experience is. It's overcoming one nagging obstacle after another. From dealing with obnoxious audience members to using convenience store restrooms while in tear-away pants. I've driven long distances with no gas money to get home. Depending entirely on the client to hold up her end of the deal. That's to say nothing of driving three hours in a g-string. There's also the matter of figuring out what and where to eat after a party out of town. Late at night, I often settle for some peanuts from a convenience store.

Washing them down with a Red Bull to keep me awake long enough to reach home safely.

I had two bachelorette parties in Conway and Little Rock, respectively, the night after seeing *Naked Fat Chick* with Rebecca. The Conway party was at a Holiday Inn Express with a group of ten girls. The bachelorette got a little too intoxicated near the end as she jumped on my back and wrapped her forearm around my throat. Almost choking me unconscious. She only weighed around 100 lbs. But that was still 100 lbs. of dead weight hanging from my neck. The other girls were apologetic as I decided it was time to wrap up. I know she meant no harm, but it's only natural that I was annoyed.

I smelled brake fluid when I returned to my truck. Sure enough, one of my brake lines had sprung a leak on the drive Conway, and all the fluid had drained from the system. I made the thirty-minute drive from Conway to my second party in Little Rock without brakes. This wasn't the first time I'd driven without brakes, and it wouldn't be the last. I traveled east on I-40 with extreme caution as I avoided getting anywhere close to other vehicles. Since my truck had an automatic transmission, things got especially tricky once I exited the Interstate. I crawled down city streets and carefully downshifted until slowing enough to utilize the parking brake as a makeshift anchor.

I arrived at my second party by letting my front right tire come to rest against the curb and straightening out as best I could. For the most part, this party was worth all the trouble I went through to get there. Much of the audience, including the client and bachelorette, consisted of excited twentysomethings who tipped generously. The client was incredibly sweet and went out of her way to make me feel at home. I gave them lap dances and Reddi-wip treatment before we all danced together.

There were a couple of horny old broads in attendance. One was a shrill and abrasive woman who got upset because I wouldn't take off my cowboy boots. Apparently, she had a foot fetish. She even tried forcibly removing my boots. I asked her what the fuck she was doing.

"I want to see your feet!" she barked as if I'd just canceled Emily's birthday party.

I've never understood the whole foot fetish thing. Like when a Facebook page posts a photo of some hot chick with rockin' tits and ass, and some asshole inevitably comments about her fucking feet. Why give a fuck about her feet?

While Becky With a Foot Fetish moped over my refusal to indulge her podiatric fantasies, an old hippie new-age woman informed me that she was reading my aura.

"Fine. Knock yourself out," I responded less than enthusiastically.

According to her, I'm an old soul. Whatever the fuck that means. With my bachelorette and her age-appropriate friends satisfied, I left to enjoy a nice and relaxing drive home with no brakes. As if proverbially trying to reach Amarillo by morning.

***

The yellow pages ad paid for itself at the beginning of each month. Our online ads were still in place and delivering on that investment. I was now receiving daily calls from account executives pimping advertising options from radio to billboards. Radio intrigued me but looked like a sure loser for Hardbodies after I crunched the numbers six ways from Sunday. The best-case scenario had us turning the same net profit we already were, and I wasn't interested in being charitable to corporate broadcasting. The mere thought of a sexually provocative billboard in Arkansas seemed like a surefire invitation for protests and death threats.

A surprising source for bookings emerged in the form of Myspace. I'll say it time and time again. Myspace in its mid-2000s heyday was the greatest social network to date. While not without its flaws, it was much friendlier and more fun overall than Facebook, Twitter, Instagram, and the rest. Not only did I enjoy fascinating conversations with people from all walks of life, including the singer from Double (they of the 1986 hit "The Captain of Her Heart"), but I picked up parties here and there. Not a lot, but it was nice to score the occasional gig from a free advertising source.

One such party came in late March courtesy of a girl named Heather for her friend's bachelorette party. Heather and I conversed regularly on Myspace. Commenting back and forth on those goofy yet addictive surveys that constantly made the message board rounds. I liked to answer mine with all manner of sarcastic, absurd, and sexually provocative responses, because of course I did. She was a sweet girl with a sharp enough wit to hold her own against me. One smart-ass joke at a time.

I was excited when Heather requested my services. Arriving at her apartment in Sherwood, of all places, to encounter a half dozen excited and tipsy young women. There wasn't anything about this booking that stood out for better or worse, whether it be an after-party threesome or some horny old broad demanding to see my feet. It was a typical performance that went like clockwork, and that alone made it a smash. I gave lap dances and consumed Reddi-wip off tits. We danced together as they fed me shots, and I hung out afterward. Like Heather, the rest of them made an impression on me for being sweet and a special group of friends.

Heather and I remained in contact via Myspace following that party. She planned to book me again for her own bachelorette party once she and her boyfriend tied the knot. This never came to pass as she and I lost touch around the time Facebook supplanted Myspace as the king of social networks. She had an impact on me. Besides her being in a relationship, I was never sexually drawn to her. Not that she wasn't without physical charms given her cute blonde in glasses look. I enjoyed the pleasure of her company online and in person. So many people have come and gone in my life. All I'm left with are memories.

CHAPTER 15

One question I'm sometimes asked is, "If you're so great, why aren't you performing in a Las Vegas male revue?" I make more money doing bachelorette and birthday parties in a place like Arkansas than I would in a Vegas stage show. Fact. And, unlike those over-glorified marionettes, I wield full creative control over my performances. Not only am I not bound to boy band-style dance moves, but I'm free to rely on humor and intellect as part of my overall sex appeal. Allowing me to win over women who normally wouldn't care for male strippers. And that's a monumental source of pride for me.

There's also the matter of specialization. Private parties are nothing like male revues and must be approached in a completely different fashion. Those Vegas guys can't and won't do what I do. They lack not only the free-spirited nature required but the sheer gumption and tenacity as well. The willingness to travel long distances and perform solo in living rooms and hotel suites for strangers. No choreographers are telling me what to do. And not even my extensive preparation can fully brace me for whatever craziness or melodrama I may encounter.

I've always been one of a handful of private party entertainers throughout the nation who travels long distances to perform. This includes handling two parties in a single night that are located far apart. I've already written about a couple such occurrences, but one Saturday night in April 2006 shows how far I go for my audiences.

It rained as I ran errands around Little Rock before my bachelorette party that night in Memphis. A nice spring drizzle that made the air fresh and clean. Not only was I thinking about my party, but also the birthday party Kyra had as well as the bachelor party each for Leah and Chantelle. Charlie and his angels would be out in full force that night. I stopped for lunch at a local restaurant. The name of which now escapes me but one that is long gone. As I sat by a window and ate my sandwich while watching the rain make everything green and lush, my phone rang.

"Our male stripper for tonight canceled. Could you possibly help us out?" a female voice asked frantically.

This party was in Fort Smith. Approximately four and a half hours west of Memphis. Booking it would require me to traverse the entire state of Arkansas via I-40. My party in Memphis was at 8:00pm. If I hit the road at 9:00pm, I could be in Fort Smith by 1:30am. That's seriously fucking late for a performance, and girls are usually dozing off by that point. I explained all of this to her. She informed me that the bachelorette was hell-bent on having a male stripper, and they planned to party all night. I booked it and immediately planned out the all-nighter now ahead of me.

The male stripper who canceled on the Fort Smith girls was Dylan. Even on his own, he booked parties only to decide at the last minute that he didn't feel like doing them. I was right to have never liked him.

But he wasn't alone. This sort of behavior is common among private party male strippers.

The drive from Little Rock to Memphis is monotonous. Running mostly straight and flat as it cuts through Arkansas farm country. Not an ugly drive. But not remarkable. The rain stopped by the time I departed for Memphis at 6:00pm. I let the music play as I cruised down I-40. Giving the volume an extra crank when I heard "My Humps" because fuck you. I like that song. Coming upon the Mississippi River, I could see the Memphis Pyramid on the other side. Built as a 20,000-seat arena in the early nineties, it now houses a Bass Pro Shop. Like we didn't have enough of those in the world already.

I made excellent time. Arriving ten minutes early to my first party located in an eighties-vintage residential neighborhood. The girls were friendly but shy at first. After enough banter and alcohol, they cut loose. We danced as they kept wanting me to lick more Reddi-wip off their tits. As appreciative as they were for me coming from Little Rock to entertain them, their minds were totally fucking blown when I informed them my next party that night was in Fort Smith. When the clock struck nine, they encouraged me to be safe. Sending me on my way with a plate of mini quiches and tiny chicken salad sandwiches.

The drive from Memphis to Fort Smith flew by over the course of four hours and change. I was a man focused on his objective, and that was enough to keep me energetic and alert. Part of me wished that Kyra was there to keep me company, but another part was glad she wasn't. She would've alternated between sleeping and complaining about the drive. As much as I liked her, she tended to whine on road trips. I once pulled over in the middle of fucking nowhere and threatened to leave her on the side of the road if she didn't stop. Her enthusiasm for every aspect of our work never quite matched mine. But no one's did.

Fuck it. I had music to keep me company. The radio sufficed for the first couple hours as I switched repeatedly between top 40, *Retro Pop Reunion* with Joe Cortez, and an eighties hair metal show. After passing through Little Rock, I got bored with all that and listened to Roxy Music's *Avalon* album twice. Two years into Hardbodies and I already had memories associated with the towns I passed in the Arkansas River Valley. Like Russellville and the bachelorette party held in a church basement. And the huge birthday bash in Ozark. Oodles more memories would be made over the years to come.

I was on a high when I reached downtown Fort Smith at 1:20am. Perhaps it was the combination of excitement and all that driving, but I felt buzzed in a way. The girls at the bachelorette party were certainly buzzed. Giving me a rousing reception when I entered their hotel suite. I was expecting them to be tired given how late it was, but they couldn't sit still as I had my fun with the bachelorette. She was a fit and perky blonde full of life. Determined to make the most of her last night of freedom.

After declaring she could strip down to her g-string as well, the bachelorette did just that. We danced together before she laid on the bed as I got on top with Reddi-wip in hand. I applied whipped cream to her nipples. Licking and sucking them a little longer than needed. She returned the favor with extra lingering included. Then I slid down between her legs and licked whipped cream from the outer edges of her pussy as she arched her back in ecstasy. That was when her friends decided to break up the action. Which was probably a good idea. After driving there all the way from Memphis like Mott the Hoople, which they all greatly appreciated, I had no reservations about getting up close with the bachelorette.

Once she and her girlfriends were satisfied and exhausted, I made my exit at 2:30am. I was too hungry to be exhausted. Heading for the nearest IHOP to load up on breakfast and coffee for the long drive home. I popped in a mix CD and hit the road as "King for a Day" by XTC played. In my world, I was king for a day at that moment. Between my parties and those of my angels, I'd enjoyed a profitable night working for myself. The sun began to peer over the eastern horizon as I reached Little Rock at 6:00am. I was finally exhausted when I reached home. That didn't stop me from leaning against my truck to watch the sunrise before dragging myself inside to crash for several hours.

***

I was now and forever the only male stripper Hardbodies had. But I hadn't abandoned my ideas for nightclub revues. Building on the positive responses Kyra and I received from performing together for couples as well as my desire to incorporate female strippers into male revues, I began exploring the possibility of creating a live show around the two of us. Chantelle loved the concept and wanted to be involved. I wasn't the only one with an idea along these lines. A couple of different club owners contacted me around this time inquiring about such a revue aimed at couples and single women. None of this went anywhere but not for lack of exploration on my part.

One potential nightclub was in the Little Rock area. The owner threw everything and the kitchen sink at trying to fill the bar night after night and wasn't afraid to push the envelope as needed. This included hosting a weekly swingers' night. Although the owner had previously floated this idea by me, I had no idea it was a go when Kyra and I stopped in one May night after she had a birthday gig. Upon entering the club, we were greeted by the sight of several creepy looking old dudes sitting around a table and drinking. Meanwhile, a group of fat, middle-aged women attired in worn and ill-fitting lingerie embarrassed themselves to "My Humps" on the dancefloor.

Someone spotted us. In the blink of an eye, Kyra and I were surrounded by hillbilly swingers desperate to make our acquaintance. Whether they saw us as gods or sacrificial lambs was anyone's guess. I think it was equal parts both.

The good news was that Kyra and I didn't have to pay for drinks because the swingers covered our tabletop with booze. The bad news was that we were afraid to drink any of it lest something had been slipped in. We didn't dare disclose our profession. Our newfound admirers comprised a swingers group based in Morrilton. A town one-hour northwest of Little Rock. They told us of their dream to open a private nightclub. Proving their ignorance by mistaking private club status for a license to do whatever the fuck they wanted in the face of liquor laws and municipal codes. Kyra leaned towards me.

"Are they going to kill us?" she whispered in my ear.

"Maybe," I whispered back while shrugging my shoulders.

She found amusement in the wives attempting to drag me onto the dancefloor. I didn't find it amusing at all. Two of the women came close to forever ruining girl on girl for me by offering to make out for my viewing pleasure.

"You'd better get yourself some of that, Stefan," snarked Kyra while having way too much fun with this.

On my way to the men's room, I asked the doorman to keep an eye on Kyra. He responded by informing me that he was already looking for any excuse to toss those weirdos. One of the husbands entered the restroom behind me. Ostensibly to relieve himself, but I knew better. He wasted no time as we stood side by side at urinals.

"Our wives really like you," he opined as if bestowing the greatest gift of all upon me.

"That's just great," I responded on the assumption he was illiterate in sarcasm.

Proving my assumption correct, he continued, "You and your old lady will have to come to one of our parties some time. They're a blast."

I didn't respond as I washed my hands and headed back to retrieve Kyra. It was time to leave. She got in her digs on the way back to her place.

"Didn't you want to stay with your new girlfriends?" she asked between giggles.

Speaking of girlfriends… It was now May. And I finally did it. I left the film production. Which would continue well into 2008 before finally being completed. This was also the end of my dates with

Rebecca, as that experience had also run its course for me. I promptly forgot about her and the film. Immersing myself in all things Hardbodies. My reward would be an action-packed summer and fall of epic proportions.

CHAPTER 16

From May onward, the year of Hardbodies was in full effect as my angels and I repeatedly crisscrossed the state of Arkansas and beyond. I was constantly on the road. Either alone or with Kyra. Though I worried about burning out the girls, I pushed them to take as many bookings as possible. Demand was so high that I was passing on parties left and right. I was booking an increasing number of parties for myself on Thursdays and Sundays to fit in as many as I could. I should've been more concerned about burning out me.

In July, I made time to participate in a handful of male revues with the Men of Whatever (I can't remember what this group billed itself) across Arkansas, Oklahoma, and Texas. I still did parties in between. I'd do a male revue in Fayetteville one night, go back to Central

Arkansas for parties in Little Rock and Hot Springs the next, then meet up with the revue the following night in Tulsa. Although I made decent money with the revues, I was using them to promote Hardbodies and expand our territory beyond Arkansas. This scored us several bookings in the short term. Even with fuel and drive time considered, this approach was cheaper and more efficient than producing a Hardbodies male revue.

   I did a firefighter routine for each show. This entailed having two women in chairs facing each other on stage. I would dance on one, the other, or both at once while flaming columns surrounded us. Filling the club with smoke and violating multiple fire codes to the ire of management. It brought back memories of my early stripping days when I'd fling a running, gas-powered chainsaw around the stage. With me, every stage performance was a pageant of toxic masculinity.

   It was an okay crew of entertainers. The one in charge was inexperienced in managing strippers. I got along with them, except for one. Some douche canoe from Indiana or wherever. One of those people relatively new to something who acted like the ultimate authority on it. Extremely insecure and posturing to convince everyone otherwise. Before one show, he delivered a self-serving lecture on how he delivers a cop performance at bachelorette parties by using the same basic intro that every private party male stripper has used for decades.

   He once asked me to rub baby oil on his back. I responded with one of the dirtiest looks anyone has ever been given. Had he been the ultimate stripping authority he claimed, he would've done what I did every night. I'd pick a girl from the audience, take her into a closet or backroom, and charge her twenty bucks for the privilege of rubbing baby oil all over my naked body. Although I'm sure this asshole would've gotten it all wrong and paid her twenty bucks, and that assumption is not without precedent.

   During my final show with these guys in Texarkana, a young woman in a wheelchair was in attendance. My cohorts and I treated her like anyone else because she was anyone else. Except to this dumbass. As soon as he caught her in his pathetic crosshairs, he lost his damn mind. Not only did he give her all his tips, but he pushed her around the venue and made a huge spectacle of her presence. It was uncomfortable as fuck. Most of all for this poor girl who just wanted to see male strippers. That was my breaking point with him. I may not have been the manager of this group, but I was about to invoke my veteran clubhouse presence status.

Once he finally left her alone for a moment to head backstage, I immediately followed and subsequently tore into him once we were out of sight from the audience. Before a small group of people, he giggled like a nervous and frightened jackass as I called him a piece of shit to his stupid fucking face for embarrassing that girl. Informing him what a worthless fucking entertainer he was. I was furious. So furious that some of the audience overheard my diatribe and applauded me when I emerged from the dressing room. It was good to know that I wasn't alone in my disgust for that ass clown.

I hung around for thirty minutes after the show as I signed naughty personalized autographs on tits and asses with black Sharpies while passing out Hardbodies business cards. Then I left what would be my final male revue performance for the next seven years.

***

Probably the least shocking revelation I'll make in this book is that performance-enhancing drug use runs rampant among male strippers. As I mentioned previously, I've never known a male stripper who used any recreational drugs other than marijuana. Given the physical requirements of the job, we're a health and fitness-oriented bunch. Shit like cocaine, heroin, and meth aren't conducive to staying in shape long term. I, for one, have always abhorred illicit drugs including marijuana. I've purchased and taken opioid painkillers without a prescription over the years but only used them when in too much pain to fall asleep on my own. Aside from being a social drinker, I've always been clean and focused on making gains.

And striving to make gains is what leads so many men, and not just strippers, to seek out anabolic steroids and human growth hormone (HGH). Within the dark underbelly of the fitness industry, the idea that it's impossible to make impressive gains without chemical assistance is pushed on both men and women. In my case, there was pressure right from the beginning of my stripping career. I was never opposed to the idea but took my time learning different steroids. How they acted individually and in various stacks. Going from 180 lbs. to 215 lbs. over the previous fifteen months proved that my body was capable of building muscle naturally at a steady pace. But I'd already injected the grape Flavor-Aid upon commencing my first steroid cycle in August 2006.

One of the biggest obstacles to ending steroid and HGH abuse is that these drugs have their own *Reefer Madness* type lies surrounding them. Chiefly, the myth that steroids will shrink your dick. That's untrue and makes no sense. Us guys who decided to juice saw this for the ridiculous notion it is. When have steroids been known to shrink muscle tissue? Mine is the same size it was before a decade of steroid use. What happens is the testicles will slightly retract during an eight-to-twelve-week cycle as they're not producing testosterone at that time. It's barely noticeable and not something any girl who had sex with me during a cycle ever spotted.

Speaking for myself, the only long term negative physical effect I still suffer from years of steroid use is a massive buildup of scar tissue in my ass from hundreds of intramuscular injections with long needles. Sometimes it aches. My hormones were all fucked up for a time after I stopped juicing for good. It took time for my insulin, cortisol, and thyroid hormone to return to normal. I also showed symptoms of prediabetes. If I'd had bloodwork done, I'm sure it would've come back a dumpster fire.

I experienced short term side effects from two of the various steroids I used. One caused massive bloating in my face along with acne on my forearms. The other left injection sites so swollen and painful that I could barely walk the day after administering it. Another issue was girls at parties smacking me right on injection sites. That fucking hurts. And yes, I used to inject steroids into my own butt. It was both the easiest and least painful injection site for me.

The biggest drawback to juicing for me was more psychological than physiological. I felt fucking amazing when on a cycle. People talk about roid rage, but I had the opposite experience. All that synthetic testosterone in my body made me feel like I was on Xanax. Everything was peachy keen during those months. Once the cycle ended, however, I'd fall into depression as my body returned to normal testosterone levels with the aid of a female fertility drug.

I also lost my passion for weight training. What had been an enjoyable and cathartic pastime became a chore to ensure I received my money's worth for these black-market pharmaceuticals. And there's the paranoia that comes with the legalities of purchasing and possessing Schedule III Controlled Substances. Crazy fast muscle gains aside, pumping iron wasn't fun anymore.

Nevertheless, I went forth. Convinced that juicing was the solution to all of life's problems. Forearm acne aside, I must admit that first cycle was pretty damn fun. Or maybe it was the parties I was getting around that time. Perhaps a combination thereof. The late summer and fall months of 2006 were the absolute peak of Hardbodies and probably my stripping career. I started August with a bachelorette party in Little Rock. It was enjoyable, but nothing special. Until a few girls asked if I would give them Arabian goggles. And I did.

I've done more parties in Hot Springs than any other town. I always love driving and performing there. Several parties took place at Clarion Resort on the Lake. With it indeed being located on the edge of a lake, there was a certain magic about stripping in those rooms. Like the bachelorette party I did there in early September. The girls had been drinking on the lake all day and were totally out of control. My client wore a yellow summer dress with no underwear. I knew this because she announced it while mooning me. I lifted her skirt myself several times as she and the other girls laughed hysterically.

The outrageousness didn't stop there. While driving to a gig later that month, I received a call about a bachelorette party in Northern Arkansas near the Missouri border. When I told her my booking fee, the girl responded by asking for a discount in exchange for letting me spend the night in her cabin. The way she said it left no doubt as to what she had in mind. Of course, I had no idea what she looked like. I probably should've asked. Maybe she was the one. Probably not if she's willing to trade sex for professional services from a guy she's never met. I politely passed on her offer.

I continued driving to my bachelorette party in the town of Shannon Hills, located along the southern edge of Little Rock. My girls were partying in an empty storefront within an old strip mall connected to a mom and pop grocery store. I saw party lights flashing and heard music blasting as I walked towards the entrance. It reminded me of throwing after-hours parties at the pool and spa dealership in Sherwood. This was a group of twentysomethings plus the mother of the groom. She licked Reddi-wip off my ass. After getting dressed and heading out, the groom-to-be showed up and was all like, "Hey, dude! What's up?" I spared him the details about his mom.

I kicked off October with a bachelorette party in North Little Rock. This was another Dylan party that he'd booked and canceled at the last minute. Once again, I marched right in and saved the day. They were a young and excitable bunch. Seeing me tear off my pants was enough to satisfy them. The brevity of this performance was a good thing as I had another bachelorette party to do that night in Hot Springs. After leaving, I stopped in Little Rock to pick up Kyra since we were booked as a duo.

We headed deep into the warm autumn night to deliver what would be the magnum opus performance of my entire stripping career.

CHAPTER 17

She was bent over the sofa arm. Her tight, round, bikini-clad ass on display. I stood behind her in musclebound glory. Reddi-wip in hand. Kyra and the other girls surrounded us. Observing with anticipation. The client held up $100 and said, "Do something sexy."

Challenge fucking accepted.

***

It was a tremendous night with a temperature in the sixties. A special feeling hung in the air as Kyra and I made the drive from Little Rock to Hot Springs via I-30 and U.S. 70. Although easier to traverse since being expanded to four lines, U.S. 70 was still a gorgeous drive. Lined with trees as we ascended the eastern edge of the Ouachita Mountains. Even Kyra, much as she loathed my truck (much as I hated performing after being cramped in her little hatchback thing), was digging the experience. Ever so slightly nodding her head to "Smack That" by Akon as I watched for reckless drivers on that long and winding road. Arkansas has its magical moments. This was one of them.

We arrived at 9:00pm. It was an expensive rental on Lake Hamilton. Our client was an attractive woman around my age. A trust fund baby from Dallas, she also had a high paying job and was single without kids. This meant oodles of disposable income, and she flaunted it when booking Kyra and me. The client wanted us to provide the bachelorette and her friends with an "extraordinary experience" at any cost. I promised her we would deliver all that and then some. And I'm a man of my word.

Kyra and I were dressed as sexy cops when we entered. The amazing open floor plan immediately caught my eye, as did the girls. It was an aesthetically pleasing group of six ladies decked out in everything from party attire to swimwear. With Kyra's assistance, I went through my cop introduction as I interrogated my bachelorette, frisked her, and placed her in handcuffs. Grinding on her as I stripped to my g-string. I motioned for Kyra to join me in double-teaming the bachelorette. Each of us straddling one leg. I moved onto the other girls as Kyra got down to her g-string and continued lap dancing solo on our guest of honor.

These girls were everything a male stripper could want in an audience. Warm, hospitable, enthusiastic, and generous with the gratuity. It was only a few weeks before Fat Joe and Lil Wayne dropped "Make it Rain" on the airwaves, but my client was ahead of the curve as she filled the air with dollar bills. Another girl fixed cocktails for Kyra and me while I returned to my bachelorette and licked Reddi-wip from her ample cleavage. I repeated this with the other girls as Kyra danced with the client. Then my partner in crime and I licked whipped cream off each other's nipples.

Although the girls were already having a rockin' time, that simple act had them clamoring for more. This was especially true of the client as she switched from dollar bills to tens and twenties. Suggesting that

Kyra lick whipped cream off my cock. The other girls squealed in delight at this suggestion. Kyra dropped to her knees and pulled down my g-string. Administering a line of Reddi-wip along the length of my cock and licking it off in a most sensual fashion. More cash came flying our way as she took me in her mouth.

I thought to myself, "Surely, we've given them more than they can handle." The fuck we had. We weren't even close to blowing their minds. The girls all gathered around us and danced liked crazy. I pulled up my g-string and covered myself as best I could, which was barely at all.

"You may as well go completely naked at this point," Kyra suggested with a mischievous look on her face.

Kyra was reading these girls well as they all cheered at the suggestion. I shook my head at her in faux annoyance while upping the ante, "Only if you do it with me."

She nodded in agreement before removing her g-string and holding it in the air to applause. I did the same and was left in nothing but my cowboy boots. We were rewarded with more tips. Fortunately, this party had no horny old broad with a foot fetish demanding to see my feet.

Kyra and I danced with these girls in all our butt ass naked glory. I continued licking Reddi-wip off their tits and saw a lightbulb go on above the client's head. She paired me with a cute blonde in blue bikini bottoms and a white t-shirt. We danced together as she bent over and rubbed her butt against my erect cock. The client positioned the blonde over the sofa arm and made her request that I do something sexy.

The only thing the client had in mind was seeing how far I would push the envelope. It was clear that the "extraordinary experience" she wanted was one of pure decadence. It was a game between us. One I intended to win. Not only against the client but her friends and even Kyra. It's a good thing I've never played a game of chicken on the road because there's no way I could bring myself to swerve even an inch. My competitive edge knows no boundaries. Nor does my stubbornness.

With the cute blonde in position, I knew what I wanted and needed to do. She looked hygienic, so I wasted no time in pulling down her bikini bottoms and applying Reddi-wip between her ass cheeks. I dropped to my knees, spread her cheeks, and licked it right off her asshole. She giggled and sighed as her friends screamed in a high-octane combination of excitement, arousal, and disbelief. As I licked the remaining dessert topping from her crack, I looked at Kyra. She stared at me in shock with her jaw nearly hitting the floor. I nodded at her with authoritative swagger as I collected my $100 rim job bounty.

All bets were off now. A brunette rocking a white men's dress shirt for some reason ripped it open to reveal her fake tits. She took my can of Reddi-wip, applied some to Kyra's nipples, and proceeded to lick and suck it off them. Kyra didn't hesitate to return the favor, after which they kissed. The rest of us watched in savage amusement as the girl dropped to her knees and lapped up Kyra's pussy. Her friends laughed, screamed, and shouted her name in faux shock and outrage. Yet no one made any effort to stop her. Not to be outdone, Kyra tossed the girl on the sofa, spread her legs wide open, and ate her pussy.

The girl motioned me towards her face so she could suck my cock while being licked by Kyra. Despite everything that had happened already, I glanced at the client, who gave me a look that said, "What? Do you need an engraved invitation or something?" I engaged in an oral threesome with Kyra and the girl as her friends knelt in a straight line and cheered us on with dirty words of encouragement. The client made it rain yet again with more singles along with tens and twenties. And a few fifties and hundreds mixed in for good measure. This went on until the client insisted that we all do a shot of tequila.

I don't know if it was the alcohol, money, sex, or overall heat of the moment, but Kyra aggressively planted her mouth on mine after that shot. Although we had a sexual relationship, we weren't particularly affectionate towards each other. And she'd never done something like this in front of others. I lingered upon the flavor combination of Reddi-wip, tequila, and pussy on her lips. Those raucous party girls instantly silenced by the spectacle. Not that they were put off by it. They wanted to know what exactly the deal with Kyra and me was. As if we'd now injected some Hallmark-style romantic drama into the mix.

We'd been there for an hour by that point but far from ready to leave. Nor would the girls have allowed us to leave that early. Or that easily. Everyone needed a break, so the client suggested we chill (so to speak) in the hot tub. The temperature was in the low fifties but felt refreshing as the girls joined Kyra and me in full nudity. I felt like Bob Guccione's vision of Caligula. Sipping Crown and Coke and eating mini quiches in a hot tub while surrounded by seven beautiful naked women. The client felt similarly as we engaged in discussion equal parts intellectualism and hedonism. It was as much a friendly battle of wits as it was a stimulating chat.

The conversation turned to the nature of my relationship with Kyra. She and I were on the same page. Describing ourselves as business partners who were also friends with benefits. The girls were polite enough to not ask why we weren't more than that. It wouldn't have been all that out of line. This was something I'd wondered myself. And I'm sure she had as well. I was fond of Kyra. I respected her. And I even cared for her. A full-fledged romantic relationship made sense on paper. Yet there was always a certain something missing from the equation. We were two cerebral individuals more adept at making decisions based on thought rather than feeling. So much alike in this way that we lacked balance between us.

That said, Kyra and I were as hot as ever for each other that night. As I basked in the contrasting sensations of hot water surrounding my body and cool autumn air on my face, I found myself reaching between her legs and rubbing her clit with my middle finger before slipping it inside her pussy. She was unbelievably tight and wet. Meanwhile, she stroked my cock while taking turns kissing me and her playmate from earlier. The other girls watched quietly and intently.

"We can put you two in a room if you'd like," offered the client.

This wasn't sarcasm. She liked the idea of facilitating sex between two people that night. I didn't think we were at that point as I responded, "Oh no, that's okay."

"So, you two are just going to fuck right in front of us?" she challenged me yet again.

The girls laughed as Kyra and I looked at each other with the same thought. Challenge fucking accepted. Before those girls knew what was happening, she and I were out of the hot tub. She bent over and rested her forearms on the edge as I entered her from behind. I've done some wild stuff at parties over the years, but this was the first and only time I fucked someone before an audience. Repeatedly thrusting my cock deep inside Kyra's pussy while our party girls cheered us on. Pounding Kyra's amazing butt with my pelvis as her playmate kissed her and stroked her hair from within the tub. Kyra and I were so worked up that we came together in an explosive mutual ejaculation.

After cleaning up in the nearest bathroom, Kyra and I returned to our audience in the hot tub and resumed talking, drinking, and laughing. It was an hour later when the girls began showing fatigue. I took that as a sign to wrap things up. These girls, who had been so unbelievably amazing to us, asked if they'd met our expectations as an audience. We assured them that they had gone above and beyond in every way imaginable. Thanking them profusely for their enthusiasm and generosity.

The bachelorette expressed gratitude to Kyra and me for giving her a final night of freedom that she never would've imagined in her wildest dreams. She also informed us that she planned to act out everything we'd done that night with her future husband. Truly one lucky bastard. As the other girls picked up our tips strewn across the living room floor, a still naked Kyra and I gave the towel-clad bachelorette one last lap dance before leaving. It was a fitting end to the night. There was something endearing about that final dance. A bittersweet farewell. And it allowed us to dry off completely before getting dressed.

Kyra and I said our goodbyes as the girls took turns hugging us on our way out the door. The client walked us back to my truck, handed us each another $100, and thanked us for the amazing show we had given she and her friends. After hugging Kyra, she looked at me and said, "I asked you for an extraordinary experience. Man, you sure don't disappoint."

"I don't fuck around," I replied with a cocky swagger.

She hugged me goodbye as if we were friendly libertine adversaries. Each worthy of the other's respect. And that's exactly what we were.

Kyra immediately dozed off as I drove through Hot Springs. A light fog rolled off the lake and engulfed the streets. Still a little buzzed, I proceeded with caution through the city as I made my way back to U.S. 70. I turned on the heat when she began to shiver in her corner, leaned against the passenger door. "It's My Life" by Talk Talk played on the boombox as I replayed that night's events in my head on a continuous loop. I knew this party would never be replicated. But the memories would fuel my naked ambition for years to come.

We made it to her apartment in the early morning hours. I walked her all the way from the truck to her bed to ensure she made it safely. Although planning to go home, I sat on her sofa for a moment to check my voicemails. Next thing I knew, it was six hours later. With Kyra sound asleep, I quietly left and drove home.

CHAPTER 18

I strutted into the lounge of P.F. Chang's in Little Rock on a Friday afternoon. My client waved to me from her seat at the bar. After introducing ourselves properly to each other, she passed me an envelope containing $200 in cash. She booked me for a bachelorette party her daughter was throwing in Hot Springs the following night. One week after my magnum opus show with Kyra. Paying my booking fee now as she wouldn't be attending. Claiming she would've felt out of place amongst all those twentysomethings.

She told me this and more as I drank a Jack and Coke. Then a second. They were on her. I think she spent that $200 less on her daughter and more on the pleasure of my company in a public place. And that was a good thing since the daughter and her friends made for a lame audience. Not rude but so easily overstimulated that they were good to go after two minutes. Despite getting paid the same no matter what, I hate when girls prematurely ejaculate in that way.

I wish the client had been at the party. It would've been better with her. She was an attractive woman around fifty. Somewhat shy, yet sassy and devious enough to essentially trick a date out of me. I didn't mind, because I liked her. She was friendly and sweet. Obviously lonely with no wedding band on her finger. I would've loved to have made her night with a lap dance or two. Regardless, I was still a little flirty with her. Largely due to force of habit, but also because I wanted to make her feel confident. My life would be so much easier without this damn compassion.

After entertaining the adult female version of *The ButterCream Gang* in Hot Springs that Saturday night, I immediately drove back to Little Rock for a birthday party performance. That one was better as it lasted longer and provided more tips. The birthday girl was not only hot but got topless so I could lick Reddi-wip off her nipples. From there, I rushed to pick up Kyra and take her to some dude's birthday party in Little Rock thrown by his wife. Afterward, I took Kyra to IHOP for a late dinner. Then we called it a night.

The following night found me in Camden for a bachelorette party. It was my first trip to this town just under two hours southwest of Little Rock. I neglected to fill up my truck in Little Rock earlier that day. Figuring I could do it at the Gurdon exit on I-30 before taking AR 53 and AR 24 the rest of the way.

I stopped at a Shell station and went inside to pay for gas. Apparently, this was the place for locals to hang out on Saturday night. Everyone turned to glare at me. As I waited on the cashier, who refused to acknowledge me while continuing her conversation with some hick, I was approached by identical twin hillbillies. Looking like extras straight out of *Deliverance,* they sized me up and down without saying a word. I don't know what they had in mind. They were so small that I, having gotten massive near the end of my first steroid cycle, was wider than the two of them side by side. Once it became clear that I wasn't welcome there, I left.

Unfortunately, there were no open convenience stores in Gurdon. I pressed on through forested state highways with my fingers crossed that I'd find gas soon. The further I drove, the less optimistic I became. Just as I was getting seriously worried, I rolled into the Arkansas hamlet of Chidester and an illuminated E-Z Mart replete with precious fuel. I gladly filled up and continued my journey for another ten miles before reaching my destination.

The memorable part of this party was a girl claiming she was going to "rock out with her cock out." After I informed her that was impossible, she replied, "Well, then I'll jam out with my clam out." I love that line and have applied it numerous times since to girls at parties. They love it too.

Then came Halloween. Some girl I met on Myspace dragged me to a costume party hosted by her sister. I did enjoy meeting and conversing with a few of the sister's friends. Particularly a hot girl named Susan dressed as a French maid. After a couple of hours, I left temporarily to go arrest a bachelorette and interrogate her friends. This was one of many parties I've done in the governor's suite at the Little Rock DoubleTree. One fortysomething woman who was clearly and understandably proud of her fake tits stuck a dollar deep inside one of her bra cups. I attempted to retrieve it with my mouth but was unsuccessful.

"Did you get it?" she asked.

I sighed, "All I managed to do with lick your nipple."

"Exactly!" she responded with a sassy grin.

Well played.

I redressed in my Halloween costume and returned to the party. It was still in full swing. Susan wanted to know all the details and I obliged. She asked me for a lap dance. I grabbed a chair from the dinner table and set it in the center of the living room. Everyone gathered around and watched with curiosity as I took Susan's hand and led her to the hot seat. The room filled with nonstop gasps and cheers as I gave her an ultra-sexy lap dance to "Pussy Control" by Prince. She eagerly followed my lead every step of the way. I buried my face in her warm pussy before slowly rising with her legs on my shoulders. I didn't strip, but she and I turned up the heat for everyone. Especially ourselves.

While everyone returned to whatever they were doing, Susan and I attempted to slip upstairs. I didn't give a damn about my date, and Susan clearly didn't give a damn about her husband who wasn't present. As if born to cockblock, some drunk fucking asshole sat down in that chair and loudly asked for his own lap dance. His name was Rusty, because of course it was. As names go, Rusty is the male equivalent of Becky. Much in the way that burgundy is just navy red. Everyone else immediately looked at him, then at Susan and I, as our clandestine plan instantly vaporized. I could've killed that piece of shit right then and there. But he received a fate worse than death when my date gave him the worst lap dance I've ever seen. That speaks volumes coming from me.

***

November came and so did the end of my first steroid cycle. My weight had jumped from 215 lbs. to 240 lbs. in a mere twelve weeks. Things were fine at first since the juice would linger in my body for a few more weeks. November is historically the worst month for booking private parties. Although business did slow down, we stayed busier than normal for that time of year. I began the month with a quick birthday performance at a Little Rock bar. In and out within five minutes.

During the writing of this book, I scored another birthday party at that same bar. Only to cancel it forty minutes later when the client pulled a Becky and attempted to renegotiate our agreed-upon price. This time, I blocked the client's number and let her figure it out on her own. No one went all Charolette on me this time, nor did I feel compelled to write an essay titled "Bobbie Stripped Bare".

My next gig was a bachelorette party in Birdtown, Arkansas. Not so much a town as it is a small grocery store and smattering of homes near a ninety-degree bend in AR 9 approximately one-hour northwest of Little Rock. As soon as I headed out, I smelled antifreeze and immediately returned home. I popped the hood to discover that a heater hose got nicked by the alternator fan. With no other option, I quickly removed that hose and rerouted the other heater hose to complete the circuit via bypassing the heater core. I drove to Birdtown and back on that chilly November night without heat.

I was glad to be somewhere warm as I entertained a group of twenty women within the comfort of the Birdtown Community Center. I've delivered numerous performances at small country venues like this one. While not as hoity-toity as a lake rental or hotel suite, these small buildings offer distinct charms for any group of friends who know how to make their own fun. It all comes down to the people involved. The girls in Birdtown were clearly a tightknit group of friends. As is the case with every great party regardless of how mild or wild things get.

I was back in Hot Springs the following week for a bachelorette party at a house on Lake Hamilton. Right across the water from the previous month's stripping extravaganza with Kyra. I was solo this time. While these girls weren't nearly as wild, they weren't reserved either. Displaying an affinity for having Reddi-wip licked off their tits. I hung around afterward to chat and drink. For some reason, I couldn't stop talking to them. To the point where they finally threw me out. Not that they hated me. They were getting sleepy. But I didn't want the moment to end.

***

Post-cycle depression had set in by December. It wasn't horrible, but I felt moodier than normal. I pushed through it as always and wrapped up the year while plotting for 2007. My final performance of 2006 was a Christmas party for the ladies of Rose Marie's grocery store in Marvell. It was around these parts where Levon Helm of The Band and *Coal Miner's Daughter* fame was born and raised. Much of the drive was on that monotonous stretch of I-40 towards Memphis. It improved once I turned south on U.S. 49 at Brinkley. Call me crazy, but there's much to be said for driving through farmland at night on a two-lane highway. Even in December as the crisp autumn air let me know that winter was but a few days away.

   The year ended with my old truck blowing a head gasket. Not willing to give up on it that easily, I disassembled the engine to discover a cracked block and burnt piston. It was time for an upgrade, so I dropped $1600 on a 1992 Chevrolet Silverado. It was a repo with a lower mileage engine swap. The dealer only charged me the remainder of the note plus $500 for the motor. It was a steal and remains my daily driver to this day. Kyra was less than impressed, but I wasn't ready to spend beaucoup bucks on expensive shit that I wasn't used to having anyway. This frugality would prove to be my saving grace in a few years.

   I was already booking parties through March of the following year and bringing in new female entertainers. Hardbodies had grown steadily in each year of its existence, and I knew 2007 would continue that trend. Between my angels, naked ambition, and newfound devotion to black-market pharmaceuticals, I was certain everything would get bigger and better. There was nowhere left to go but up. Or so I thought.

   My entire world was about to crash and burn. Once again, I would stand alone.

DON'T DREAM IT'S OVER

2007 - 2012

CHAPTER 19

Growing up in Las Vegas during the eighties, there was a dude who owned and operated a commercial window washing business on my side of town. He was a regular sight as he traveled from store to store on a yellow moped. Upon which was mounted a homemade yellow wooden box that carried his cleaning supplies. I'm sure most people paid him no mind. Some probably laughed at him. With entrepreneurial wheels already turning in my mind during those formative years, I thought his one-man operation was fucking cool. The moped was a brilliant touch, given the low overhead of a vehicle he could easily service and repair himself. He was his own man. Answering to only himself. I found that more impressive than the idea of sitting in a cubicle all day and enduring office politics bullshit. That dude will always be cool as fuck in my book.

***

2007 picked up where 2006 ended, and January was busy as fuck. The year began with Kyra and me entertaining well to do couples at a fiftieth birthday party in Little Rock. The birthday girl was enamored with me throughout the show. That always makes me feel incredible. I'm a sucker for flattery, and compliments never get old. Kyra teased me about the birthday girl afterward, but that was Kyra being Kyra.

A few days later, I took Chantelle to a birthday party in Little Rock. There were a few different guys she normally used for security, but none were available that afternoon. Making this a rare occasion when I went with her to a booking. This was for a doctor and small group at Baptist Health Medical Center. Needing to be clandestine as Baptist management would've flipped their shit if they knew, Chantelle rocked sweats over her stripper wear. I carried a gym bag containing her heels and my boombox. We were in and out within minutes as she totally made the good doctor's day.

My overall mood had improved since the end of my first steroid cycle. I worked out like a madman six days per week. Striving to maintain my gains and shed a little fat as I found myself caught in the vicious circle of bulk and cut. A perpetual loop that would dog me for years to come and one of the worst aspects, physiologically and psychologically, of steroid use. I still rocked bleached blonde hair but now resembling less Billy Idol and more Brian Bosworth. Despite my gains, I wasn't satisfied. Biding time until my next cycle in March.

With every expectation of Hardbodies reaching greater heights, I brought on new entertainers in January. Despite my best efforts, all were female. This was okay since any of my angels could quit without warning. They could all quit at once. I recruited a perky twentysomething blonde named Ashley, who in turn referred to me an attractive Latina by the name of Ciara. There was also a girl much like Kyra on the surface whom I'd courted on Myspace for some time.

Tall, busty, and into girls. She even had a friend for two girl performances. Unfortunately, she wouldn't amount to much.

There was no shortage of applicants, but most were garbage. I received email upon email from guys knowingly wasting my time and girls who had overrated themselves. One of the most frustrating experiences for me as both a talent agent and halfway decent human being was my pursuit of female talent. I had no qualms about approaching a woman and inquiring about her interest in being a private party entertainer. I encountered numerous attractive women who were flattered by the suggestion. Admitting to having already pondered and fantasized about the idea. Despite how beautiful and charming they were, they'd immediately disqualify themselves. Claiming they weren't good enough. On the other hand, nasty women inside and out had no qualms about offering forth their services. And always with an attitude.

My success throughout the region convinced me that I could expand my empire into other states. I commenced working on a new agency named BodyRoxxx Male + Female Strippers that would represent top-flight private party entertainers from coast to coast. This wasn't an original idea by any means, but I was so confident in my abilities as a talent agent and salesman that it seemed like the next step. Between everything else, I spent January authoring my business plan for this ambitious venture.

But first I had to drive to Weiner, Arkansas for a bachelorette party. Yes, Weiner. This small farming community approximately two hours northeast of Little Rock has been immortalized in countless articles listing places with funny or strange names. This was my first road trip in the new truck. Which meant that the electronic climate control module died two days prior. Without time to replace it, I bundled up on that late January night and hit the road. It wasn't too cold on the drive there. Mostly a straight shot up U.S. 67. Cruising along as Nelly Furtado said it right.

My 11:00pm arrival time was on the later side. The event was replete with lap dances, Reddi-wip, and mini quiches. The living room floor was covered with balloons and I inadvertently popped more than my share. The temperature had dropped significantly by the time I departed shortly after midnight. All that bundling wasn't enough this time as I spent the next two hours shivering and shaking. I couldn't get home fast enough. Once I did, I immediately cranked the heat, took a hot shower, and got into bed. Although warmed up, I felt a little off. Worried that I'd gotten sick. But I awoke several hours later feeling fine.

It was four years prior, a few months before moving to Arkansas, when I experienced my first bout of pneumonia. Life in Denver had turned to shit after being laid off from my day job. Bookings were scarce as I scrounged for every bachelorette and birthday party I could across a four-state territory. I'd lost weight due to malnourishment, although I kept pumping iron. My diet consisted mainly of El Monterey frozen burritos because they were cheap as fuck considering the protein and calories they packed. I even dated girls who worked in restaurants solely for free food. All that stress and exertion caught up with me as I spent an entire month sick as a motherfucker. It probably would've cleared up faster had I not kept performing, but I had no choice.

I felt okay after the Weiner party. Until the following Monday afternoon when my well-being nosedived. And I knew what it was. Despite eating more and healthier than four years prior, I'd once again pushed myself way too hard and obliterated my immune system. The next few days were spent in bed. Attempting to keep down food while doing my damnedest to sound upbeat on the phone. Yes, I was still taking calls for bookings. Someone had to do it.

I pursued business as usual while severely ill during February. Making time for rest when I could. It was during one of those scheduled rests that I discovered Wikipedia and spent an entire afternoon reading about serial killers. Other breaks were spent catching up on films ranging from the French New Wave classic *The 400 Blows* to the sleazy exploitation romp *Class of 1984*. I couldn't bring myself to get up one morning, so I watched *To Live and Die in L.A.* instead. Something about the high-class sleaze of William Friedkin's 1985 crime saga makes it a fitting metaphor for Hardbodies at that time.

Not only did I escort Kyra to a couple of her parties during this month, but I continued performing as well. Along with being weak and feverish, I did these parties on an empty stomach to avoid vomiting. Apparently doing a fine job of hiding my illness as no one asked me if I wasn't feeling well. A horny old broad at a bachelorette party in Sherwood, of all places, had the nerve to remark that my work was "easy money." I responded with a lecture on all the times I'd driven long distances and performed through pain and sickness as I had that night.

She wasn't the first person to accuse me of making easy money and sure as fuck wouldn't be the last. That's often the case for entertainers of all mediums. What we do isn't "real work" according to assholes who hate their jobs and probably their lives. That's somehow my fault since Hardbodies, despite the headaches it brought, was a labor of love for me. There is no law nor rational thought that states an individual can't both enjoy his or her work and demand top dollar for it.

And though I was self-aware of this at the time, I still let it get to me. I have no one to blame but myself for buying into the idiotic notion of hard work as a virtue. It's a virtue signal. Another gold medal event in the Oppression Olympics that selfishly places obligations upon others with, "I work hard, so everyone else needs to kiss my ass." And what the fuck is hard work anyway? Have you ever heard of soft or easy work? No, because it doesn't exist. And neither does hard work. Either shit gets done or it doesn't. I'm wary of any person who boasts of efforts expended rather than objectives achieved.

I possessed the confidence to take off my clothes for strangers and could seduce attractive women. Yet I lacked the confidence to give myself full credit and set greater personal expectations. I had fun but all too often allowed internalized Calvinism to deny myself the pleasure I'd earned. Constantly increasing my quota for output without the promise of rewards. Something like PussyQuest 2005 seems not so sleazy given how far I pushed myself day after day. Night after night. I had the ability and means to embrace a hedonistic philosophy by working smarter instead of harder. But I held back.

February ended and so did my pneumonia. I woke up one sunny morning feeling refreshed. Treating myself by going to McDonald's for a chocolate milkshake. It had been forever since something tasted so good. As I sat in my truck and sipped my decadent breakfast while watching the morning traffic fly by, all I could think about was getting back on track with everything. Hardbodies, the BodyRoxxx project, hardcore workouts, and my next steroid cycle.

It was a few days later when I made a milkshake of my own. A Jose Canseco Milkshake as it's sometimes called. I couldn't believe how comforting it felt to insert that long needle deep into my flesh and slowly press the syringe plunger. It was like reconnecting with an old friend I'd sorely missed.

CHAPTER 20

Booking a male or female stripper is a shot in the dark. The biggest reason being that most, if not all, the photos on a given agency's website are not of actual entertainers available for your event. Many of them aren't even strippers. Just random photos of hot guys and girls used for marketing purposes. Often in violation of U.S. copyright laws.

The typical scenario for many agencies goes like this: The client calls and is told whatever they want to hear. Then instructed to pick their top three (or five, or whatever arbitrary number) strippers from the website and told that one is guaranteed to show.

Here's my guarantee: the stripper from any of these agencies who shows up (if one shows up at all) will not only NOT be one of the entertainers the client chose but won't even be featured on the website.

This isn't to say that the mystery stripper is a bad entertainer. He or she may be a great entertainer. I know because I've been that entertainer working through such agencies back in the day. They also lied to me as my audiences often weren't what I'd been told to expect.

And the entertainer you receive could be far worse than you'd ever imagine. We're not talking about expecting a blonde guy and having one with dark hair show up. In early 2007, one of these agencies briefly undercut my booking fees with some guy, most likely a Hardbodies reject, they brought on board. As per two accounts I received, he arrived in regular clothes, stripped completely naked, and jerked off. That's what he thought exotic entertainment was. And the agency – whose name I don't recall, or I'd totally share it – sent him to at least two bachelorette parties. Meaning they sent him to at least one more party knowing what he'd do.

If you're wondering how they continue getting away with this, it's because they only charge $50 to $100 per booking on their end. No one is going to small claims court over that amount of money. Your bank is less likely to reverse such a charge and more likely to lecture you on trying to book a stripper. The only pragmatic recourse for clients is to chalk up the ordeal as a lesson learned the hard way. Resulting in these clients never again trying to book a stripper. Hurting all honest entertainers and agencies from coast to coast.

There are legitimate reasons why some agencies don't feature actual entertainers on their sites. In Hardbodies' case, this was due to our presence in a small market prone to good ol' Southern gossip and backstabbing. Many of my strippers refused to be featured on our website for this reason. The few who didn't changed their tune quickly after being recognized by some asshole who'd harass them and tell his friends. I filled the Hardbodies site with a combination of stock photos (which I purchased) and images of porn star acquaintances (with their permission) from other parts of the country.

But I was transparent about this practice with prospective clients who contacted me. This being Arkansas, most understood why I did that. If the would-be client was legit, I'd email photos of the entertainer(s) available for their event and go from there. No harm, no foul. The only people who voiced a problem with this method were mainly of the poor white trash variety who couldn't afford our services anyway. In that sense, keeping my strippers off the site allowed me to better qualify prospective clients.

***

I roared into March like a lion on steroids. Stacking more juice on this second cycle. So much that I was injecting into my shoulders along with my ass. Immediately after shooting up, I'd badly want to pump iron. And I would like crazy. I was making up for being sick throughout February. Feeling like I'd failed myself by getting pneumonia. Guilt swept over me at the mere thought of allowing sickness or injury to slow me in the slightest. This was not an option for me. I had to be perfect at all costs.

Business remained steady through March. Awaiting that explosion I believed inevitable. Although nothing special occurred, I enjoyed excellent bookings as did Kyra and Chantelle. Leah was increasingly less available, and I knew what that meant. With the writing on the wall, I began pushing my new recruits to up their game while continuing the search for even more talent. For all my tireless effort, however, I wasn't discovering new girls on par with my angels. At least I was finding decent girls. Which is more than I can say about the guys I encountered. All attitude. Zero talent.

I launched my talent search for BodyRoxxx and enjoyed a nice head start as those porn star acquaintances agreed to come on board. They were always up for making extra cash between shoots, and the porn thing afforded them a certain caché with prospective clients. I spent countless hours scouring profiles on adult talent websites. And I saw a lot of scary men and women. I could probably write an entire book on that experience if I could remember all that I saw. My favorite had to be this *Troll 2* looking motherfucker who wanted to do incest themed porn, because of course he did.

And what's with all the weird and degrading porn these days? Can't people just watch two hot girls fuck anymore? Maybe I am an old soul when it comes to porn.

I recruited approximately thirty entertainers for BodyRoxxx that month. Proving this project was truly a large-scale version of Hardbodies, only two were dudes. The girls were more enthusiastic, driven, and willing to give me a shot. Nearly all the guys I spoke with acted like divas and made ridiculous demands, because of course they did. A few girls did too. Like one who insisted I pay for her boob job. Still, the ladies were overall more willing to hear out my proposition through a filter of sensible thought.

Along with adult video performers, my class of recruits included glamour and fashion models as well as a professional wrestler. There was even a *Penthouse* Pet. A fucking *Penthouse* Pet! I was pushing my gigantic ego around in a wheelbarrow. I'd become so cocksure that I rejected a female applicant who would achieve moderate fame on a VH1 reality show. I didn't find her attractive in the slightest and had no idea how to sell her.

I built the BodyRoxxx website in conjunction with all this talent scouting. Creating a logo and color scheme that relied heavily on red. This contrasted Hardbodies for which electric blue had become the primary color.

While the BodyRoxxx project came together there was plenty to do in the here and now around Arkansas. It was around this time when Hardbodies began scoring local mainstream attention. Not in the sense that we were the subject of interviews and news features. Rather, that media people were talking about us and asking me for favors. I quickly learned that such favors would never be repaid. The exception to this rule was a guy named Blake, who was promotions director for the local Clear Channel stations. He always offered me something of value upfront in return for my assistance with any event he was producing.

Given that money talks and bullshit walks, the main reason media folk began reaching out to me was to sell advertising. As discussed earlier, radio made no sense financially. I did experiment with running ads in local print publications. Resulting in many inquiries but few bookings. I lost hundreds on those print ads, but that's better than losing thousands to radio.

Others tried selling me services including photography, web and graphic design, and technical writing. I never took offense to those people cold contacting me. They were trying to earn a living, and it takes guts to reach out to someone. What I didn't appreciate were those assholes who pitched me by insulting my existing operation. The Hardbodies website wouldn't win any awards but was informative, easy to navigate, and loaded quickly in an era when many prospective clients were still using dialup. It was inexcusable in 2007 for one web designer to call it a "piece of shit", but it's laughable in 2019 given that he was trying to sell me a Flash site.

Incoming calls and emails increased yet business remained steady. This got underneath my skin. Learning the hard way that increased exposure and brand recognition doesn't automatically result in increased sales. Many of the new inquiries were from people who couldn't afford our services and responded by being ugly. Countless "working men" criticized me for targeting a higher-end clientele with my female strippers. Well duh. Every strip club in Arkansas is a cesspool of drugs, prostitution, and overall mediocrity. Our clients were people who wanted adult entertainment that was classy and safe. As with anything else, you get what you pay for.

Guys mistaking Hardbodies for an escort agency was always a thing but out of control now. They were rude and far too arrogant for motherfuckers who'd relegated themselves to paying for sex. And they made no bones about what they sought. I would've racked up beaucoup busts had I been an undercover vice cop. Probably my favorite was the dude who left a voicemail saying he was "wanting a blowjob" and "don't give a fuck what she looks like." There was a local media personality who contacted me about finding a woman for sex. And more than one church pastor called me from his office phone as if I didn't know how to Google.

On the other end of the weirdness spectrum, a random guy emailed me of his own volition to inform me that he would never do business with us because he was a good husband, father, and Christian. I guess he was struggling with personal bullshit and that was somehow my fault, because of course it was. Would it have been asking too much of him to be a fucking man and to grow a pair? As for the Christian part… Who did he think most of our clients were? Zoroastrians? Please.

But all this new craziness did nothing to disrupt business as spring arrived. I accepted it as part and parcel of being in this industry. Dealing with these weirdos was my version of paying tribute to a hypothetical mafia. I pushed myself forward along with Kyra, Chantelle, and the new girls with mixed results. God, so much pushing. Even looking back after all these years leaves me overwhelmed physically, mentally, and emotionally. 2007 is the hardest year to write about. The one I least want to revisit. I was already coming apart at the seams by March. I didn't notice due to my steroid-induced state of euphoria. But even that wouldn't shield me from the maddening darkness just around the corner.

CHAPTER 21

I wrote about legitimate private party male strippers being scant as few guys are willing to put forth the effort required. That's only part of the story. The other part has to do with self-confidence, or lack thereof. It's a rare breed of man who can enter an unfamiliar place and entertain a group of women alone. My attempts over the years to turn novice entertainers into bachelorette party superheroes failed for this reason. When it came time for them to put up or shut up, not a word escaped past their lips. This is also why group dance numbers are the de rigueur of male revues. Most male strippers can't take to the stage alone.

Widespread abuse of performance-enhancing drugs among male strippers is a direct result of rampant body dysmorphic disorder throughout the industry. I was no exception as my years of steroid use stemmed from my own body dysmorphia. At least what I perceived as body dysmorphia. I'm not so sure now, but I digress. While it seems contradictory for people holding aesthetic related anxieties to become strippers, it makes sense in a fucked-up way. These guys are seeking affirmation from women. A quest for personal self-worth. Even at my worst, I never sought affirmation. I just wanted to entertain and connect with audiences. That's always been my passion. In my case, I took that passion too far.

My entrepreneurial drive and desire to entertain combined with an adventurousness sometimes bordering on recklessness served to override my anxieties and allowed me to take private parties by storm. Regardless, flattery from the opposite sex has always meant the absolute world to me. On the other hand, some women feel justified to criticize my physique based on individual tastes. I've been told that I have too much muscle and not enough. The same goes for fat. While both my body fat and lean mass have fluctuated over the years because I'm a fucking human, my physique has always been above average. And no, my price of admission does not afford anyone the right to pick apart my body.

Yet another reason I canceled my performance at Emily's birthday party. Given Becky's issues with the booking fee and the crazy stunt Charolette pulled trying to get me back on board, I was anxious that these two and others would point out every flaw on my body. Maybe I jumped the gun, but it wasn't a risk I was willing to take after what happened in April 2007.

***

The month began with Leah bowing out as expected. She'd accumulated a nice little nest egg and wanted to spend more time with her husband. They kicked things off with a trip to one of those Hedonism resorts in Jamaica. It was an amicable split. She said she might be back, but I knew better. As would happen with Kyra and Chantelle, Leah proved to be irreplaceable. The new female strippers filled those bookings with mixed results. A definite "it" factor was missing with these girls. Being a bachelor party ninja, she left behind some mighty big platform heels to fill. And they were never truly filled.

I forged ahead with Kyra and Chantelle in tow as I took bookings for April and June but not May. I hadn't received a legit inquiry for a male or female stripper in May and was getting worried. May had been a hugely profitable month for Hardbodies the prior two years. I was budgeting my personal and business expenses around a repeat of this in 2007. There were rumblings about rampant subprime mortgage lending coming back to bite the economy in the ass. But surely this wouldn't affect us. Right?

Mid-April found me performing at a bachelorette party in Oppelo, Arkansas. Name aside, nothing is amusing about this depressing community located in a heavily meth-infested area one-hour northwest of Little Rock. The party was mediocre. Not a disaster, but I've had better. Tips were meh. Half the girls hid in the kitchen. There were a handful of enthusiastic partygoers I chatted and drank with afterward. And that was the end of that.

Until the following Monday, when I received an email from a woman named Vanessa, who claimed to have been at the party. Although I didn't recognize her Myspace photo, I knew she'd been present due to her email. A hateful diatribe about me being hideously unattractive and the worst stripper ever. She chastised me for charging too much and not having a "little swimmer's build." Being large framed, I can't have a little build of any type. I also don't shred easily, even with steroids, so I mostly never bothered with it. Getting too lean causes me to lose my booty, and we most definitely can't have that. I was probably bloated that night from one of the steroids I was on and never used again after that cycle but far from the "fat disgusting slob" she accused me of being.

I somehow managed to keep my cool and replied. Asking Vanessa to elaborate on her issues with me. She responded with pathological lies about how I'd trashed the bathroom and broke some items in the living room. Given that my performance took place in the living room, I fail to see how I could've damaged anything without someone noticing and saying something. And I never mishandle the property of others. It's that whole Golden Rule thing by which I live. She claimed that the girls who were friendly to me hated my guts and talked mad shit after I left. This woman was clearly off her rocker. Attempting to bring me down to her level of misery and self-loathing.

And it worked. I was willing to believe her claims of me being unattractive and those girls hating me. Willing to believe this about every party I'd done. Much in the way that I'd worn myself down physically to the point of demolishing my immune system and catching pneumonia, I did the same thing to my mental and emotional state. I was susceptible to entertaining negative thoughts and feelings about myself, and that's exactly what happened. It didn't matter that this unsavory cunt was a lying sack of shit. I'd run myself so far into the ground that anything was possible.

A few days after my conversation with Vanessa, I lost a retail merchandising side gig I'd had for the past year. I was asked to start handling late-night assignments that required extensive travel. This was clearly not an option for me, so I split. On the plus side, it meant I could reduce the number of cell phones I carried from three to two. Losing that extra income wouldn't have bothered me as much if I'd had bookings lined up for May. But still, nothing. Not for me. Not for anyone. I couldn't understand it. Maybe I was a fraud and somehow everyone knew it. That didn't explain the bookings we were getting for June and July. But my mind was hardly in the right place anymore.

I had another bachelorette party the following Saturday. For the first time in my career, I was nervous. Resulting in a performance best described as reserved. It was fine by any technical standard as I said and did all the right things. But I refused to open up. I failed those girls because they thought they'd failed me as an audience. They were willing to like me as much as I would allow them to. But I was more than willing to believe they secretly hated me and couldn't wait to tear me to shreds behind my back.

My newfound irrational beliefs were reinforced when Vanessa emailed me the following week to ask me if I'd ruined any more bachelorette parties. And to accuse me of stealing jewelry. This was now a thing. And it wouldn't end anytime soon.

***

May 26, 2007. A warm and humid Saturday night. Alone in my garage. A mostly empty space illuminated by red and black lights. A folding metal chair sat in the center as I sat, stood, paced, and repeated. I was in an eighties' industrial music mood as "Lovely Day" by Front 242 blasted at one hundred watts:

"He walks through empty lanes

Cold anger, bursting veins"

This was the final weekend of May. I'd failed to book a single party for the entire month. Not only for me but for everyone. There were calls, but everyone was booking for June and beyond. It was insane. No one contacted me about May. Except for lowlife degenerates like the one who called me that night. I turned down the music and forced a pleasant greeting into the phone.

"You need to have one of your girls call me back," a gruff voice instructed me.

"Go fuck yourself, you dickless piece of shit," I responded to this disrespectful request as only I can.

Back to the music. Things slowed down with "Neun Arme" by Einstürzende Neubauten. Music was the only company I wanted. I didn't want to go anywhere, and that was unlike me. Despite the lack of bookings, my bills were paid with money to spare. I could've treated this downtime as an impromptu vacation. But I didn't see it that way. BodyRoxxx, on the other hand, landed its first two bookings in May. One in California. Another in Indiana. That was cause for at least a tiny celebration, but I was hung up on the four BodyRoxxx bookings I'd rejected due to no entertainer availability.

Chantelle was gone. She wanted to spend more time with family. I didn't doubt that being part of the reason, but I could tell she saw Hardbodies as a sinking ship. That left Kyra as the final angel, and I found myself leaning on her more than ever before. She didn't handle May well either. Taking every opportunity to make her unhappiness known. That pissed me off. I'd spent the past two years making her a top priority within my agency. I couldn't believe how ungrateful she acted over one bad month. The remaining girls called me constantly to ask if I had anything for them. With them being relatively new, I didn't know if they were buying this month as an outlier or thinking my entire operation was a lie.

The musical paced increased with "Assimilate" by Skinny Puppy. Speaking of dogs, Vanessa was now a full-fledged stalker in my life. Along with hateful emails, she was calling me from prepaid cell phones. Hanging up if I answered. Leaving ugly voicemails if I didn't. She even mailed a handwritten letter to inform me that she knew where I lived. This began the agoraphobia that still affects me somewhat to this day. If she believed all these awful things about me, who was to say that everyone else didn't?

I had no one to confide in regarding Vanessa, but I'm not sure it would've mattered. As a man being stalked by a woman, I could already hear people making light of the matter and questioning why I would complain. I was also far too proud to admit what was happening. Besides, she was a wife and mother with a respectable job at an established local company. This made her "good people" by Arkansas standards. What was I? A juiced-up pretty boy whose profession wasn't "real" work.

The industrial dance beats continued their relentless pounding as I turned on the strobe light. In slow motion, I took another pull from my huge bottle of Jack Daniels. Not even the bliss of synthetic testosterone coursing through my system was enough to overcome my despair. I recalled seeing my bottle of whiskey on the kitchen counter the previous afternoon. Next to a box of sleeping pills. For one crucial moment, the thought of consuming the entirety of both seemed like a plausible idea.

This might've been a good time to get out, but I had no other option for earning enough to pay my bills. The side work stuff was something I did more out of boredom than for money. Stripping was my bread and butter. I had to keep doing it whether I wanted to or not.

CHAPTER 22

It was back to business as usual in June. At least on the surface. Beginning with a bachelorette party on the first Friday. Booked by an existing client with whom I'd enjoyed a successful bachelorette party in Benton two years prior. I had great expectations for this one despite it being thirty minutes east of Little Rock in Lonoke. The location of no good party ever. This time was no exception. The bachelorette proved herself an ungrateful twat by running outside and crying. While this had nothing to do with me per se, my new state of mind coerced me to believe otherwise.

I took the Kyra clone and her friend to a bachelor party in Morrilton the following night. After whining the entire way, the girls delivered a so-so performance. I couldn't get too upset with them as the audience was nothing special either. They resumed their whining and crying about anything and everything on the drive back. There was some bullshit about one of them wanting to date the other's brother. Or maybe it was one of them wanting the other to date her brother. How I kept from intentionally smashing head-on into a semi was beyond me.

Fuck, I was depressed. Anxious beyond belief. As if everyone in the world was coming for me with a freshly ground ax. This wasn't narcissism. I readily believed that Vanessa's influence was far-reaching. Deep down, I knew better than that. But it was easier to believe otherwise. I'd also wrapped up my second steroid cycle and knew my depression was about to get worse. There were lots of bookings coming up. Both solo and with Kyra. How was I going to get through these?

I'd always prided myself on walking into every performance stone-cold sober. Whether it's a private party or male revue, so many male strippers require a buzz before showtime. I often have a drink or two with my audiences. Occasionally more than that. But I'd never consumed alcohol before a performance. Until now. I hated myself for it but couldn't see any other way to get through this.

And it worked. My first buzzed performance was a birthday party in Hot Springs on a Thursday night. I prepared on the drive there by drinking watermelon Bacardi Silver while keeping an open bag of watermelon Jolly Ranchers on the seat next to me. Should I get pulled over, artificial watermelon flavor on my breath would be much easier to explain away than that of beer or liquor. Not only was I literally drinking and driving, but I was chucking glass bottles out the window. I'm not proud of any of this.

The birthday girl was an attractive older woman who took to me. I gave her an intense alcohol-fueled lap dance. Her husband didn't mind at all. There was an obvious cuck quality about him. It wasn't the first time I'd encountered a husband with a cuckold fetish. And it sure as fuck wouldn't be the last. This is something that normally makes me feel uncomfortable, but the booze helped this time. Buzzed or not, however, there was no way in hell this went any further than a stripping performance. I repeated this alcohol-induced formula the following night at a birthday party in Jacksonville.

Kyra and I headed to El Dorado that Saturday for a bachelorette party duo performance. It was a gorgeous late spring evening. The sun still shone as we winded through the lush, green scenery of AR 35 and U.S. 167. I'd wondered how she'd respond to my drinking on the road. To my surprise, she didn't bat an eye and joined me. She was clearly as burnt out as I was. We talked and laughed while reminiscing about our prior travels together. She even helped me book a bachelorette party at the end of the month. Taking the phone and collecting information from the client.

We reached El Dorado as night fell upon us. I already possessed fond memories of this town between several excellent bookings and the local nightlife. This night was no exception. Kyra and I had wild and crazy fun together as we entertained our audience. They particularly enjoyed watching us lick Reddi-wip off each other's nipples. So much that she and I went through an entire can. Finishing it off as "Party Like a Rockstar" by Shop Boyz played. Wasn't that the truth?

Kyra dozed off as I drove out of El Dorado. I didn't know it then, but that night would be the final time I performed there. Southern Arkansas was about to become a nonfactor for Hardbodies. The region already had economic issues, and the coming recession would only make things worse. My phone rang about halfway back to Little Rock. I didn't recognize the number. It was late, so I let the caller go to voicemail. It was Vanessa. She just wouldn't stop. Instead of contemplating taking my life, I began entertaining the idea of taking hers. The world would be a better place without her presence.

Kyra and I amped up the raciness two weeks later at the DoubleTree in downtown Little Rock. Two girls from Southern Missouri were in town to celebrate one's birthday. Much like that insane bachelorette party in Hot Springs the previous fall, these ladies wanted an amazing experience. Kyra and I were totally game. We went with a cop theme and placed the girls in handcuffs. I danced on the birthday girl as Kyra took the client then switched. We had the girls lick Reddi-wip off our nipples. Then we sat side by side on the edge of the bed as the birthday girl sucked my cock and the client ate Kyra's pussy before switching. Sharing our respective sexual experiences all the while. These girls didn't have many between them and used this weekend as an excuse to travel out of state and try new things.

I spent my days desperately seeking new talent. The new girls weren't up to the standards set by my angels, and I knew the Kyra era of Hardbodies was coming to an end. Surely there had to be another Kyra, Leah, and Chantelle out there. Each had seemingly fallen into my lap. It only made sense that, should I beat my brains out hard enough, I could replace them. Yet another example of me attempting to work harder instead of smarter. Although working smarter wouldn't have saved me here. The talent I sought did not exist. Not in Arkansas.

The BodyRoxxx project whimpered along as I booked out of state parties here and there. Some of the amazing entertainers I initially recruited weren't that interested in taking private parties after all. Others, such as my prized *Penthouse* Pet, were too busy with other projects. Over the coming years, BodyRoxxx would be comprised of female strippers throughout the country finding us and doing some parties for a while before drifting away. It was income, but a far cry from the fortune I envisioned.

The Great Escape was a film I often had on TV during this time. The character I relate to most is Big X. I appreciate the equal parts glory and burden of being the person everyone looks to for solutions. Besides having always been a sucker for a good prison escape story, it was a fitting movie for where I was at the time. I wanted to make a bold and daring escape of my own. To where? I had no fucking clue. I wasn't even sure from what beyond Vanessa. As much time as I'd spent in 2004 wanting more for Hardbodies, the simplicity of those now halcyon days left me longing for them. They weren't a perfect time. But far preferable to where I was now.

Pining would have to wait as I drove to Fayetteville for a bachelorette party on the final Friday of June. The three-hour drive afforded me ample time to build and sustain a nice buzz. A little more buzzed than the girls. We took a break halfway through to chat and drink as they caught up with me. I don't remember much about this party other than the bachelorette being hot and having a sexy voice. Kind of raspy and sensual. She also shared my absurd sense of humor. I resumed my performance and spent the rest of my time with her as we laughed incessantly.

The following night had me closer to home with a bachelorette party in Alexander. A small town bordering the southwestern edge of Little Rock. I was buzzed again, as this was now a pre-party ritual. As a firefighter, I predictably failed to put out the fires I'd been summoned to contain. Along with my usual showmanship, I encouraged the girls to flash their tits at me repeatedly. This was something they'd kept hinting at. I merely gave them the okay to do it.

All those pretty titties were trying to tell me something. It should've been obvious while half-straddling, half-sitting on the bachelorette's lap while she lounged on the sofa and pulled down her tube top, time after time. Why would these girls invite a strange man into their home and be this forward with him? Because I wasn't just any strange man. They wanted to like me for me. And they did. Far more than I liked myself in that moment. Despite the war waging inside me, I forced myself to push forth the excitement and warmth that made me an exceptional entertainer. Aggressive and overtly sexual. Providing my audience with the judgment-free security to express themselves as they pleased in the company of the opposite sex. If only I could've seen it then.

I dropped off my gear at home and headed out to a Little Rock nightclub. Meeting up with some Myspace girls. We alternated between dancing and drinking as I regaled them with stories. I was interested in one particular girl. We bumped and grinded on the dancefloor as angry looking dudes stood around the perimeter with arms folded. Why is that always a thing at nightclubs? She was dumber than a box of rocks. Even for a one-night stand, I require stimulating pillow talk. I was also uncomfortable being out, so I called it a night.

And that was it for June. Hardbodies stayed busy throughout the month, and I made a lot of money. But I was fucking miserable and getting worse by the day. The combination of Vanessa, runaway self-criticism, and lack of elite stripping talent to fill the platform heels of my angels was an albatross of epic proportions. We already had bookings lined up for July and August. And there would surely be more to come. Could I hold it all together?

CHAPTER 23

I burned through the summer of my discontent with alcohol-soaked intensity as everything that could possibly go wrong did so and more. Hardbodies stayed busy through July and August, but there was no growth from 2006. In fact, we were back to 2005 numbers. While this meant that I was earning decent money, I was absolutely devastated by the regression. Tough economic times ahead were already affecting us as well as the ever-concerning lack of quality entertainers. It appeared that the Arkansas talent pool had dried up after blessing me with Kyra, Leah, and Chantelle. No one else matched those three.

Ciara came the closest. I escorted her to a bachelor party outside Conway on the first Friday of July. She was an excellent tease and capable of intelligent conversation. I was more disappointed with the audience. They seemed to take her for granted and were more interested in playing poker. There's no excuse for that anywhere. Even less so in Arkansas with its god-awful strip clubs. It seemed like guys would book female strippers only to resent them. Lending credence to my long-standing theory that some "working men" are bigger drama queens than the average teenage girl.

I had a bachelorette party the following night at the Peabody (as it was known then) hotel in downtown Little Rock. Previously named the Excelsior, this was the setting of the alleged encounter between Bill Clinton and Paula Jones. It was a brutally hot and humid Arkansas summer night. The air conditioning was out at this prestigious establishment. Along with tipping $13, my audience had the nerve to criticize me for sweating as I performed in what felt like a fucking oven. Meanwhile, Vanessa left an ugly voicemail. I went home and drank.

Because Ashley bailed on me at the last moment and Ciara wasn't available, I pushed Kyra into service for a bachelor party several nights later. It was in the Morrilton area. Near where Vanessa lived. Part of me wanted to tell Kyra about the entire ordeal, but I remained steadfast in keeping it to myself. This party also sucked. One of these assholes had the nerve to call her thick. She was offended and rightfully so. I must have looked like I was going to kill someone because the client wasted no time in trying to calm me down. I was at my peak weight of 260 lbs. at the time following my second steroid cycle. The combination of being jacked as shit and angry at the world made me scary as all fuck.

That was the funny thing about my steroid use. I'd make tremendous gains in a short period of time yet was never satisfied with the results. Steroids did amazing things to my body but weren't the miracle drugs I'd anticipated. The constant cycling prevented me from achieving consistency. To be fair, some of the problem stemmed from my embrace of conventional fitness wisdom. A lot of this is bullshit. And anyone who claims that doing tons of crunches won't help shrink your midsection deserves to be shot in the face. Repeatedly.

I could no longer stand to be home with my thoughts and spent many nights drinking while driving the backroads of Arkansas. I'd become familiar with all the speed traps and hunting grounds of various sheriff's departments, so I had no worries. Despite everything, I hadn't lost my passion for cruising along U.S. routes and state highways on hot summer nights with the windows down as music blasted from my speakers. Even shrouded in darkness, the lush Arkansas landscape relaxed me with its undeniable beauty. Occasionally, instead of going home, I'd stay at a motel. Although never sleeping well in strange places, this contributed to my escapism.

I'd do this following parties as well. Like the night in late July when I drove to Marshall for a bachelorette party. This town approximately two hours north of Little Rock is (as of 2019) home to one of the last operating drive-in movie theatres in the country. I don't remember much about the party. It must've gone well since I was there for a couple of hours as we all drank in the hot tub following my performance. Not finding the Interstate all that romantic, I took the long way home. These few hours were my calm before the storm because I knew Kyra was about to leave Hardbodies and me any day now. At that moment, however, I was all out of fucks to give.

***

Kyra quit the following Friday afternoon as I prepared for a bachelorette party that night in fucking Sherwood of all places. She resigned by calling me to bitch about the recent parties I'd booked for her. Aside from that shitty bachelor party, there was nothing wrong with any of them. I was present at many. She earned solid to excellent tips and had a blast with her audiences. The reality was that she was all stripped out and wanted to do other things. I understood but wished she'd been honest about it. What truly set me off was what she said about me.

"You need to get out of this business and do something else," she instructed me in a bitchy tone.

I was incredulous as I asked, "What the fuck is that supposed to mean?"

"It's not working. And you're just moody all the time. I don't even want to call you anymore," she replied without hesitation.

"Go to hell," I responded as only I could at the time.

And just like that, an era had ended. I entered 2007 with high hopes and my angels in tow. Now, not even three-quarters of the way through the year, it was all gone. I suddenly found myself left with a couple of average female strippers, a nationwide agency bringing in nothing more than extra spending money, lowlife motherfuckers constantly asking for favors, shattered self-esteem, and a fat, ugly pig who wouldn't leave me the fuck alone. No wonder I was drinking so much.

Kyra wasn't wrong in suggesting that I move onto an entrepreneurial venture in a different industry. I could've ended Hardbodies at that time after a successful three-and-a-half-year run. Far exceeding every would-be competitor who came before and after as not one lasted beyond ninety days. Although I had a few abstract ideas for other businesses in my head, I refused to throw in the towel. Not only because I'm stubborn as a mule, but also because I refused to go out this way. Most importantly, this was how I earned a living. I had no immediate replacement for that income.

I know some reading this are still wondering why I didn't attempt to forge a legitimate relationship with Kyra. I had a hard time locating her while researching this book but finally found her on Facebook. She's a wife and mother far from Arkansas. Living a lifestyle that I couldn't and wouldn't. Although still attractive, I wouldn't give her the time of day if I met her now for the first time. If we'd attempted a relationship, it definitely wouldn't have lasted.

I soldiered forth that night in Sherwood and the following night at a bachelorette party on Lake Ouachita. The latter took place in a cabin near the town of Mount Ida. Not far from Hot Springs. I put everything else out of my mind and enjoyed the scenic drive as I loaded up on watermelon Bacardi Silver. Even at night, the westward drive on U.S. 270 away from Hot Springs was stunning. As is the entire Lake Ouachita area. A popular retreat for Texans as per all the license plates I saw that night. I should've thought to camp on the lake afterward with my phone off. No strippers, clients, or Vanessa. Just me and nature.

The cabin was amazing. Set off the road and surrounded by towering pines. I entered to discover a spacious interior that blended rustic charm with modern comfort and convenience. It was a great party with a fun audience. The standout for me was the client. Her name was Anna. Along with being a beautiful blonde in her twenties, she was the sweetest person I'd encountered in some time. Authentic in her doting over me, the bachelorette, and her girlfriends. Her kindness meant so much to me in that moment. Why couldn't I meet someone like her who wasn't already taken? I would ask myself that again when I performed at her bachelorette party a few years later.

***

Business hadn't exploded the way I anticipated, but Hardbodies was still getting requests for strippers. When a girl named Bambi contacted me about coming on board, I was all too eager to give her a shot. She was attractive enough with her petite yet busty physique. And she said all the right things. My questions about her previous experience were satisfied by her responses. The only thing that bothered me was her claiming to be Jared Leto's secret girlfriend. Since everything else checked out, I chalked this up to nothing more than an especially goofy celebrity crush.

I wasted no time sending Bambi to a birthday party. And she totally fucked it up. According to the client, Bambi arrived looking so unkempt that she paid her just to go away. After apologizing profusely while refusing to reimburse the client (because she shouldn't have paid that skank in the first place), I called Bambi to get her side. She informed me that, as Jared Leto's secret girlfriend, she didn't have to take shit from anyone. If a crazed fan really did send him their severed ear, I'll bet I know who it was.

Now totally apart at the seams and barely holding myself together on a Saturday night in late August, I drove to a "fun" party in the farming community of Moro, Arkansas. Much of the ninety-minute drive east of Little Rock took place on I-40. I took the Brinkley exit and cruised down AR 238 while drinking myself into character. The road zigzagged through farmland as I tossed empty bottles out the window. I remember telling myself, "I can't keep doing this."

The party consisted of several middle-aged women gathered in a double-wide just outside town. It was fun. The lights were already dimmed when I entered, and I engaged my audience with lap dances and conversation. There was a certain coziness about the whole thing. Enough to make me not want to leave. I mostly just didn't want to go home, and I was too exhausted to drive around all night. I left after an hour as they were getting tired as well.

Despite being beat to fucking hell upon arriving home, I couldn't bring myself to be alone in bed with my thoughts. I grabbed my Jack Daniels, collapsed on the sofa, and turned on the TV just as Martin Scorsese's brilliantly absurd *After Hours* began airing. I couldn't stop dwelling on all that had happened over the past several months and where to go from here. I was bottling up so much within me because I had nowhere to turn. It felt like I was drowning in slow motion as no one noticed. Part of me hoped I would doze off that night and never awake. At the same time, I was far too stubborn to ever give up on myself.

I made it through the entire film. Just when I thought I'd never fall asleep, a repeat of a new show called *Chelsea Lately* came on. That did the trick.

CHAPTER 24

I didn't get many bookings for September but started the month with two parties on a Friday. The first was an easy afternoon birthday surprise at a Little Rock law firm that had me in and out in ten minutes. So easy, in fact, that I did it sober. But I got my buzz on while driving to a bachelorette party in Bismarck, Arkansas that night. Just over an hour southwest of Little Rock. Not far from spectacular DeGray Lake. You bet your sexy butt I have a story about a party there several years from now, but I digress.

It should've been a great party given my audience of lively and fun-loving twentysomethings. There was also an obnoxious, middle-aged woman who made it her mission to constantly Becky her way into my performance. She'd seen a male stripper perform at a bachelorette party in California years prior and relentlessly critiqued my performance for not being exactly like his. She couldn't nor wouldn't grasp the radical notion that private party strippers have their individual ways of doing things that are neither right nor wrong. Even as I walked out the door, she kept harping on about this guy.

"Fuck him and fuck you," I finally responded as only I can.

I took the scenic route home. Crossing over Lake Hamilton and cutting through Hot Springs National Park. Rocking out to Killing Joke's *Night Time* album. Breathing in clean late summer air as I drove through one of my favorite areas of Arkansas helped me to relax. Not just from the stress of California Becky but the stress of everything. Although nominally concerned about the lack of bookings for the next couple of months as I increasingly heard talk of layoffs and other economic woes, part of me was strangely relieved. Perhaps this could be the breather I so desperately needed. I just wish I hadn't felt so fucking guilty even fantasizing about it.

Bambi had the nerve to call me the following Sunday and ask if I had any work for her. I coldly informed her that Hardbodies no longer required her services and hung up. It felt fucking amazing. So amazing, in fact, that I immediately canned everyone else and canceled all upcoming bookings for female strippers. And just like that, I was back to square one as Hardbodies' sole entertainer. I also turned down male stripper bookings for a brief period while I pulled myself together. It was the right decision. This saved not only my business in the long run but also my sanity and perhaps my life.

My timing was perfect as the phone barely rang that fall. Save for booking the occasional BodyRoxxx party around the country, I took a much-needed convalescence. On top of not stripping, I eased up on both my workouts and eating habits. I occasionally took advantage of living within spitting distance of a Kroger and various fast food restaurants. If I found myself in the mood for burgers or ice cream, then I went and got some. Despite my recent drinking binge, I wasn't an alcoholic. Regardless, I largely abstained from alcohol during this time.

It was a dark and rainy autumn. Providing ideal ambiance for days when I did nothing but watch television. I discovered, no pun intended, shows like *MythBusters* and *Dirty Jobs* as well as *Good Eats*. Especially notable was my introduction to Anthony Bourdain via *No Reservations*. He's the closest thing I claim to a writing influence. Showing me how to embrace my own attitude and swagger and make them central to my narratives. Like Bourdain, sometimes I too would bear witness to the unspeakable culinary atrocities of Rachael Ray and Sandra Lee around this time.

I also played NES games on PC. Finally getting the chance to beat *Super Mario Bros. 2* and *3*, *Contra*, and a few others. As a kid, I beat *Super Mario Bros.* without cheats while playing through every level on my original life and never touching a single enemy. I also indulged in some Denver nostalgia as I watched the Colorado Rockies execute their infamous Rocktober run before being swept in the World Series. For the first time in years, I rarely thought about or did anything stripping related.

Aside from goofing off, I commenced work on a business venture in a different industry. Despite not being the writer that I am now, I could already tell an entertaining story. And I cooked up the idea of producing a monthly print publication. Titled *Exposé*, it would explore arts, entertainment, culture, and more throughout the region. I envisioned it as a sexy, edgy, and stylish alternative to the existing free local rags. All of which sucked and continue sucking to this day. With no idea what I was doing, I threw myself headfirst into learning about everything from publishing software to advertising sales. It was an ambitious project that temporarily satisfied my naked ambition.

Unlike Hardbodies, *Exposé* developed a buzz practically overnight. It was like I posted about it on Myspace one day, and people were talking about it the next. Would-be advertisers and contributors came calling along with people who wanted to be featured. With so much free time on my hands, I said, "Fuck it," and began working on the debut issue set for March 2008. I wrote a few features including one about a local woman trying to launch a fantasy maid service. A business idea that's popularity far exceeds its market demand. When not writing, I sold ads and got familiar with Adobe InDesign.

It all began moving too fast. And that wasn't a good thing for me at that time. I intended this as a slow burn business venture. Ideal considering my current state of mind. I was inundated with emails and Myspace messages from people I didn't know telling me I should do this or that. I quickly discovered that finding decent contributors for a publication was just as maddening as finding decent strippers. One guy ignored my mission statement when he pitched a feature on a new Ruby Tuesday location. There was nothing about *Exposé* that even remotely screamed, "We publish features on chain restaurants!" He got all butthurt over that rejection, because of course he did.

If nothing else, I ran with *Exposé* as a form of escapism. It distracted me from Hardbodies being dry-docked for the moment as well as from Vanessa. Her harassment slowed to an email or two per month. They were still ugly as fuck, and so was she. And it still affected me. I was mostly a shut-in during this time and rarely ventured outside for anything beyond food and tanning. For the first time in my life, I felt like staying home. It was incredibly cozy as the weather and the world at large grew ever colder outside. So, I went with it.

Inevitably, I pulled the plug on *Exposé*. It was getting overwhelming as I handled every aspect by myself. Which meant that recent history was repeating itself. Fuck that. I was trying to pull myself together. Not further beat my head against the wall. I refunded my advertisers and shelved the project. A good idea considering the current plight of print publications. I would revisit the *Exposé* premise as an online publication multiple times over the following decade but never go anywhere with it. I finally accepted that were I to author something of epic scope, it should be a book about my life in stripping. And here we are.

***

December arrived. I began plotting the return of Hardbodies in 2008. After nearly three months of non-stripping related shit, I was ready to get back in the game. There was no choice. I couldn't afford to stay on vacation forever. Along with getting myself back in shape both physically and mentally, I contemplated where to find new female strippers. I invested time in studying Arkansas and the cultural geography of the state from region to region. County to county. I don't know what edge I was looking for specifically. I just wanted to better understand my surroundings. Spending many nights learning more about the state while enjoying the impressive oeuvres of Japan and Gary Numan.

I agreed to help Blake from Clear Channel on a promotion involving some band in town. It was like Creed with a different singer. I think. They played a show at a now-defunct Little Rock nightclub that was previously one of those hemispherical movie theatres from back in the day. I pulled myself together as best I could and headed out to hang with Blake as he played his drunken Santa character. He still shows people photos of us together at that event. This embarrasses me since I didn't look all that great. My downtime had left me bloated and my muscles looking depleted. It was due time to get back on top of things and prepare for a new steroid cycle in January.

Things quickly fell back into place. I cleaned up my diet and upped the volume and intensity of my weight training sessions. Even booking a bachelorette party in North Little Rock for December 29. My birthday. This was perfect. Not only would I close out the worst year of my life on a high note, but this comeback would provide me with positive momentum to carry me into a new year and beginning. Stripping was once again exciting to me. I'd built Hardbodies out of nothing once. I could do it a second time with the added benefits of experience and wisdom.

My birthday arrived along with my redemption party. And it was arguably the worst booking of my career. Unlike the Vanessa party, which itself was mediocre but not disastrous until after the fact, or the relentless drama surrounding Emily's birthday party for which there was no performance, this party was horrendous in and of itself. The audience was a fucking disgrace. Rude and disrespectful from start to finish. I was so eager to please that I put too much effort into righting a sinking ship. I should've left after five minutes. Not only did they barely tip, but those bitches had the nerve to try and reclaim that money afterward. Why the fuck was I even there?

There were only 48 hours left in that god-forsaken year. That still seemed like an eternity. 2007 could not end fast enough for me even if it had ended six months ago. Why wouldn't it die already? Just fucking die, you pig! I had no fucking clue what 2008 had in store for me, but I was willing to believe it had to be better than this. I'd fallen so far in such a short time that I was still catching up with everything. I was so unbelievably sick and tired of it all. There may have been only two days left in that year, but it seemed like two years. If I could've slept through the rest of 2007, I would've.

But I survived those 48 hours like I'd survived so much else that year. I sat home and waited for the ball to drop with more anticipation than Dick Clark and everyone in Times Square combined. When the clock struck midnight, I let forth a massive sigh. It was finally over. 2008 was officially here.

Now what?

CHAPTER 25

I drove to the Little Rock suburb of Maumelle on the second Saturday of January 2008 to perform at a fiftieth birthday party. Maumelle has been the setting of numerous performances over the years. I took AR 100 to Odom Boulevard. The same route I've taken to every Maumelle booking before turning into any one of the various housing developments along that street. Prior to Hardbodies, I sold a few hot tubs to people in this neighborhood that sits along the Arkansas River and contains several small bodies of water including Lake Willastein.

My client was a sweet, middle-aged woman who was as concerned about showing me a good time as she was her guests. That's how I'd describe everyone in attendance. A fun and friendly group of middle-aged women with neither a Becky nor Charolette in sight. My birthday girl was also a recent divorcee, so there was that to celebrate as well. Due to the high neckline of her top, I brushed aside her hair and licked Reddi-wip off her neck while "Low" by Flo Rida blasted from my speakers.

"Don't give her a hickey," one of her friends interjected humorously with faux caution.

I shook my head and reminded her, "This isn't high school."

After my performance, I had a drink with my party girls as we chatted. This was the first drink I had that night. My pre-party boozing now behind me. The client beamed at me with appreciation as she asked me innocent questions like:

"So, how's business?"

Luckily, she made me feel good enough to easily maintain my composure.

"It's going well," I responded cheerfully.

I made my exit and drove home to the sounds of Duran Duran night versions. While lacking scandalous delights such as titty fucking or girl on girl, it was an enjoyable experience for all involved. I left my client feeling as if she'd received the bargain of the century. I hadn't felt that level of gratitude in months. It's the party I would've loved for my birthday two weeks prior. An excellent way to kick off a new year and fresh start.

***

2008 immediately washed away the sins committed by me and others the previous year. Business stabilized and remained consistent over the next two years but not at 2006 levels. My angels were gone. Vanessa popped up occasionally to remind me how awful I was. Hardbodies returned to underground status. The inquiries from people either wanting favors or trying to sell me something slowed to a trickle. Lonely guys also stopped calling en masse at all hours of the night, thank fuck. My advertising focus was on yellow pages, internet, and word of mouth. I refer to this time as Hardbodies Lite.

I made no effort to seek out male talent. Not only did I require all male stripper bookings for myself to make ends meet, but there weren't enough bookings to have even one other guy. Many requests were specifically for me based on my reputation as an excellent and provocative entertainer. I picked up new female strippers here and there to handle bachelor and birthday parties. While I avoided weirdos like Jared Leto's girlfriend, there were no standouts. All were along the lines of Amber or slightly better. I didn't get to know any of them. Much less partner with anyone as I had with Kyra. The lineup of me and a couple of serviceable female strippers at any given time would comprise Hardbodies for the next five years.

There was no shame in running a steady yet unspectacular business. But I didn't feel that way at the time. Although Hardbodies was still alive and kicking after all it and I had endured, I saw myself as a failure. Contributing further to my newfound shut-in habit. My home gym remained a place of solace as I began the new year with another steroid cycle. I wasn't at all the stay at home type, but this was easier than attempting to trust people or talking about my business. Bachelorette and birthday parties became my social life. Providing me with the perfect outlet for my histrionic tendencies. And I got paid for it.

***

I had a busy spring that began with a bachelorette party at the Best Western in Southwest Little Rock. An unusual location due to being in one of the many bad parts of town. These girls didn't know any better. They'd come down from Russellville and planned to spend most of their night at the nearby Electric Cowboy. That representing the high life to them.

Gratuity was so-so. I suppose on par for a dozen women packed in a cheap motel room. The only notable thing about this mediocre affair occurred as I worked my way around the cramped room. I reached an obnoxious, middle-aged woman and dropped my head close to her lap. Immediately I was overwhelmed with a stench not unlike road kill baking in the August sun. I've been fortunate enough over the years to have encountered but a few instances of vaginal infection while stripping. But each one made me want to cut off my nose.

This woman was totally into me, because of course she was. That made matters worse in so many ways. She was fucking odd with her frumpy, sixties-esque fashion sense. The floral print dress, pantyhose, and short perm didn't do it for me. Nor did whatever the fuck had crawled up her snatch and died. This alone was worth at least a second booking fee. If only I could've forced Vanessa to go down on her at gunpoint. I spent only a few seconds on Sixties Becky With Twat Rot before moving onto a more hygienic girl.

I was in Morrilton for another bachelorette party the night after Vaginapocalypse Now. The client for this party was a woman named Karen. She was the mother of the groom. Unusual but not unprecedented. Even more unusual was how I got to know her somewhat before the party as she stayed in touch with me throughout the weeks prior. Her marriage was falling apart as she and her husband divorced not long after this, and she understandably struggled with this. We had several lengthy phone conversations. Talking about things I cannot recall. I went along with this not only because I'm truly that nice but also due to my own need at the time for a friend. Our respective feelings of being lost and alone were all we had in common. That was good enough.

Much like I'd done the previous fall with my magazine project, Karen clearly threw herself headfirst into organizing this party as an escape. There was no doubt she wanted to show her future daughter-in-law an amazing time. But it felt more like Karen's party than anyone else's. Although I was on schedule, I remember her calling with an impatient tone while on my way. The anticipation on her part was that great. She'd rented out a nightclub for the event. Balloons were everywhere. I arrested my bachelorette and danced all over her as Karen took photos. She continued capturing my image as I made my rounds with all the guests.

It was Karen's turn as I made her take a seat. Despite being the girl most excited over my presence, she was also the most apprehensive about being close to me. No more stalling. It was time to get down to business. Although I was never into her personally, the experience was thoroughly exciting for me nonetheless. She had an absolute blast receiving that lap dance. It truly meant a lot to her. In that moment she forgot all her worries. The dual stresses of ending a marriage while holding everything together. Enjoying life for herself and no one else. That's what it's all about for me as an entertainer.

The audience split and went their respective ways. Karen asked if I wanted to hang out with her. Feeling adventurous, I said yes. I had no idea what she had in mind. It turned out that neither did she. The sun was setting as I hopped into her vehicle. I was starving, so she drove to Sonic. Not my first choice, but I was too hungry to care. After eating, she took me to a bowling alley. Despite being Saturday night, this place was fucking dead. Instead of bowling, we sat at a table and talked about mostly nothing. We went to another bar and did the same thing. I finally called it a night and she drove me back to my truck. The drive to Little Rock afforded me time to ponder the night's events. I felt bad for Karen and recognized the agony of her world falling apart. If hanging out with her for a couple of hours helped, then I was more than happy to have obliged.

***

I had a bachelorette party in Batesville a couple weeks later. A storm was moving in, and I hoped to make it before the downpour. It was one of those hauntingly beautiful gray spring evenings as I made the two-hour drive from Little Rock. My audience was satisfied after one song. The client was happy as she slipped me an additional fifty bucks on my way out. All hell broke loose once I made it out of town. The rain hammered upon my truck with no mercy. It wouldn't have been so bad if my wipers hadn't suddenly died. A parade of would-be reckless drivers accumulated behind me as I carefully descended U.S. 167 towards Bald Knob.

My vision through the windshield was so impaired that I rolled down the driver's side window and stuck my head out for a better look. This left me soaking wet, but that was better than running off the road. I'd had enough of this by the time I reached Bald Knob. Dropping that bonus fifty on a motel room. Luckily, I got a first-floor room with an empty space in front. I quickly unloaded the truck and sought solace in my over-glorified storm shelter. As I warmed up in a hot shower, I kept looking at the tiny bathroom window. Covered by a flimsy metal grate coated in the same paint as the walls. I tried to imagine someone using that window to sneak in or out of the room. Not me, because I would've gotten stuck.

I didn't know what to expect as I dropped my towel and climbed naked into a strange bed. This wasn't the first time I'd done that, I suppose. I grabbed the remote and searched in vain for something to watch. It was an election year. What can I say? The Padres were playing the Astros and I settled on that. This was at a time when smartphones were still catching on. Although my flip phone had internet, it was slow and limited. But I enjoyed my stay. It was nice to take a short break from everything without feeling like I was running away from shit. I even managed to fall asleep.

It was a dream like no other. So unbelievably vivid that I still remember it like it occurred five minutes ago. I stood naked on a stage before an audience comprised of women who'd crossed my path over the past decade. Not unlike what Guido Anselmi fantasized in Fellini's *8 ½*. My physique was impressive but not the steroid-fueled one I had at that time. This one was pure and natural. More like the post-steroid body I'm rocking now. Perhaps my body was trying to tell me something, but I was several years away from listening. I was rock hard in every way imaginable. Stalking the stage like a wild animal. Awash in fog and multicolored lighting.

Every member of my audience looked to me for leadership. But I didn't merely want to tell them what to do. I wanted each woman to find the courage to do exactly as she desired in that moment. For me to stand before them physically, mentally, and emotionally naked required total confidence without a shred of self-doubt. Each girl took a piece of my confidence, made it her own, and chased her respective sexual muse. Many danced and joined me in being naked. Some performed sex acts with me. And some with one another. A few chose to derive pleasure from watching the debauchery surrounding them. No matter her persuasion, it was all good

CHAPTER 26

April showers brought May parties. Hardbodies wasn't exceptionally busy, but things were certainly improved from the previous May. Not that it could've been worse. It was hard to believe that a year had passed after spending an entire month in a continuous panic attack. Things were improved. Time had managed to somewhat heal those old wounds. If only time could've done something about Vanessa, who began the month by sending me yet another hateful email. Now accusing me of stealing multiple iPhones. It would've been a neat trick on my part since that party occurred nearly three months before the first iPhone hit the streets.

I drove to Hot Springs one afternoon for a birthday party at a medical clinic. It was nice to take a ride out there and back during the day to enjoy the natural beauty along U.S. 70 and in Hot Springs itself. That warm and partly cloudy day did not disappoint. The slight drizzle I encountered here and there only enhanced the mood. It was sexy weather perfect for stripping. If only I could have an afternoon party in Spa City every spring day.

The clinic was open for business. This was a quick, in and out affair between appointments. It was cloudy when I arrived, but sunlight quickly poured through the windows as I straddled my handcuffed birthday girl. I truly wanted to make her day extra special, if only for a moment. Before I knew it, I was back on the road. I stopped for lunch at a nearby Chili's. Sitting alone near a window, I reflected upon the performance I'd delivered only minutes earlier. This pondering over a post-performance meal is something I've done countless times. The privilege of entertaining others is the ultimate high. I often experience a moment of clarity afterward.

But it was different now. Hardbodies was only four years old. Yet I'd already experienced a lifetime of dizzying highs and destructive lows during that time. I'd become increasingly reflective by the spring of 2008. Not that I hadn't previously, but I was now making a point of thoroughly savoring every special moment. Every future memory in real-time. I still had a long way to go in this business but didn't know that at the time. I'd already gotten a taste of how quickly it could all be taken away from me. These experiences meant more to me than ever before.

***

My sex life was also scaled back during the Hardbodies Lite era. That had to be expected given how closed off I was to the world. I wasn't meeting as many women I wanted to fuck, unlike a few years prior. Was it them? Or was it me? But I was still game to make my move on any girl who caught my eye. As happened at a June bachelorette party in Bentonville. The home of Walmart.

I made the three-hour drive on a Saturday afternoon. The sun shone brightly as I cruised along in good spirits. I was due in Bentonville by

7:00pm. That's early for a bachelorette party, but there would be several older women in attendance. I felt a good vibe from the client over the phone. She and the bachelorette were in their early thirties. As were a couple of other girls. I would have some youthfulness to play off during my performance. Although I travel to every party with optimism, I couldn't help but think this one would be extra exciting.

It was an older neighborhood. Each side of the street aligned with a row of small and mismatched minimal traditional homes. Most were blue or white. A couple rocked the boat in pale yellow. Front yards were covered in vibrant green grass by virtue of this being June in Arkansas. A variety of trees loomed over the neighborhood, but the sun nevertheless broke through as it began its descent into the western horizon. I got the impression that most residents were elderly and had already settled in for the evening. A deafening silence filled the hot and humid air.

As I put on the rest of my cop costume on that quiet street, I looked up to see an attractive blonde walking towards me. This was my client, Nicole, and her Myspace photo didn't do her justice. She was tall. In flats, she was nearly as tall as me. Her painted-on designer jeans accentuated long, shapely legs and an incredible ass. Add in her off the shoulder top, and she fit in this neighborhood as well as I did. There was a ring on her finger, but so what? For the next hour, she and the rest of the women in that small, white house would only have one man in their lives.

I read much from Nicole's body language and tone of voice as we squared up on the booking fee and went over details before I made my entrance. For some clients, the mere act of booking a male stripper is a thrill in itself. There's an air of danger and uncertainty about the whole thing that makes it exciting. The outside possibility that I'd take her money and run makes for a risk-taking exercise that can get a female motor running. Nicole was everything at once. Enthusiastic, nervous, intrigued, and slightly defensive about it all. To me, it was fucking hot.

Made even hotter as I watched her walk back to the house. Dat ass indeed.

The bachelorette was about to marry husband number two. This gave my performance an advantage right out of the gate. Now over the mystique of first love, the second time bachelorette is a pragmatist about matrimony. She loves this new man in her life but knows better than to view him as the be-all, end-all of her existence. My bachelorette that evening was no exception. She welcomed my presence with open arms and legs. As her hands kept busy grabbing my ass, she was reminded of her fiancée.

"I love him, but he doesn't have an ass like this," she proclaimed in pragmatic, second-time bachelorette fashion.

Not only did she enjoy having me all over her, but we engaged in conversation and joked around throughout my show. The rest of the audience was enjoyable as well. The older women weren't interested in lap dances but were polite and encouraging. And the gratuity was generous. My only complaint early on was that Nicole hung back in the kitchen. She watched, and I felt her eyes on me the entire time. I constantly looked over and, as if trying to communicate with her telepathically, tried to give her what I thought were inviting looks. I wanted her in on the action.

It was time to bust out the nuclear option on Nicole. I retrieved a white bath towel from my duffle bag and wrapped it around my waste. Everyone watched in shock and awe as I removed my g-string and was now clad in nothing but cowboy boots. Not only did this excite my bachelorette even further, but Nicole could no longer keep her distance from me as she made her way over to us. As the three of us danced together, the other women could take no more and stepped outside for a smoke break. I flirted with Nicole if for no other reason than the sheer fun of it.

After a few minutes of dancing in this party girl sandwich, the bachelorette also headed outside to take seven minutes off her life. This afforded me some one on one time with Nicole.

She didn't disappoint as she leaned in and whispered in my ear, "Do you ever get hard while doing this?"

I was already getting hard and this truly made me stand at attention.

"Some girls bring it out of me," I replied with a wink and a nudge in my tone of voice.

We continued dancing as she slipped her hand underneath my towel and stroked my cock. Instant chills all over my body. I tried to maintain my composure as she flashed a smile that was equal parts sassy and seductive.

"I want to feel you inside me," she sighed heavily.

Was she for real? Or was this some form of role-playing? If this was legit, I was totes down for it.

"Let's do it. When and where?" I demanded.

Her face lit up like a fucking Christmas tree as she told me the name of the hotel where she was staying and the room number.

"Does ten work for you?" she asked.

I smiled and said, "Ten is perfect."

We separated as the other women returned. I wrapped up things while chatting with my audience. Most of them didn't know that I'd driven all the way from Little Rock and were shocked that I was driving back that night.

Meanwhile, Nicole headed for another room. I watched as she walked away and tried to contain my excitement over getting to peel those tight jeans off her firm, round butt. I had to wait two hours for that but needed to eat first anyway. Dinner before dessert. I said goodnight to my bachelorette and her friends. They wished me a safe trip home as Nicole walked me out.

"You're not going to stand me up, are you?" she asked nervously.

I shook my head.

"I'll be there," I replied with authority.

"See you later," was all she could push past her lips in that moment.

Night had fallen as I drove off in search of something to eat. I spotted a Village Inn and thought to myself, "Fuck it. That'll work." It conjured memories of me and my old Denver crew enjoying our weekly early morning rendezvous at Village Inn back in the day. I thought about that as I ate my dinner. When I wasn't thinking about fucking Nicole's brains out. I wanted her so badly I could taste it.

Expectations ran great on my drive to the hotel. The night air felt refreshing on my face as I cruised along with the windows down and "Dance Hall Days" by Wang Chung blasting from the speakers. I was cool on the surface, but the anticipation had my stomach in knots. That I felt this way for the first time in seemingly forever was exciting. I'd been closed off from the world for so long. If anyone needed some no strings attached pussy that night, it was me.

I wasted no time when Nicole greeted me. Pushing her back and shutting the door behind me. I grabbed her by the hips and pulled her tight against me. We locked lips as my tongue explored her mouth and vice versa. I squeezed her butt and grinded my crotch on hers as our lips remained pressed together. She let herself fall back onto the bed and pulled me along. Kissing as I laid on top of her. She was now grabbing my ass. I broke my lips from hers to kiss and lick her neck and shoulder as the fragrance of CK1 filled my nostrils. The room was dim. Only the lights of the city outside illuminated us via the window.

I removed her top and bra. Her round, C-cup tits were warm in my hands. Contrasting the subtle bite of the air conditioner fighting the muggy heat that night. Chill bumps covered her smooth skin, and I wrapped my arms around her. I placed my mouth on each of her nipples and swirled my tongue on them. She arched her back and shook as I pressed my tongue against each nipple before sucking harder and flicking my tongue over them. I kissed my way down her torso until reaching her jeans and unbuttoning them.

She decided I was wearing too many clothes. Pushing me off the bed and standing next to me. I lifted my arms as she removed my t-shirt and tossed it into a corner. After she played with my nipples as I'd done to hers, I dropped to my knees and turned her around. Slowly, I pulled down her skintight jeans to reveal her sexy ass in a lacy red thong. I couldn't help but smack and lick each cheek as she giggled and moaned. Upon removing her thong, I was delighted to discover that her pussy was totally shaved. I don't like pubic hair on myself or anyone else. It's not aesthetic, and there's no good reason to keep it.

I was more motivated than ever to push her back on the bed, spread her legs for days, and dive in face first. God, she was sweet like candy. I opened her lips to dance my tongue over her clit and suck it while inserting one, two, and finally three fingers inside her soaking wet pussy. She moaned and squirmed incessantly as I massaged her g-spot and tasted her rapidly flowing juices. There was something pure and innocent about this. I couldn't remember the last time I enjoyed the pleasure of a woman's company without the specter of drama casting its long and ominous shadow upon me. Only she and I existed in that moment as I brought her to multiple orgasms.

My tongue and fingers needed a rest. Nicole took this opportunity to roll me over and return the favor. She was magic as she took my rock-hard cock in her mouth and worked it ever so delicately with her tongue. I lied back and let the rest of my body go limp as if soaking in the sun on a tropical island. Perhaps I should've been livelier, but I think she knew I was enjoying her spectacular fellatio skills. She revisited her hand job from earlier while teasing my frenulum with her soft, wet tongue. I was overwhelmed with the sensation of falling gently through infinite space without a care in the world.

Nicole slid her tits up my body and hovered her pussy over my cock. She lowered herself until I was deep inside her. The initial penetration was so mind-blowing that we both remained still for a moment and enjoyed simultaneous orgasms. Contrary to what some have stated, men can experience multiple orgasms without ejaculation. For me, it results from embracing the sensual, full-body aspects of sex, and not merely focusing on getting myself off. If I want a quick release, it's much easier to do that by myself with the help of girl on girl porn.

She rode me softly at first while I caressed her sexy, naked body with my hands. The feel of her curves made my fingertips tingle with electricity. I grabbed her ass with both hands. Lifting her up and down as she tossed her head back and breathed heavy. We worked together rhythmically. Thrusting my cock hard inside her soaking wet pussy every time she brought it down on me. The night grew hotter with every move until we couldn't wait anymore. She leaned forward. Pressing her tits against my chest as we embraced each other for dear life. I fucked her fast and furiously. Our unbridled moans filled the air. Once I knew she'd reached the point of no return, I let it all go deep inside her as we came together explosively.

We held each other for the longest time until she finally rolled off me. Few words had been spoken between us to this point and that didn't change following our sexual tour de force. We looked at each other for a while. It was all the conversation we needed. That was the nature of our relationship. And yes, it was a relationship. One that lasted only for a night. We were both in the same existential place at that time. Fate allowed us to comfort each other through equal amounts of carnal give and take. It was what it was and helped keep me going through it all.

I dressed and left. Not interested in spending the night, and she didn't offer. Our farewells were generic. I wished her goodnight. She told me to be safe on my long drive home. That was it.

I was on such a high that my three-hour journey flew by. My mind analyzed the events of the past four years and all I had experienced. That night's party and subsequent sexual encounter with Nicole proved time would forgive my past mistakes. If only I could've forgiven myself. But I couldn't. Not even for things I hadn't done. And that was the worst feeling of all. It made no sense, but that's the way it was.

A scan of radio stations just south of Fayetteville resulted in "Amarillo by Morning" by George Strait himself oozing from my speakers with its haunting words and melodies. I wasn't rich like I'd expected, But, Lord, I was free.

CHAPTER 27

The second half of 2008 was steady if unremarkable. That's why I can relegate it to a single chapter. I stayed busy. Audiences ranged from okay to great. Vanessa still emailed occasionally to inform me how awful I was. More steroids were injected. This was a routine and I'd settled into it. I was going to write that I can't complain, but I should bitch myself out for becoming subdued in every aspect of my life. It wasn't me, and I knew it. Yet I couldn't help myself. The brutality of my detractors became more influential than the enthusiasm of my champions. I didn't see it until now.

Outside of bookings, I wasn't up for excitement. I didn't feel like it. An example of this phenomenon in motion could be seen at an August bachelorette party in Sherwood. Yeah, good ol' Sherwood. It's always felt like a homecoming even if I've never lived there. Not even Becky could take that away from me. This group of polite, enthusiastic, and generous women included an attractive young lady with an incredible ass. I know that because she lifted her skirt and showed me her thong-clad booty in all its spankable glory. I applied Reddi-wip to the length of her crack and slowly licked it off from bottom to top. A soft moan forced its way past her lips, followed by giggling.

This went over smashingly with my audience. Even at the most conservative point in my life, I still had the gift of being sexually aggressive in a zero-pressure fashion. It's something I've been complimented on numerous times. Lending credence to my belief that the easiest way to get laid is to not give a shit whether or not I get laid. A quality lost on nearly every male stripper applicant I ever encountered. Their sole motivation was meeting hot girls and getting laid. Perhaps it was partly a guy thing that was supposed to impress me. It didn't. I was trying to run a successful business. Not a precursor to Tinder.

Much like those "nice guys" who rack up "sex points" through being a girl's personal doormat, too many male strippers believe all the gym time and drugs they've put into their bodies entitles them to pussy. It becomes a major issue at private parties when such an entertainer screams obscenities and storms out when he doesn't get his dick sucked. It is asking too much of some male strippers to entertain a group of excited women, have fun, and make money. Should a potential hookup opportunity for later present itself, then that's gravy. There is perhaps no bigger turnoff than someone placing their sexual desires as an obligation upon others. No man or woman with self-respect wants to fuck someone out of obligation. I don't care what a girl looks like. I'll tell her to go to hell if that's the case.

Getting back to Miss Bootylicious… She was single. Everyone else made a point of letting me know that. I found her charming. She felt comfortable enough in my company to let me lick whipped cream off her butt in front of others. I considered pursuing her for later but decided against it. Maybe it would've been a different story if this were like the party with Nicole. Three hours from home and no expectation of further interaction. I was in no shape to tackle a local girl who might've wanted to talk the next day. Along with feeling broken from all the negative shit I'd experienced, I was consumed with the sensation of being trapped. Trapped in solitude and distrust. And though I still enjoyed it, trapped in stripping. Even a friends with benefits situation was too much for me at the time. So, I drove home, got myself off to fresh memories of dat ass, and fell asleep on the sofa watching that fucking stupid ExtenZe *Sex Talk* infomercial. You know, the faux talk show that used to air on late-night cable between spots for Girls Gone Wild? Yeah, that.

It wasn't my only brush with trash TV around this time. I kicked off September with a bachelorette party in Oceola, Arkansas. This town of over 7,000 sits on the Mississippi River in the northeast corner of the state. Just under three hours from Little Rock. It's an uninteresting drive taking place entirely on I-40 and I-55. The party itself was good, and I was tipped well. It was late for a booking as I arrived at 11:00pm. I recall my performance taking place in the dining area next to the kitchen for some reason. The wood paneling made me feel as if I'd traveled back in time to the seventies to do this party. It was a friendly if conservative audience. After an hour, I was back on the road.

I began feeling hungry after leaving Osceola. Normally, I would've stopped somewhere. Another thing I don't like about I-40 between Little Rock and Memphis is the lack of dining options. Limited to McDonald's, Taco Bell, and Waffle House late at night. I would rather starve than eat at any of those places and have many times. Memphis was nearby but crossing the river just to eat something wasn't worth the hassle. I stopped for gas in West Memphis, where I grabbed some peanuts and a Red Bull before getting the hell out of there. It's an odd and creepy town. Not surprising given its sordid history of wrongful murder convictions. And no, I've never had a party there.

My snack tided me over for a short while, but I became increasingly hungry on the drive back to Little Rock. As soon as I got back, I stopped at the nearest IHOP. That's my unofficial go-to restaurant for late-night road trips. Both food and service have always been good in my experiences. Denny's was okay too, but I see fewer of those over time. Waffle House is fucking gross. My first and last Awful Waffle house experience was in Nashville, Tennessee near the airport. Food and services were substandard, and the coffee was the worst I'd ever tasted. This was especially a problem as I drink my coffee black. It was fucking nasty. Like they never changed the filter or grounds.

I was sitting in my booth and sipping respectable coffee. Waiting for my breakfast sampler when the phone rang. It was 3:00am. The caller ID read Chicago. With the restaurant packed, I knew I had a few minutes before my food arrived. My curiosity was peaked, so I answered and was greeted by a surprisingly chipper female voice:

"Hi. I'm a producer with the *Jerry Springer Show*. I'm calling to see if you'd be interested in helping us put together an episode about strippers. Something wild and crazy."

I was aware that television producers work long and odd hours, and I appreciated her enthusiasm. However, I politely declined her offer. I was not in the right place for getting involved with something like that whether or not I'd be on camera. And I'd already done the *Maury* thing. Providing a strong sense of "been there done that" for me. I wanted to fly under the radar as I ran my business in peace and solitude. That probably didn't help Hardbodies long term but was all I could manage at the time.

What annoyed me was a call I received from a producer with the series *Bridezillas*. She pitched me the idea of staging a disastrous bachelorette party in Memphis that included me turning in a horrible performance. Culminating in an ugly shouting match between the girls and me. I wasn't rude but let her know that I didn't appreciate the idea and asked that no one from the show contact me in the future. Plenty of people are eager to make fools of themselves on television, but I'm not one of them. Saying nothing of the potentially destructive impact a stunt like that could've had on my career.

That brings me to a trend I noticed at the end of the decade for which I believe reality television was to blame. Some clients seemed disappointed when I delivered a top-notch performance. As if they were hoping for me to ruin the party. These girls didn't explicitly express dismay with my "failure" to act a fool but seemed thrown off by my mad entertaining skills. This phenomenon repeated itself at a dozen or so parties during 2008 and 2009. I was not amused by this. I'd invested a fuckload of time and effort into entertaining every audience to the fullest and in the most positive manner conjured from deep within me. No way in hell was I about to play fucking court jester.

Aside from that minor inconvenience, the remainder of 2008 rolled forward without a hitch. Even the pre-election mortgage crisis didn't slow down Hardbodies. At least not any more than it already had in 2007. There weren't any standout parties but no train wrecks either. Not even browsing through notes of my parties during this period sparks any entertaining anecdotes. I remember nothing about any of them. Hardbodies Lite was truly in full effect.

I do remember a call on Thanksgiving afternoon about a birthday party that night. Since I had nothing going on, I informed the prospective client that I was available and quoted my fee. She had the nerve to ask for a holiday discount. I told her, if anything, I should be charging more on a holiday. She nervously cackled like a fucking idiot and hung up.

And I recall talking to a creepy, middle-aged woman around this time. There was a Charolette-like quality about her as she refused to tell me anything. Choosing instead to ask a series of cryptic questions in a passive-aggressive tone. As I attempted to pry information from her, she asked me about alcohol. Followed by something about sex. That's when I ended the conversation. For all I know it could've been Charolette. I wouldn't be surprised.

***

I celebrated my 30th birthday by waking up at 4:00am with what I thought was a heart attack. Feeling as if I'd been stabbed in the chest, I could barely breathe as I jumped out of bed and wondered what to do. I went outside. The crisp December morning air was a relief. I walked over to my neighbor's front porch, where she often left her cigarettes and lighter sitting out overnight. In a panic to calm down, I helped myself to one. At the risk of endorsing smoking, it brought me down as my chest pain gradually faded. I went back to bed. Later that day, I discovered that I'd experienced my first serious bout of acid reflux. Something that would affect me for the next few years. As if I needed that on top of everything else.

CHAPTER 28

Spring 2009 was monsoon season in Central Arkansas. Each day brought a rainstorm. Be it one hour, all day, or any length of time in between. Often without warning. Sunny skies would abruptly give way to dark clouds and a relentless downpour. Should the sun return just as quickly as it left, an ocean of steam filled the air. All this humidity did wonders for the vegetation. The lush, green landscape couldn't have been lusher or greener. Throw in the area's generous supply of insects and venomous snakes, and many days it felt like living in the Amazon.

It was during 2009 that I took up running on a near-daily basis at the park. An interesting development since I've always disliked running. Nor did it ever properly serve my overall fitness objectives. However, running afforded me an outdoor activity in a relaxed setting. The park was enclosed within a paved walking and running trail. There were basketball courts and dining amenities as well as a playground, gazebo, and field. A small park at under five acres but packing a certain charm. Hidden away from the nearby hustle and bustle in every direction.

I'd commence each lap at the park entrance and run past the empty field on one side and middle-class homes on the other. Past the basketball courts typically occupied by neighborhood teens. The trail rounded north and took me through a small wooded area that hid me from the world for about ten seconds. I'd turn another corner and run alongside Rock Creek. A popular spot for people working nearby to smoke weed on their lunch break. On more than one occasion, I looked over to spot a water moccasin proudly swimming twenty feet away. Its unmistakable blocky head held high. After passing the sad, tiny, and rarely occupied gazebo, I'd wrap around the playground and its green and yellow equipment before returning to my starting point.

This routine was a literal proxy for the figurative running in my life at the time. I wasn't so much running from the past as I was running towards the future. It was time to put the drama of Hardbodies' past behind me and hit my own reset button. I still wasn't sure what exactly I was chasing and wouldn't until a decade later as I write this. My undying vision. The dream I had in that Bald Knob motel room a year prior. A basic instinct that has haunted me since I first became conscious of the world around me circa 1981. My naked ambition is more than a set of personality traits. It's a philosophy. A way of life. I've asked myself countless times if my involvement in this crazy business was a mistake. If anything, it probably saved my life.

I kept running as April showers gave way to more showers in May. Even in the most relentless of downpours, I ran. The air thoroughly cleansed of pollen and exhaust by sheets of water from gray clouds hovering close in the low Arkansas sky. That same rain left my clothes drenched and glued to my skin. My body never broke a sweat. It didn't need to. I was surrounded by storms. But my mind was clear as I executed my routine around the park. This wasn't an escape from my problems but rather a confrontation. I was so close to a breakthrough that it was like acid in my mouth. But that coveted moment of true self-awareness remained a decade away…

***

Year two of Hardbodies Lite was in full effect from beginning to end. Business remained steady if unspectacular. I knocked out bachelorette and birthday parties throughout the region while scoring female stripper bookings here and there via both the Hardbodies and BodyRoxxx brands. Outside of being the year of the cancellation (as I endured an extraordinary amount of booking cancellations by clients), 2009 produced solid parties left and right. No standouts but no dumpster fires either.

Stefan Lite was also in full effect. I remained in exile as a self-imposed homebody. The agency should've been renamed Homebodies Entertainment of Arkansas. Along with parties, I picked up short-term retail merchandising projects on occasion. That aside, I rarely ventured anywhere beyond the grocery store and tanning salon. Running in the park didn't count. It didn't require me to interact with others. There was no place I wanted to go. No one I wanted to see. Partly due to my frustrations with Central Arkansas nightlife after being spoiled by Denver. But also because of how uncomfortable I felt in my skin.

Except when I was performing. Something about being the center of attention always brought out the best in me. So much of it that I had to share this with my audiences. This has always been my driving force as an entertainer. If I can make myself a sexy and unstoppable force of nature, I can bring out the best in everyone around me. My vain and attention-seeking ways were never intended to one-up others. I've always led by example in attempting to make others feel good about themselves. It's never been my modus operandi to take affirmation from others without giving an equal or greater amount in return. If anything, I have a bad habit of giving too much of myself to others.

Lots of time was devoted to experimentations in writing and photography. Along with maintaining my LiveJournal account, I played around with other blogs intended for profit. This included writing journalistic pieces about local culture as well as stories about my stripping experiences. I was also paid to write album reviews for a website. I didn't earn much from any of this. Making money from writing requires shameless self-promotion. I was already self-promoted out with stripping. And I hadn't settled on a singular direction or worked up the nerve to truly write what I know.

I took countless self-portraits in 2009. Many for business purposes but not all. The master bedroom became my portrait studio. Taking advantage of its large bay window. Not only did the afternoon sun provide me with plenty of light, but the Venetian blinds allowed me to adjust and diffuse it to artistic taste. My go-to spot illuminated me entirely, and the shadow-filled corner background lent depth to every image. No place I've lived since has afforded me such a convenient location for shooting quality self-portraits with little effort.

My life settled into a simple routine as I chased for something bigger and better. While cooking lunch one February afternoon, I received a phone call about a bachelorette party. The prospective client's name was Becky, because of course it was. This event was to take place in the small farming community of Hoxie in Northeast Arkansas.

Although certain where that was, I asked to make sure, "Next to Walnut Ridge, right?"

"Uh, yeah," she rudely confirmed.

I immediately lost all interest in doing business with her. Because I'm too damn nice, however, I remained polite and told her my booking fee for that area. She responded with an icy, "Okay," and hung up. With that problem having apparently solved itself, I went about preparing my meal.

Not even two minutes later, I received a call from another woman about a different bachelorette party. Unlike Becky, this caller was friendly and respectful on the phone. I was excited to book her party.

But Becky wasn't done as she called back while I spoke with my new client and gathered information. Since I think it's impolite to put a prospective client on hold and take another call, I sent Becky to voicemail. She called again. I sent her to voicemail again. Then it happened again. And again.

Becky called me eighteen fucking times as I booked that party. The client offered to let me take that call, but I said absolutely not and told her what happened. We continued our conversation as Becky kept hanging up when sent to voicemail and immediately hitting redial. My phone beeped mercilessly, and I was still cooking lunch. It was enough to take a booking while preparing fish and pasta, but the actions of that skank in Hoxie were too much. After getting off the phone with my new client, I waited for that next call. I didn't have to wait long.

I unloaded on that fucking bitch, "How fucking dare you pull some bullshit like that when I'm on the phone with a client? Don't you ever fucking call here again!"

And she never did.

***

I performed for my largest private party audience in March. A fiftieth birthday party in Heber Springs. Located on beautiful Greers Ferry Lake approximately ninety minutes north of Little Rock. The birthday girl's husband spared no expense in assembling this event with approximately 200 guests in attendance. I was paid $300 to drive to Heber Springs, perform a single lap dance, and drive home. It was intoxicating to hear a deafening wall of cheers from that many people directed solely at me. Even the men appreciated the entertainment aspect of my interaction with the guest of honor. Having that many people applaud me upon completion was a special moment indeed.

And before I knew it, I was back home in solitude. I don't remember what exactly I did later that night, but it probably involved falling asleep on the sofa while watching a film on Turner Classic Movies. Much like running in rain or shine, this was a common ritual. I've always had trouble falling asleep regardless of how exhausted I am because I have a difficult time shutting down my mind. My waking hours are dominated by rapid-fire thoughts filling my brain faster than I can process at once. I'd hate to think of all the good ideas I've conjured and lost in the blink of an eye.

***

It was around the second anniversary of Vanessa coming into my life that she left. Her final correspondence was an email with one of my recent self-portraits attached. She asked why I couldn't have looked like that at her friend's bachelorette party. I was leaner than two years prior, but the difference wasn't drastic. Ten or fifteen pounds lighter. After all those hateful emails and voicemails over the past 24 months, I finally responded to her:

"It wouldn't have mattered because you still would've hated me."

I never heard from Vanessa again.

With that chapter closed on paper, but not in my psyche, I continued running. The conditions didn't matter. Not even when a barrage of giant raindrops pelted my face. I ran at full speed while avoiding a slip and fall on that wet track with every stride I took. The dragon I chased wasn't in sight, but I could feel it within my grasp. Mocking me incessantly. I was long past the point where most people would've given up, but I couldn't bring myself to do the same. Quitting isn't in my DNA. I couldn't have given up if I wanted to. There was no choice but to stay the course even if it took forever. And that's how it wound up feeling.

CHAPTER 29

Writing about 2009 ten years after the fact has opened my eyes in many ways. As much as I dreaded writing about 2007, I didn't realize that 2009 was also a downer year until now. It doesn't pack the "Stefan goes off the deep end" batshit insanity of two years prior. But I was clearly ending the decade in a state of depression. There truly was no place I wanted to go. And all I wanted to do was rise above everything at any cost. My on and off steroid use didn't help matters, but what was now an old habit would ultimately have to die hard.

Cliché as it sounds, there are countless things I would do differently in retrospect. I would've retired the Hardbodies and BodyRoxxx brands and gone solo as an independent entertainer. Still working with female strippers as I saw fit without being married to constantly seeking parties for them. But I still hadn't accepted the fact that I would never again represent another male stripper. I may have been depressed, but my glass was stubbornly half full. The widespread obsession with quantity over quality regarding male strippers is so omnipresent that even my rebellious ass wasn't immune from this groupthink that grew from Vegas casinos resenting guys like me entertaining their guests without receiving a cut.

Before the right audience, I am an outstanding entertainer who never fails to bring down the house. The key phrase is "the right audience" though. I'm the perfect stripper for many women but not all. Nevertheless, I tried in vain to be the universal male stripper in Arkansas. The one who was a great fit for every audience. Given my role as a talent agent and my failure to recruit other male strippers, I felt an obligation to please anyone and everyone. This is the greatest sin I've ever committed as an entertainer. Had I not been married to Hardbodies, I could've spent my days shamelessly promoting myself as an individual entertainer and discovered more audiences tailor suited for my act.

I could've rejected booking requests from less than optimal prospective clients. Those who exhibited qualities ranging from contempt to sexual repression. I am often contacted by women with requests like not removing my pants and not being sexual in any way. I can't make up this bullshit. In the early stages of writing this book, I received a call from a middle-aged woman about a birthday party. Her name was Becky, because of course it was. She wanted a "male stripper, but not really." That was code for "I'm too uptight to appreciate your bare butt." Given that my butt is one of my best physical assets, asking me to not show it off is like asking Babe Ruth to not hit home runs. Why even have him in the fucking lineup?

Being the first male stripper for many of my audiences, I often educate prospective clients when they contact me. Many ask for this education and I'm happy to oblige. These women have the right attitude and possess the open-mindedness to absorb everything I feed them. It's a positive sign that makes me optimistic about an upcoming party. But I have a problem with those women who call with an attitude, show disinterest in what I tell them, or tell me how to run my business. They obviously have low expectations for me or any male stripper they find. And it's impossible to deliver a successful performance to an audience that has preemptively decided I suck. The money is never worth it.

At some point during the summer of 2009, I received a call from a woman about a bachelorette party. I don't remember her name, but I'm assuming it was Becky. She had the fucking nerve to ask if I could perform a Hawaiian luau style dance in a grass skirt. I informed her that I don't offer such a thing, have no interest in offering it, and that she should find someone who does. She was incredulous in her response and argued that I could easily purchase everything I needed and spend time learning how to perform a luau dance in time for her party. Because I should totally spend money and time, which is also money, to deliver a performance I don't want to do and finish in the red.

I should've told her to go to hell. Instead, I wasted valuable time trying to sell her on my exotic performance. One may think I was doing my duty as an aggressive salesman, but I was executing an exercise in futility. This woman was not only more frigid than Antarctica as she outright rejected my pitch but accused me of being unreasonable in refusing to honor her request. I explained to her that booking a male stripper to perform a traditional ethnic dance was akin to expecting a jazz trio to play country songs. It's not what I do. But it all came down to the fact that she had zero respect for me and assumed I would do anything for money. Even if I'd managed to sell her on booking me as a stripper, she would've ensured that my performance was an epic disaster.

Some people assume they can woo me with all sorts of insulting nonsense. Like the woman who wanted to book a female stripper for a birthday party. Boastfully willing to spend "up to fifty dollars."

Likewise, you have Becky and Charolette trying to entice me with the brief and tightly supervised pleasure of Emily's company. I don't understand why anyone would attempt to do business with someone for whom they hold a low opinion. I guess it's an asshole thing. What else can I say about people who feel justified in displaying blatant disrespect towards others?

And while horny ol' Becky was the first client to offer me less money after the fact, numerous individuals have attempted to negotiate with me upon initial contact. I learned way back in my Denver days that giving in to such demands is a guaranteed recipe for disaster. The client and audience will have no respect for me. Because they can't. On the other hand, if I stick to my guns on price and score the booking, all will inevitably sing my praises by the end.

But some would-be clients refuse to see all the preparation and overhead that goes into each performance. Like the young woman in the summer of 2009 who wanted to book me for a quick birthday lap dance in Fayetteville. Given that six-hour roundtrip, my booking fee for that area is double what it is for Little Rock. Yet she argued, "But it will only take you five minutes," as she willfully ignored the facts.

Even Emily's birthday party would've required three hours of prep and drive time sandwiched around the actual performance. Not to mention all the time spent playing out the performance repeatedly in my head in the days leading up to it. In Emily's case, there would've been the additional mindfuckery of figuring out how to play it cool.

I shouldn't have been nice to everyone. The clients and audiences who appreciate all that I do for them are more than worth it. But it's a different story for those who take me and everything I give them for granted. I know that now but didn't in 2009. My confidence as an entertainer would be boosted by an excellent audience. Only to be lowered days later by a mediocre one. That was my fault for believing I could please everyone. Case in point is two bachelorette parties from June 2009.

The first occurred in Memphis on falsely advertised Mud Island. A peninsula bordered by the Mississippi River and Wolf River Harbor. After crossing the river into Tennessee via I-40, I turned north by that Bass Pro Shops pyramid abomination and reached my destination five minutes later. The neighborhood was a collection of well-maintained row houses and lawns that achieved an island aesthetic. If you had to live in Memphis at the time, that was probably the best part of town in which to reside. These days, I wouldn't advise living anywhere in Memphis.

It was a beautiful late spring night. Summer only a few days away. The house looked tiny compared to its neighbors but turned out to be quite spacious once I was inside. I made my entrance as a firefighter to a small group of twentysomethings decked out in their best party and clubwear. I always enjoy seeing my audiences make sexy fashion statements. It's a good sign they're ready to have a blast. There were no hand jobs or hookups, but it was a successful performance. My audience engaged me every step of the way and tipped generously. I hung out afterward to have a drink and converse on a variety of topics.

The girls gave me a bachelorette party gift bag as I left. Other than a bottle of water for the drive home, there wasn't anything I wanted. But the gesture showed the positive impact I'd had on them, and it meant a lot to me. I held my dick with both hands all the way from Memphis. The expectations for me were great, and I exceeded them in every way. This party is a textbook example of why girls wanted me at their parties. They wanted an out of this world experience. I delivered in fucking spades. Earning all the self-adulation I could shower upon myself that night.

Six days later, I was at a bachelorette party on the outskirts of Roe, Arkansas. This tiny community an hour east of Little Rock is in farm country. It's also mosquito country for much of the year. I'm glad I rarely do parties in that area for this reason alone. I was hell and gone from Mud Island as I drove to a mobile home on a gravel road in the middle of nowhere. This is not me piling on rural folk. I'm game for entertaining any group of women ready to appreciate all that I offer. The client for this party was a sweet, middle-aged woman who wanted to make the young bachelorette's last night of freedom one to remember. For that alone, I had respectable expectations.

It wasn't a bad party, but it was mediocre overall. I was attacked by mosquitoes upon getting out of the truck. Ever the perfectionist, I was bothered about performing with fresh insect bites on my skin. It was so hot and humid that the air had a sticky quality about it. I again made my entrance as a firefighter but to a less enthusiastic response this time. Both the client and bachelorette were on the shy side. As were many of the women. They were friendly for the most part, although gratuity was lacking. I knew they didn't have much money but did everything I could to make their night.

Some old bag informed me that they didn't have much money. No shit. In true "too nice for my own good" fashion, I warmly informed her that everything was fine. She showed her gratitude by telling the other women in a snarky tone, "I told him we don't have much money, but he said it's fine." I beat myself up slightly for not having said the right thing, but there was nothing I could've said that would've prevented her response. She was dead set on being a victim at my expense. Justified from her lopsided perspective. I was looking down upon them in her mind when nothing could've been further from the truth.

Additional unpleasantness followed courtesy of a woman either in her forties or the product of hard living. Motivated by a Miller Lite buzz she vigorously rubbed her denim-clad ass against my cock. I can't even begin to describe how irritating the friction of jeans feels on my junk when it's concealed by only a thin layer of fabric. It can be painful, and this was one of those instances. Being too polite for my own good, I kept nonchalantly easing away as she refused to take the hint and humped my leg. That felt awful on my freshly shaved bare skin and ran the risk of causing ingrown hairs.

I wrapped up my performance and left. My exit was amicable on the surface, but I sensed resentment towards me. The old battle-ax psychologically projected her personal feelings of inadequacy on me. And country girl can survive couldn't fathom why I wasn't rock hard for her. There must be something wrong with me if drunk and aggressive trailer trash painfully rubbing against my cock doesn't get my motor running. To her credit, the client made every effort to keep me happy. It wasn't the worst party I ever did. Not even in my bottom ten. But still the sort of booking I should've been avoiding all along.

Hindsight truly is 20/20.

CHAPTER 30

Autumn 2009 brought me back to Tennessee for another bachelorette party. This time in the town of Millington. Twenty minutes north of Memphis. I guess Justin Timberlake has ties to Millington, so my condolences to its citizens. The most memorable aspect of this party occurred when the bachelorette fed me cake on the front stoop while another girl told me about her Christian faith. Not in a preachy or evangelical fashion. Just as casual conversation. I was still in my g-string, but the other homes showed no signs of life. The night air felt amazing. Fall had quickly chased away the relentless summer heat. Something so simple that part of me never wanted it to end. Yet another Lynchian moment I added to my collection.

The remainder of the decade was full of surrealism that would make David Lynch proud. If pressed to choose a favorite film of all time, I'd go with *Mulholland Drive*. A metaphor for where I was at that time compared to five years earlier. As if I were not what I had once appeared to be. That wasn't true, but I'd lost sense of who I was. I occasionally wondered if I was Diane masquerading as Betty. Was I truly a fraud? Or had the past few years distorted my vision? Deep down, I knew I was Betty fooled into thinking I was Diane. It would be a long time before I allowed myself to accept this.

I've always been a sucker for films in which the line dividing two distinct characters is blurred. Along with *Mulholland Drive*, two other favorites of this flavor are Ingmar Bergman's *Persona* and the joint Donald Cammell and Nicholas Roeg project *Performance*. This narrative initially reflected the conflict within me as I struggled to balance the libertarian and authoritarian tendencies equally consuming my soul. I would go from being Ami Perrin one moment to invoking John Calvin the next without warning. I hadn't accepted that hedonism was a net gain of pleasure. That my inherent self-discipline was not only acceptable but a necessity for me to achieve true pleasure.

This narrative structure also reflects my oft-contemptuous relationship with the world around me. Even at my lowest, the fact that I refused to give up allowed me to still exude enough self-confidence to polarize everyone who encountered me. Some would gravitate towards me via motivations either honorable or not. Others would ignore or attack me either as a cry for help or an outright rejection of my never say die mentality. There are good and bad people on both sides of this equation. Sussing out the diamonds in the rough from the worthless lumps of coal was never an easy task. It would've been less difficult had I given myself the credit everyone else, even my detractors, is quick to bestow upon me.

I performed at a birthday party on Mount Nebo. Approximately ninety minutes northwest of Little Rock, this state park is off I-40 near the town of Dardanelle. It was a clear and crisp Saturday night in

November as I ascended to the mountain's 1350-foot summit. As I do when I can't see house numbers, I looked for the home with several vehicles parked outside. I texted the client. She snuck outside to pay me. Asking for five minutes before making my entrance.

What happened next was the only time this has occurred in my eighteen years of stripping. Dressed as a cop, I pounded on the front door and announced myself as the police. My birthday girl, also the homeowner, answered in a total panic. Thinking I was a real cop. The other girls laughed hysterically as I barged in and walked towards the living room. She was having none of that.

"You can't come in here like this!" she protested vehemently

"I can do whatever I want," I scoffed.

She shouted at her friends, "Don't laugh! This isn't funny!"

That, of course, only made them laugh harder. She figured it out at that point, and a sexy time was had by all.

***

I cut back on my physical running at year's end. But I was still charging full speed ahead as I sought to lift myself from the doldrums. It was time to leave behind the ghosts of stripping past and make another run at exotic entertainment glory. I was older, wiser, and smart enough not to make the same mistakes twice. Late 2009 was a period of creative fertility. Ambitious ideas bounced nonstop off the walls surrounding me. I believed I could replace Kyra as well as Leah and Chantelle. Part of me wanted to believe I could find male strippers on my level. Even if I had to build them from scratch. I designed an over the top male revue that would build Hardbodies' reputation far and wide. But it was naïve in the sense that no venue would give two shits about my long-term professional needs. Even if my plans would've benefitted them long term as well. It seemed only I considered profitability tomorrow and beyond.

Facebook and Twitter became marketing considerations around this time. No social network would benefit Hardbodies the way peak Myspace had. I experimented with allowing prospective clients to book entertainers via texting. An instant disaster as I was swamped with texts that read simply "How much?" or "What you got?" Um… How much for what? This would've been scrapped quickly on that basis alone. But the decision was expedited by some creepy asshole mistaking us for an escort agency and asking if I'd be receiving a "shipment" of Asian girls soon. Not digging the human trafficking connotations of his question, I texted him the phone number for the Arkansas Sex Offender Registry office. He texted again a few minutes later. Unimpressed with my sense of humor. Fuck him.

December took me back to Memphis for a birthday party. At 74-years-young this birthday girl set a new record for me. Seventy being the previous mark. What's great about entertaining women of that age is they honestly no longer give a fuck what anyone else thinks. They're going to have fun, damn it! This time was no exception as my birthday girl, so full of life and energy, held her own with me every step of the way. Typical of a coed birthday party audience, everyone was good after a couple of songs. I immediately left for Jerusalem. Jerusalem, Arkansas, that is.

While not as extreme as the drive from Memphis to Fort Smith, it was still a three-hour trek. Mostly on I-40. A straight shot from the Mississippi River to the Arkansas River Valley. My journey became more scenic once I turned north off the Interstate for the home stretch. This area also has communities by the names of Macedonia and Cleveland. There's also a place called Lick Mountain. That's kind of naughty. Jerusalem is only fifteen minutes north of Hattieville. Site of the first Hardbodies booking in April 2004. Now I was back in the area for the final Hardbodies booking of the decade.

My audience was a Christmas party for the female employees of a husband and wife owned restaurant located on a popular Arkansas lake. He was the client for this booking and, save for one of the girls, no else one knew I was coming. Not even his wife. Having already been paid in full a couple weeks prior, I arrived and pounded on the cabin door. Announcing myself as law enforcement. Although knowing I wasn't a real cop, the wife was caught off guard by my presence. Because she threatened to kill her husband for this, I placed her in handcuffs for my initial lap dance. She had no complaints. Neither did anyone else.

***

After all the reinvention I endured in 2009, I hit a lull by decade's end. If only I'd possessed the strength to excuse myself for that. I was in a mood decidedly strange yet oddly soothing all at once. I continued to make progress in the development and revision of business strategies for the coming new year and decade. Much of this would amount to trial and error, but such was the nature of my naked ambition at the time. I'd had enough of Hardbodies Lite and was once again primed to turn the world around me upside down.

I was ready to come out from underneath my personal shell. The chronic loneliness was crippling by this point. I had subjected myself to more seclusion than is healthy for an extrovert. Wanting so desperately to feel alive once more. A random girl I spotted in the local Kroger confirmed I wasn't dead yet. She was hot. Her tall, athletic physique accentuated by yoga pants and a long-sleeved lycra top. It was a warm day for December in Arkansas. She was a "really pretty" girl with long, dark hair and cheekbones that could cut glass. It was enough that I could once again feel an immediate sexual attraction to a woman after so long. More accurately, I allowed myself to feel it.

New Year's Eve found me in solitary confinement as I listened to early Depeche Mode. Specifically tracks from *A Broken Frame* and *Construction Time Again*. The latter is best known for the song "Everything Counts". A classic, to be sure. But the album contains excellent, lesser-known tracks including "And Then...", "The Landscape is Changing", and "Two Minute Warning". Looking upon the cold, gray, and bare treed landscape outside my window made for a surreal contrast to the comforting warmth and dim amber glow of my interior surroundings. The cold and metallic sound of DM tying together these two disparate environments with soothing melancholy perfection.

I should've been out living it up on the final night of the decade. The first full decade of my adult life. But there was no place for me. No place I wanted to be. Except in the bittersweet embrace of self-imposed isolation. I wasn't interested in making out with a poor man's Marylin Monroe at this stroke of midnight. It was at this point I realized the wall I'd build to protect myself was too high. And yet it was somehow redundant at the same time. As I knew there wasn't much on the other side. I'd gone to an extreme in shielding myself from the haters and failures of recent history. Now institutionalized within its long and ominous shadow.

It didn't matter because I had grand designs for the next day and beyond. All my months of running had brought me to a Zen-like state of balance and clarity. A state my intuition told me would not end anytime soon. In a pragmatic sense, I was now doing all the right things to achieve both the short-term and long-term objectives I desired. That I'd be wise to stick with the plan. I was once again just that good. Fuck that. I was better than ever. I was about to grab the world by the throat and mercilessly throw it to the ground. As Tony Montana would say, it was a great big pussy just waiting to get fucked. And my dick was bigger and harder than ever.

I wish I could say that's what happened, but the truth is not even close. If I thought 2007 through 2009 were trying, they weren't shit compared to the next three years. I would've sold my soul to the devil in exchange for more Hardbodies Lite if I believed in that sort of thing.

CHAPTER 31

I felt positive after beginning 2010 on a high note. The latest bachelorette party in the governor's suite at the DoubleTree in downtown Little Rock. After admitting she wouldn't be heading to the altar a virgin, the young bachelorette confirmed this by wrapping her legs around my back as if second nature. Due to the chilly weather on that early January night, there wasn't much cleavage available for Reddi-wip action. Since the client and mother of the bride was the only one rocking a low-cut top, her expensive titties received all the attention they deserved.

Against all odds, I tried for some mother and daughter action later that night. But I did well regardless. No group of women would offer me their best liquor or refer to me as a "sexy son of a bitch" had I not made their panties soaking wet. Proving that, despite all I'd endured, I hadn't lost a step. Even allowing my ego to swell a little as I'd earned that self-adulation. I was returning to prominence in every aspect. Believing that I was rising like Phoenix, Arizona from the desert in the first days of a new decade.

A steep climb awaited me, but I was ready to end my Brian Wilson lifestyle and start running up that hill. Parties were aplenty in early 2010. Even booking requests for female strippers. Mostly now handled by Cheyenne and would be for the next three years. There's not much to say about her. She was attractive, experienced, and drug-free. Good enough at that point. I had the feeling her primary motivation was to catch my eye, but I just wasn't into her. Other girls applied. I waded through everything from unrealistic demands to spread eagle photos of some of the scariest looking bitches ever captured in jpeg. Male applicants were nonexistent. That was fine since I needed all the parties I could get.

It was an ideal time to end the Hardbodies and BodyRoxxx brands, but I couldn't do it. I viewed such an act as a surrender even though my name was more prolific than Hardbodies by then. I couldn't see that it was the logical evolution of my career to emerge from behind my business entities and go solo. Still representing other strippers as I saw fit. I probably would've arrived at this conclusion soon enough had these good times lasted beyond a few months. I even toyed with the idea of leaving Arkansas. My creative juices were flowing like crazy.

The bookings kept coming and had me driving all over the region. Two parties stood out during this period. The first was another bachelorette party in downtown Little Rock. This time at a smaller home in an older neighborhood. Both packed oodles of charm. Maybe it was the cozy weather on that Saturday night in April. Just warm enough to negate the need for a jacket. City lights filtered through the leaves of tall, old trees. Casting shadows upon front lawns and cracked sidewalks. Magic was all around and inside me as I went inside to arrest my naughty bride-to-be.

I liked all the girls, but the client was my favorite. Not only hot but incredibly sweet to boot. And married. I never meet this type of girl when she's available, and that's what I've always wanted in a nutshell. So caring and giving. The girl I'd bend over backward for not out of obligation, but because I'm dying to repay every wonderful favor in spades. She was so committed to ensuring that I felt at home that I get a little choked up thinking about it. The anti-Becky, if you will. I took care of my bachelorette and made sure the client received special Reddi-wip attention as well.

The second gig was also a bachelorette party and my first trip to Eureka Springs. Located three and a half hours northwest of Little Rock, this resort town attracts people from all over for its beautiful Ozarks scenery and (allegedly) haunted old buildings. I'm not a huge fan. Maybe because I prefer Hot Springs and can be there in under an hour. Also, the streets in downtown Eureka Springs are narrow and a bitch to navigate. The town seems to shut down early. Even on Saturday nights.

This night was notable for being the bachelorette party of the client for a previous such event in 2007. I wrote about it. What? You don't remember? For shame. To recap… The client was a girl named Anna, who also packed that delicious combination of sweet and sexy. Her kindness was indispensable to me during the descent into madness that was my Summer 2007. I had no idea she was the bachelorette this time. She had no idea I was coming. Upon making my entrance, we both were overcome with excitement and awkwardness.

The experience provided insight into where I was in early 2010 versus a few years prior. Along with Anna, roughly half the girls at this party were present at that previous show. They voiced a consensus that I looked better than last time. Not only aesthetically speaking but that I seemed more energetic, full of life, and in better spirits. On my way out, Anna gave me a copy of the souvenir booklet created for her party. Much like receiving a gift bag, this meant a lot to me. I may still have it somewhere.

It was a late party. Uncharacteristic of me, I was too exhausted to drive back to Little Rock. I grabbed a room at the creatively named Motel 62 located on – wait for it – U.S. 62. After a few hours of light sleep, I was on the road at 6:00am. This allowed me to see the Ozarks in all its stunning glory as the sun rose from the east. The price of the motel room was worth the experience. My spirits were better than ever as optimism swept over me. "I've got this," I told myself. How was I supposed to know what awaited me just around the corner?

***

Business screeched to a halt in May. It wasn't a carbon copy of May 2007 and its zero bookings. But it was close with only one. This wasn't a one-month fluke, however. It was the beginning of a trend that lasted through 2012. I'd go days, sometimes weeks, without a phone call. Everything stopped without warning or explanation.

The beginning of this prolonged slump coincided with the implementation of the Patient Protection and Affordable Care Act. I don't believe this to be a coincidence. Many potential clients were now short on disposable income due to skyrocketing deductibles and the loss of existing healthcare plans. Jobs were lost. Hours cut. Small businesses went under. Numerous clients told me as much. Adding insult to injury, I still couldn't afford health insurance.

I was always far from wealthy but now found myself living hand to mouth. I didn't go crazy as I had three years earlier. At least that was all out of my system. I once again sank into depression. But, as always, I never gave up. Against all odds, I would keep myself afloat. Constantly analyzing the situation. Searching high and low for a solution. Any solution. I slashed my standard booking fee by 25%. People still bitched at me for being too expensive. I knew they were frustrated and struggling, but I was too. I noticed that culture overall was changing for the worse. Anger, snark, and hostility became more widespread as the flamboyant inclusivity of Myspace was supplanted by the cold distance of Facebook and political soapboxery of Twitter.

Nothing did more to preserve my sanity during these years than higher education. I pursued my interest in filmmaking. Enrolling in a two-year college and majoring in film and video production. But first, I had to earn my high school diploma. Throwing myself headfirst into studying for the GED exam. My efforts paid off so handsomely that I graduated with the highest GPA for that year's graduating class. Not only was I a high school graduate at 31 but also a high school valedictorian.

***

I had two parties in December 2010. Each notable for different reasons. The first was a bachelorette party in Memphis that remains my final Memphis booking to date. Because Memphis is a crime-infested shithole now. It was one of those parties where the girls lost their minds en masse upon my entrance, threw all their tips at me in stacks, and couldn't take anymore after that. My entire night was little more than a drive to Memphis and back, but the money was totally worth it.

The other gig was a going-away party in Little Rock. My audience of female coworkers possessed more stamina than the Memphis girls. I found myself gravitated towards the client. Her name was Jennifer. A tall and shapely blonde around forty. Rocking that leggings and long sweater combo I find alluring on the right physique. She totally had the goods with her busty attributes and legs for days. And she exuded kindness. Something I needed as badly as money. The return of my world to shit had pushed me back into isolation.

Multicolored party lights illuminated the otherwise darkened living room. Red and blue streamed across a mostly gray and minimalist aesthetic. One downside to the subdued sexiness of Jennifer's fashion statement was that it made Reddi-wip play impossible. We clicked on a personal level, and I used our mutual attraction to my performance advantage. With some girls ducking outside for smoke breaks, Jennifer remained seated on the sofa. I wrapped a white towel around my waist, removed my g-string, and grinded my rock-hard cock on her warm pussy. The towel hiding our naughtiness as I let it fall in the rear. She squeezed my bare ass with both hands and tightly clenched my cock with her firm thighs.

We danced together and made bedroom eyes at each other. Neither of us sure where this was headed. If it was simply the moment, then she and I lived in it to the fullest. The other girls too intoxicated and otherwise preoccupied to notice the sexual tension filling the room. Finally, the guest of honor wised up and took it upon herself to break the spell between Jennifer and me. I got dressed and headed out. She walked me to my truck. I could see she was emotional about something and asked if she was okay. She teared up and hugged me. Telling me how much she was going to miss her friend. I comforted her as best I could before I vanished into the night.

There was more going on behind Jennifer's bright exterior than her friend moving away. It takes one to know one. "What is going on with the world?" I asked myself while driving home. Along with imagining what a sexual encounter between us would be like, I wondered if it would've been a good or bad thing. Would we be comforting or using each other? Perhaps they're the same thing. I'd held back so hard that I ejaculated acid before going to sleep that night. But I had cash in my pocket. That was worth celebrating more than ever those days.

CHAPTER 32

Not only were there not many parties in 2011, but there's not much to say about them. Only one is worth writing about and for all the wrong reasons. The others range from good to mediocre and offer nothing I haven't already covered. There were a couple of memorable callers. Such as the asshole who requested a female stripper with a "fat ass" and didn't understand why I had a problem with that. Or the guy who mumbled incoherently. When asked to articulate, he responded by shouting incoherently. Apparently, speaking loudly and speaking clearly are six of one in his world. Still not sure what he wanted. It probably involved a fat ass.

2011 saw my directorial debut with a short film promoting the campus library. I'd made the acquaintance of the library staff soon after beginning my first semester. The library director showed me entertaining short films other colleges had produced to promote their libraries. Sensing an opportunity, I offered to produce and direct a short narrative film with the assistance of my fellow film students. The next step was selling the film program's instructor on my idea. He immediately jumped on it as a project for the Video Production I course during the Spring 2011 semester. My film was officially greenlit.

In true film snob fashion, I wrote a screenplay inspired by Fellini's *Juliet of the Spirits*. That may seem like overkill for a student film about a campus library, but I was making the most of my opportunity. An entertaining story about a student receiving a tour of the library and all it has to offer while being greeted by everything from a literal bookworm to a vampire. I was excited about my charming mix of fantasy and humor, and so was everyone involved. As a testament to how expensive filmmaking is, this three-and-a-half-minute film utilizing free equipment and labor still cost me $500 to produce. Even with things so tight financially, I couldn't say no.

An opportunity to work with people both talented and reliable was alone a healthy return on investment. I'd spent years trying to convince people to go out and make money, yet these kids were eager to give 100% in exchange for experience. While this project was a class assignment, no one coasted through it. It was amazing to see each student take charge of his or her crew position. Allowing me to focus solely on producing and directing. This was such a novelty for me after dealing with the likes of Freaky Tales, Jared Leto's crazy pretend girlfriend, and other scary-ass motherfuckers.

The first position I handed out was to an eighteen-year-old girl named Carly. Her title was assistant director, although she was probably more of an associate producer. She made my life easier by handling all the scheduling duties and serving as a liaison between me and others while I directed my actors. Proving that I have an eye for all kinds of talent, she excelled in this role despite not being an obvious choice for it. I knew she had it in her. I felt more comfortable with her than any of my other classmates. I had an infatuation with Carly in a kid sister sort of way that I had no idea how to express. My biggest fear was that it might come across as sexual. It probably did on an occasion or two. Please excuse me while I crawl under a rock and die.

The film turned out nicely. I edited it over my first spring break. Which I also spent replacing the transmission in my truck. So much for partying. I also composed an original music score and recorded additional audio. The library director loved my film, and it was featured on the school's website for some time. And if anyone reading this is curious, they can watch it on my YouTube channel – Stefan Diamante – under the title *LRC (2011)*. I make a cameo appearance as a strapping firefighter rescuing a damsel in distress played by Carly along with being an extra in another shot.

***

Without school and filmmaking to distract me, the summer of 2011 was especially cruel. I sold off many personal possessions to make ends meet. Nothing I've missed, so I'm better off without them. I scored my first party ever in the Southwest Arkansas town of De Queen. Too bad it sucked. The best gig of 2011 was a bachelorette party in, of all places, Sherwood. A high energy blast of unbridled enthusiasm and generous tipping. I hung out with them afterward to chat and drink. Something I rarely did around this time. God bless those girls for being the highlight of my summer.

To see if agencies besides Hardbodies were suffering, I applied as an entertainer to several nationwide outfits that advertise services in Arkansas. Some responded by admitting they weren't receiving any inquiries from my territory. Others balked at my base pay and travel fee demands. Indicating to me they were practically giving away bookings while attempting to stay afloat. Many of these outfits would go under during the early 2010s. One agency by the name of Hunks and Babes didn't reply to my email, and I quickly forgot about them.

I spent my days watching my savings slowly dwindle. Throwing anything and everything at the wall to see if something would stick. I invested in online advertising that netted me a whopping four bookings over the next twelve months. At $240 annually, this came out to $60 per party and a horrible return on investment. I still couldn't fathom what was happening. It was so fucking dead. I kept telling myself, "Any day now, it's all going to turn around." But week after week, month after month, any day never came. I continued beating my head against the wall as I waited for the fall semester to commence.

My wish was granted in late August. One of my courses this time was Video Production II, which allowed me to direct my second short film. *The Crisis* (also available to watch on my YouTube channel) was a simpler production consisting of two shots and one scene. It also gave me the experience of directing someone else's screenplay. Unlike *LRC*, everyone else was involved from the start. I also edited the film as well as shot and inserted photographs of lingerie, handcuffs, a blindfold, a bullwhip, a handgun, dollar bills, and an empty Jack Daniels bottle. The droning, Throbbing Gristle-esque score was also my creation and added to the sinister vibe of the film.

***

I wrote several chapters prior of a suspicion that I was occasionally booked by clients who were hoping my performance would be a laughable dumpster fire. While any evidence to support this is anecdotal at best, there's zero doubt that some prospective clients contact me with only the lowest of expectations. Why is this a problem? Because audience expectations cannot be met, much less exceeded, if no expectations are set. An audience with great expectations is easier to satisfy for exactly that reason. They've already made up their minds that I'm going to be great. On the other hand, my greatness is an impossible sell to an audience that has already branded me ignorant, dude-bro trash looking to score a quick and easy buck.

For years I made every effort to win over that audience. Not until recently did I recognize the futility of those efforts and say, "Fuck 'em all." Becky and Charolette represented the final straw of this madness. The latest in a long line of women who have no respect for me or what I do and clearly aren't nice people. None would be happy with anything I did because they'd preemptively decided they weren't. This is the live entertainment equivalent of arguing with ignorance. It can't be done. And it's not fair to my good audiences if I let the bad ones get to me. So, I don't anymore.

But it was still getting to me in December 2011. And that brings me to the booking I teased at the beginning of this chapter. This one a girls' Christmas party at a beauty salon in DeWitt, Arkansas. A ninety-minute drive southwest from Little Rock, the town is the seat of Arkansas County. You can tell someone put a lot of thought into that name. According to that bastion of truth Wikipedia, DeWitt is best known for being the hometown of a member of the greatest southern rock band ever. That's right, 38 Special. But I digress.

Unfortunately, I wouldn't be rockin' into the night this time. The client's name was – wait for it – Becky, because of course it was. This party sucked from beginning to end. My audience was mostly frumpy and uptight middle-aged women who spent the entire show looking down their noses at me. It felt like I was there so they could try to hate themselves a little less. Enthusiasm and gratuity were mediocre. The one saving grace was a small woman in her eighties. A total sweetheart. The one to whom I gave the most attention. Because she was worth it. The rest could go to hell.

Tragedy struck when my favorite party girl fell and hit her head on a cabinet. I was on the other end of the salon and immediately rushed to her aid. Asking her if she was okay.

One of those frumpy bitches immediately took a tone with me, "No, she's not okay!"

I could see the consensus was that I had no right to show concern for this woman's wellbeing. I was the lowlife stripper begging for dollars.

They were good people. I was trash. How dare I breach the barrier they proudly and defiantly constructed between them and me? I had forgotten my place. A place that existed only within their collective world of low self-esteem. The late, great Frank Zappa once claimed that there's more stupidity than hydrogen in the universe. I claim there's more low self-esteem than stupidity. Let's see any of those bitches quote Zappa. Didn't think so.

With the party at its conclusion, I quietly dressed, packed my stuff, and walked out without acknowledging anyone. Not that anyone noticed. As I walked to my truck, I overheard a woman on her phone telling someone that the little old lady had "tripped over the stripper's duffle bag." It took everything to keep me from exploding on that skank. All my stuff was at the opposite end of the salon from where my favorite girl was for the entire duration of my performance. There was no good reason for her to lie about this other than to stroke her sad, pathetic shred of an ego at my expense. After all the time, effort, and near nudity I'd given them, this was how they thanked me.

I rode out what remained of the year by looking towards 2012. My final semester of film school would be upon me before I knew it. Along with another steroid cycle. I was still using from the massive stash I'd accumulated before business went to hell. There wasn't even a semblance of fitness objective or strategy anymore. I'd juice for a few months and not juice for a few months afterward. Then repeat. I couldn't see any significant advancements being made. But to challenge this method would've been sacrilege. The fitness gods told me I was nothing without drugs, and I believed them. If I wasn't getting the results I wanted, that was all on me. Not the drugs. Never the drugs.

I kicked around more ideas for Hardbodies as well as other potential business ventures. The thought of an online publication crossed my mind as it did from time to time. No matter my approach it always ended with me not finding the right subject matter for my vision. A vision rooted in sex appeal. Sex sells, but only if one knows how to sell it. When on my game, I can sell it like nobody's fucking business. My biggest gift and burden. Significantly limiting my professional opportunities and personal relationships. My greatest talent is also my greatest curse. Anyone who criticizes that statement shall validate it.

CHAPTER 33

One other thing I did in 2011 was respond to an email request from an Arkansas-based author. She was including a male revue scene in her latest novel and asked for a general play by play she could use as a template. I obliged and promptly forgot all about it. Cut to one year later, and I'm getting messages from people who just read my name in a *New York Times* review for a book titled *Deadlocked*. I had no idea who Charlaine Harris was or that she was such a big deal. Now I knew.

***

2012 was a near carbon copy of the previous year. The exception being zero parties of note. Not even a smidgen of Becky drama. This isn't to knock the bookings I scored that year. There was a fortieth birthday party that was lots of fun along with a bachelorette party comprised of girls in lingerie. But even those didn't offer anything outlandish for better or worse. So, fuck it. Let's discuss the 2012 summer schlockbuster, *Magic Mike*. Or, specifically, the film's impact on male stripping.

Did it have an impact on me? Yes and no. It's rarely brought up amongst my audiences. When it is, women fall into three categories: those who haven't seen it, those who hated it, and those who enjoyed it but correctly assumed it an unrealistic Hollywood portrayal of male strippers. For me, the film is largely inconsequential. My clients and audiences don't consider it relevant to me and what I do. Nor do I. Its massive hype in the media is horribly overstated from my vantage point, but that hasn't stopped my contemporaries from clinging onto that hype like it's the land of milk and honey.

A handful of prospective clients have used it as a tool of criticism against me. But these women still wouldn't have booked me if the film didn't exist. They're also clients I don't need. One woman bitched me out due to Hardbodies not having a male stripper who looked like the film's title character. Because I manufacture strippers in my garage, I guess. I don't know what she was thinking. The truth is she wasn't thinking at all. Still too nice for my own good, I tried in vain to sell her on booking me. But she wasn't having any of that.

"If you're so great, then why aren't you already booked on that date?" she sneered in a tone that made me want to reach through the phone and backhand her.

I pounced immediately with, "If your hypothetical male stripper is so great, what makes you think he'd still be available on that date?"

She responded by telling me to stop harassing her before hanging up. Bullet dodged.

While writing "Emily Stripped Bare" during autumn 2018, I did a fiftieth birthday party in Little Rock. The birthday girl wasted no time informing me in her snottiest tone that she would be seeing the Magic Mike show in Las Vegas the following week. Her point being that I wasn't worth her time or attention. This was inexcusable behavior not only towards me but to her husband (the client) and their friends. I hope she had fun at a boring stage show while constantly having insanely overpriced merchandise shoved in her face. Not to mention that none of those guys would ever give a woman her age the time of day no matter how good she looked. The joke would've been on her if she weren't too fucking stupid to get it. Bitch.

I've never watched *Magic Mike* and have no plans to. It was made by an overrated director who rose to prominence on the back of James Spader's thespianic brilliance. Due to my limited free time, I already have a backlog of films I mean to watch. Like *Terminator 2*. As in Bruno Mattei's *Terminator 2*. But I know the gist of *Magic Mike* from my party girls. A bunch of male strippers get rich and addicted to coke. Horseshit on both counts. A few women have flippantly accused me of recreational drug use on this basis. If this film were accurate, it would've tackled anabolic steroid and human growth hormone abuse among male strippers. That, however, would also be an indictment against the same epidemic among contemporary Hollywood actors.

Despite its mostly nonimpact on my stripping career to date, *Magic Mike* does bother me for a few reasons. Along with the drug thing, the film is a product designed for consumption by the lowest common denominator of male stripper enthusiasts. These are the women of low expectations I discussed in the previous chapter. The women who bitch me out because there isn't a male strip club in Arkansas where they can watch hot guys without having to tip them. Women who resort to whining and ad hominems when something isn't to their standards rooted in ignorance. One of the many wonderful things about the women comprising my ideal audiences is they would never attack anyone over differing tastes in anything.

While this helps weed out bad clients and audiences, it also widens the gap between them and me. It's one thing to skip the obvious troublemakers altogether, but I want the chance to close a sale with prospective clients who are on the fence. A big part of booking parties for me and other strippers is education. Many of my callers are booking a stripper for the first time. A daunting process for some due to the uncharted territory into which they have ventured. It's vital that I educate them, encourage them to ask questions, and instill them with confidence in me. But when I have a woman on the phone who has accepted *Magic Mike* as the be-all, end-all gospel on male strippers, any attempts to educate fall on willfully ignorant ears.

I could criticize the film for its depiction of male strippers, sans cocaine, but I'm critical of other male strippers myself. This is where I'm torn. It's not representative of me and the handful of guys left in the world who operate similarly. That's the hard thing about being an exception to the rule. Much like the women to whom it most appeals, the film celebrates the lowest common denomination of male stripper. And that's most male strippers these days. Starring a guy who, by all accounts, is a failed male stripper. He should not be considered an authority on the subject, because he isn't. One of the many motivations behind this book is to rightfully claim this authority status for me.

Magic Mike can be considered an attack not on male strippers but pretty boys in general. This fits in with the longstanding plot device of having an unattractive guy chasing after a hot girl. The audience is supposed to cheer when he wins her away from that douche of a hot guy or cry when she rejects him. It's that old and tired as fuck, "It's what's on the inside that counts," argument. He's insecure and unconcerned with his physical appearance. Therefore, he's a good person. If so, then why is this broke dick dog only chasing after some girl for her looks? That's a rhetorical question. A lot of films are made by the real-life versions of these pathetic characters. I explored film and video opportunities upon graduating in the spring of 2012 and found myself stonewalled by such assholes. The common feedback I received was, "Well, I'd think you'd want to be in front of the camera." Fuck you, too.

In the way many attractive actors are quick to play asshole versions of themselves under the direction of some loser who should still be getting his head shoved in toilets, it seems like every male stripper not named Stefan Diamante has jumped brown nose-first onto the *Magic Mike* bandwagon. Nearly everyone is coopting that name to sell their male review and private party bookings. It was always bad enough to see photos of guys in matching pants, haircuts, and steroid cycles. Now they're also wearing matching tank tops with the *Magic Mike* logo. I'm guessing most of this usage is unlicensed because fuck intellectual property laws and shit. And what the fuck constitutes a "*Magic Mike* tribute show" anyway? Are the entertainers doing blow onstage? That would be honest within the context of the film's lies. Go all the way with it. I didn't pretend to lick a girl's butthole at a bachelorette party once. I fucking did it.

The success of the Magic Mike brand has furthered emasculated male stripping in the style set forth previously by Vegas casino shows. That boring and vapid boy band-esque performance of nameless and faceless juicers allowing themselves to be exploited financially. In exchange for low pay, peer approval circle jerks, and the possibility of tail. I can't imagine why many of the women I've entertained who've been to these shows once, and only once, speak of the experience with nary a shred of enthusiasm. These shows do everything to strip (no pun intended) male exotic entertainment of the piss and vinegar that attracted me to it and drives my performances.

This rant makes me love even more my individualistic, rock and roll approach to stripping. It's fucking gorgeous. To anyone arguing that I wouldn't make the cut for any Vegas show, you're goddamn right I wouldn't. I'm far too creative, adventurous, cerebral, daring, and sexy as fuck inside and out to be anyone's onstage boy toy. The further along I get with this book, the more obvious it becomes that I am to male strippers what Camille Paglia is to feminists. And that statement coming from a male stripper proves itself.

***

I graduated in May 2012 with an associate's degree in film and video production. Going from high school dropout to college graduate in under two years. A college graduate with honors. Summa cum laude with a 4.0 GPA. I wasn't joking when I said pursuing this degree was my escape from everything. With this project completed, I was back to working full time at getting my business back on track.

During the fourteen years I operated Hardbodies, several would-be competitors popped up briefly to challenge us. It's easy money, right? Apparently, it isn't. Not a single competitor lasted beyond 90 days. CallGurlz was no exception.

What the fuck is CallGurlz? An attempt at an exotic entertainment agency featuring male and female strippers run by KeysDAN. What the fuck is KeysDAN? A DJ for hire in Central Arkansas. I discovered him when I saw an online ad for CallGurlz consisting of Hardbodies marketing copy stolen verbatim save for the agency name and contact info. Because, as I stated before, fuck intellectual property laws. I find it hard to believe that someone who works with music in any capacity doesn't know about that, so he's a blatant fucking thief.

I don't like KeysDAN. Along with being a thief, he's a fat, pervy-faced sack of shit who looks like he sweats Crisco. Talking to him on the phone is even worse. He reminds me of a guy in Florida named John who operates a dubious stripping operation under a gazillion different names. Vulgar and overly aggressive at times for which none of that is called. After a shouting match during which KeysDAN made multiple physical threats, and for each I instructed him to put up or shut up, he agreed to stop stealing my marketing copy. In true chickenshit fashion claiming that he only stole it to get my attention in the hope we could collaborate. Really? He couldn't just call or email me with a business proposition? Yeah, sure.

It didn't take long for CallGurlz to go the way of Hog Wild Dancers. This was somehow my fault in the mind of KeysDAN, because of course it was. It couldn't have been the fact that this is not an easy business, or that he didn't have the first fucking clue as to what he was doing. Or the fact that hardly anyone was booking strippers during this time. The CallGurlz name and its ghetto chic nomenclature were also a problem. It looked as if he were representing two-bit whores. That part was true as his roster only ever consisted of a few girls from the local strip clubs. But no, it was that mean ol' Magnum being all greedy and shit. I wonder if he and Becky are friends. No, seriously.

***

I was getting desperate by the end of 2012. Not desperate enough to work with KeysDAN, but there was a definite sense of urgency. Maybe things would never turn around in Arkansas. I gave serious thought to setting up shop somewhere else. I considered returning home to Las Vegas and going head to head with the casinos in attempting to build a private party stripper empire in the American Southwest. I was certainly fearless and crazy enough to do it, and it came close to happening. In hindsight, that adventure would've been equally fraught with its own brand of problems. Not unlike had I relocated to New York City in 2004.

Everything needed to change. I proved how far I was willing to go with change as I stared at my blonde hair in the mirror. The hair color I'd rocked for the past decade. I went blonde early in my stripping career. It immediately became one of my defining features. Some women were vocal in their dislike of it, but that only endeared me further to the blonde cause. There was an edge that being blonde provided me for years. But that edge was gone. The blonde hair was now simply blonde hair. Nothing more. I took one final look before drenching it in black L'Oréal Preference.

I wasn't hopeful about 2013 given the past few years. They had left me a shell of a man. But at least I wasn't KeysDAN. Or a *Magic Mike* scab. Because of this, my never say die attitude was about to be rewarded. A Hardbodies resurgence was on the way. Complete with interesting new strippers. I would even start dating again. And, perhaps most important of all, I was about to meet the close friend and confident I needed far more than I still care to admit. Oh, and lots of hot girl on girl action. Future halcyon days were on their way and not a moment too fucking soon.

Just like this book right now, my life then needed a major tonal shift…

MORE THAN THIS

2013 - 2018

CHAPTER 34

Lesbians!

The city was alive on Saturday night. Electric. It wasn't the people out and about for a good time. No, there was something else in the air. My own version of napalm in the morning as I smelled victory close at hand. Getting there would be no cakewalk, but I was no longer operating in seclusion from my remote Cambodian outpost. The tide was turning. I could feel it. Taste it. The anticipation steadily rose. Like when a girl and I both know we're going to fuck and keep escalating the tension. Increasing the explosiveness of that inevitable carnal release.

Bruno Mars pounded from my truck speakers. I couldn't speak for him, but I was no longer locked out of the heaven I badly wanted.

Everything was changing quickly and for the better. A rush of dizzying highs one day to the next. It was overwhelming in the most amazing way. My intuition worked overtime. I still lost sleep, but now over excitement instead of stress. All guns cocked, locked, and ready to rock. Hardbodies was back, foxy buns. God, I felt so fucking alive.

2013 wasted no time starting with a bang. My first booking was a lesbian bachelorette party. The client wanted to do something special for her bisexual fiancé. Getting a male stripper for her last night of freedom seemed like the right idea. It was. As unsuspecting patrons in a downtown Little Rock bar sipped their drinks, sexy shenanigans were happening in the private party room. I focused heavily on entertaining my bachelorette. But the client and other audience members, all lesbians, were down with receiving their own lap dances. They were good to go after thirty minutes. A fun crowd and positive start to the new year.

This wasn't my first stripping encounter with lesbians nor my last. Most are game to engage me during performances with lap dances and even some Reddi-wip action. I feel like I'm making a big deal out of this, but it's incredibly flattering. Even humbling. I've invested so much time and effort into entertaining women and delivering the best male exotic entertainment money can buy. That women who aren't into men can appreciate and enjoy my performances means a lot to me.

***

After two years of Hardbodies Lite followed by three years of Hardbodies Dead, I had no ideas for my agency entering 2013. I was still leaning towards leaving Arkansas and had invested more time into tooling with the BodyRoxxx brand in anticipation of moving. Any bookings scored by Hardbodies would be gravy. I'd gained some noticeable bulk after spending the latter part of 2012 on a heavier steroid cycle than I'd done in the past few years. In a potentially dangerous move, I only waited a month before commencing a second cycle to preserve my precious mass as I starved away excess fat via cardio and carb cutting. It worked at the time but wouldn't sustain.

Rapid fat loss while preserving muscle is the most common objective of anabolic steroid and human growth hormone use among men and women. Including all those self-styled internet fitness gurus. Just because someone doesn't possess an exorbitant amount of muscle doesn't mean he or she isn't juicing.

Still not getting a clue about the inconsistencies of juicing aside, I came into the new year with newfound wisdom and experience. I'd still make mistakes, but they were ones I hadn't made before. My attitude and outlook were thoroughly refreshed as if it were 2004 all over again. The sins of 2007 through 2012, committed by me and others, had washed away. There truly was a sense of better days ahead. And damned if I wasn't going to make the most of them. The night was still young within the Hardbodies lifespan, and I was hungry for action.

Bookings rolled in at a pace that was spectacular by the standard of the previous three years. It seemed like my target demographics had finally stabilized financially and were once again in the mood for fun. The only downside was that I was turning down bookings due to lack of entertainers. Cheyenne bowed out in January in favor of a new boyfriend. So, it also felt like 2004 all over again as I was Hardbodies' sole entertainer. I immediately got to work on fixing that as the calls kept coming.

My proposed move to Sin City was quickly in doubt. If a Hardbodies renaissance was indeed happening, then it was more practical financially to see where that went instead of pursuing uncertainty in another region. No matter my choice, I wasn't moving anywhere just yet. I was having a blast knocking out party after party without multiweek gaps in between.

***

The Hmong are an ethnic group historically located across China, Laos, Thailand, and Vietnam. Many relocated to the United States from the seventies through the nineties due to persecution from the communist regimes that assumed power in Laos and Vietnam. This stems from the vast number of Hmong men who fought against the communists in the Vietnam War and Laotian Civil War. Regardless of one's opinion on American involvement in these wars, there's no arguing that the Hmong stuck their necks way out for us. Fighting their hearts out against the evils of communism. These are people for whom we have a moral obligation to accept into our country.

Northwest Arkansas has a Hmong community numbering just over 2,000. I've performed for Hmong girls a few times over the years. They pulled out all the stops when it came to parties. Event space rental, PA systems and lighting, and plenty of food and beverages. I relate to that over the top approach to partying. Go big or go home, I always say. Even with a limited budget, there's nothing that a little creative thinking can't do to take any shindig to the next level. Not unlike how I'm constantly on the lookout for anything I can utilize to make my performance more personable for each audience.

I entered March with a birthday party in Fort Smith for a group of twentysomething Hmong girls. Upon arriving at the event center rented for this party, I spotted a group of guys hanging around the entrance. Figuring they'd been ushered outside ahead of my appearance, I was a little apprehensive that they might be resentful of my presence. I know how young men can be if their girlfriends are about to go crazy over a male stripper. But these guys were cool as shit. As I headed inside with the client, they joked to her about going easy on me. One of them held the door open since I had both hands full. Another little thing that meant a lot to me.

If you'd told me in 2001 that someday I'd be plugging my cell phone into a P.A. to provide the music at a party, I'd have been all like, "Fuck you." But here I was in 2013 doing exactly that. My party girls looked terrific. All glammed up and ready to follow my lead. It wasn't a large crowd. Maybe a dozen girls. But they were oodles of fun and tipped generously. I was still coming out of my shell of the past few years, and this was another excellent audience that helped me step out further. My birthday girl was so sweet and not ready for me to leave, but they had an itinerary to keep.

Before making the drive back to Little Rock, I searched for a place to eat. There was a Village Inn. Instantly feeling nostalgic for my Denver days, I didn't hesitate to make that left turn. It was somewhat busy yet rather quiet. The tabletops were sufficiently illuminated in the otherwise dim dining room. Providing the perfect ambiance for my thoughts as I sipped coffee, ate my skillet breakfast, and watched cars fly by from my window booth. Damn, I was a long way from Denver.

I desperately wanted to return to those days many times over the past few years. This night was different. Some company would've been nice, but I'd been doing without company for a long time. My mind was attempting to grasp this sudden turnaround. Was it really happening? Could I build upon this? And could I find entertainers to help execute a new breakthrough for Hardbodies? After nearly a decade of ups and downs, was Hardbodies finally maturing to fruition? I should've done then what I should've done in 2009. Dissolve the agency and go solo. Despite being in better shape physically and mentally than four years prior, I still wasn't ready for that.

Regardless, there was renewed interest in Hardbodies and me. I was amped to exploit that for all it was worth. It felt good to be busy again. Fuck, it felt good to feel good again. I could finally confront the ghosts of stripping past. After it all fell apart in 2007, I had pushed everyone and everything from the past out of my mind. Not allowing myself to think about it or look at photos. Now I could analyze my past mistakes honestly while making plans for bigger and better things. Go big or go home indeed. I was done staying home all the time.

The sudden influx of cash afforded me the chance to improve my truck. Replacing worn components and the old stereo along with adding new tires and wheels. A worthwhile investment as I'd be driving lots of miles over the next few years throughout Arkansas and beyond. Sliding around on concrete underneath my truck as I bled my upgraded braking system felt oddly refreshing. Even as I raced to finish before darkness fell. Things were coming together, and I knew it.

I booked parties for March and April at a brisk pace. The search for new talent was also underway. Moving to Vegas was becoming less an option. I couldn't leave now. There was money to be made. Next up was a birthday party in Hot Springs courtesy of the birthday girl's husband. One of those parties at which I'd be in and out within fifteen minutes. I'd done so many of these already. One or two songs and they'd be good. Why should I expect this party to be any different?

It was Saturday night in the middle of March. I got in my refreshed truck and drove to America's First Resort. Spring was a few days away, but winter lingered with a slight crispness in the air. I felt cocksure as I rolled into town. This was the sort of performance I could do in my sleep. My only disappointment being that I wanted a greater challenge than a wham, bam, thank you ma'am birthday quickie. On the bright side, I'd be home before I knew it.

I never would've imagined that I'd stay for four hours.

CHAPTER 35

A light fog swept off the water as I pulled into the driveway of a home on the shore of Lake Hamilton. Not an eerie or sinister fog. More like being on stage as I rocked out with my cock out. I got out of the truck and texted the client. While waiting, I put on the rest of my firefighter costume, added some more cologne, and popped a Tic Tac. The client appeared and we discussed my entrance game plan. I would enter through the front door once he turned off the outside light.

"Yeah, these girls might get naked for you," he said with subdued excitement.

Having no idea what any of them looked like but knowing they were all a decade or so older than me, I tried my damnedest to sound enthusiastic about that prospect. Fuck it. I'd be gone long before that came close to happening. He went back inside as I grabbed my gear and walked towards the tiny front lawn to wait for my cue. Getting closer, I could see someone dancing alone in the middle of the living room through the front window.

Fuck me running. Here was this stunning woman in a short, tight, zebra print dress. She had bleached blonde hair, a hot body, and fake tits. There was a Bo Derek quality about her in terms of skin tone. A natural beauty accentuated by her subdued approach to cosmetics. There was a fierceness about her. An, "I'm doing my thing and don't give a fuck if you have a problem with it," attitude as she lost herself in both the music and moment. And there was an element of me at my best that I saw in her. I was transfixed. Doing my best to stay out of sight while keeping my eyes glued to her.

I desperately wanted her to be Tori, my birthday girl, and to shower her with attention. But she didn't look old enough to be the woman I was expecting. I'd work it out somehow. And I'd have no problem with her getting naked. I continued watching her dance like no one was watching. Only for a minute, but it felt like an eternity. The light went out and I walked towards the door. It was then I knew this would not be the typical couples' birthday party performance. Something huge and life-changing would come my way once I entered that house.

Numerous bachelorettes and birthday girls have lost their minds over me at first sight. It's perhaps the ultimate form of flattery for me as an entertainer. And it gets me a little choked up every time. Not only was my newfound dancing queen indeed Tori, but I'd never seen a woman more beside herself with excitement to see me. Remembering how she raised her hands to her face as if she'd just been crowned Miss America still gives me chills. She was all smiles as the client introduced me to everyone. Two other couples were present, but my entire focus was on the birthday girl. She was too good to be true. And it only got better.

It was apparent once I began giving Tori her first lap dance that there was amazing chemistry between us. We'd just met but were already lifelong friends. That's the best way I can describe it. I ripped the black tank top from my torso and wrapped it around her neck as I bumped and grinded on her lap. If not for the steady stream of camera flashes in the dimly lit living room I would've forgotten anyone else was present. Tori apparently did too as she devoted her undivided attention to me. She grabbed the waistband of my tear away pants as I stepped backward out of them. I didn't hesitate to press my nearly nude body tight against her. She was technically a stranger, yet this was the first time in years I felt close to someone. It was easy for me because she made it easy.

I followed this shameless display of shamelessness by giving lap dances to the other women. Diane, like Tori, rocked fake tits on an athletic frame. She was a brunette and somewhat shy but an enthusiastic participant in my sexy games. I'd encounter her several more times in the future. Tori and I always trying to extract her from her shell. I honestly don't remember anything about the other girl other than she was blonde. She wasn't all that into me and our lap dance consisted of her tolerating me for a couple of minutes. That was fine because she's no Tori and I'd never see her again anyway.

Back to Tori, whom I quickly learned had trouble keeping her clothes on. She was back in her chair and wearing only a g-string. The other women also got topless, but I was fixated on my birthday girl's impressive rack. I've seen and felt a lot of breasts in my life. Tori has arguably the most impressive pair I've ever seen, real or fake. Not only are her 34D tits perfectly proportioned and symmetrical, but they show not a trace of scarring. Even her nipples are the ideal size, shape, and color go along with the rest of her amazing aesthetics.

It was time to break out the Reddi-wip on those bad girls. And before anyone says, "But her husband was there," this was clearly acceptable. I've encountered lots of couples into all kinds of stuff over the years. God knows I get enough calls from guys wanting to watch me fuck their wives. Not a service I offer by the way. I could see that Tori was something of a "hotwife." Free to engage in light fun with others.

Nominally into girls for this sort of thing but obviously hot for me in that moment. More camera flashes went off as I applied whipped cream to her nipples before licking and sucking them clean.

It was time to up the ante as I announced, "I have something for you."

I retrieved a white bath towel from my duffle bag, wrapped it around my waist, and removed my g-string. What's interesting about the towel gimmick is that it's less revealing than wearing a g-string. The appeal is due to the towel not being tightly fastened to my body. It's not something I break out at every performance. I must feel totally comfortable with my audience to do it. And it would be too much for some girls. This night, however, was perfect for being daring.

Save for cowboy boots, I sat butt ass naked on Tori's lap. Bumping and grinding on her nearly naked body with only a towel between us. Her delicious titties pressed against my chest. She smelled very sexy. As in the Victoria's Secret fragrance Very Sexy. I couldn't shake the feeling that I'd known her forever, and I'm sure it was mutual. There was something comforting about being in her company. I could allow all of me to come through my performance. I could be myself.

I put the g-string back on as we took a break. I could've left then, and everyone would've been satisfied. But not only could I not pull myself away from Tori, she couldn't remove herself from my side. We were Siamese twins joined at the hip. Conversing amongst ourselves and with others. Despite how friendly everyone else was, all I could focus on was the birthday girl hanging on me the entire time. We were a sexually deviant duo keeping each other warm as we stood on the back deck in the cool late winter air. I didn't question why it felt so right. I just went with it.

Back inside, Tori and I slow danced for what seemed like an eternity. We talked about so many things and forgot that anyone else was there. Like that orgiastic bachelorette party several years earlier, this was a once in a lifetime gig. It stands to this day as the best birthday party performance of my long and extensive career. It's not every night I encounter my anima incarnate. Her shameless self-confidence and sexually provocative ways told me I was indeed dancing with Girl Stefan. We had so much in common, from our love of nudity to hatred of pubic hair. She opened up about her sexual curiosity for girls as well as her shyness about it and struggles to find anyone to fully explore with.

There was nothing one of us could say that would cause the other to be taken aback. It was all good. And she was all good. It was obvious how unbelievably sweet, kind, and caring she is. Not a single malicious bone in her body. It was her birthday party, yet she prioritized making sure that I felt at home. I reminded her that all she needed to do tonight was enjoy herself. But she reminded me that this was her house and that she had an obligation to every guest including me. We discussed our shared disdain for people who choose to exclude themselves from fun when they are more than welcome to take part. We concluded that life is too short for needless drama.

I wasn't sure how to describe these feelings for my newfound BFF and confidant, but Rhianna was present to lend a hand:

"Not really sure how to feel about it

Something in the way you move

Makes me feel like I can't live without you

It takes me all the way"

I fell in love with Tori that night. Who wouldn't fall in love with her? She's so sexy, ditzy, and wonderful. I couldn't and still can't get enough of her free-spirited nature. She says and does what she wants without embarrassment. I badly needed exposure to that attitude. Although on the road to self-improvement, I still walked into this party a shell of the person I'd once been. Tori quickly helped me return to form. Every little thing she does is indeed magic. Such as when she asked me the question we still laugh about to this day.

"Would you warm my ass?" she requested matter-of-factly.

She was completely naked by this point. The cool air from outside kept creeping in as some individuals took smoke breaks. But I loved the innocence of her request. Her butt was cold, and she wanted me to warm it with my hands. It was that simple with no ulterior motives. I was more than happy to oblige as I squeezed and caressed her firm, round cheeks. We continued slow dancing as if we were the only two people on the planet. Finally, we realized there were others present as they began dozing off. This wouldn't be the only time we were the last two standing.

Four hours after I arrived, I managed to pull myself away and head home. It wasn't easy by any means. I spent the entire drive home wondering if I'd ever hear from her again. We'd covered so much ground yet barely scratched the surface of what a friendship between us could entail. That was it. She was the friend I'd desired insatiably for so long. I'd just met her, and this was crazy, but I felt like I could tell her anything. I was sure she felt the same about me. What if she was too shy to get my number from her husband's phone and text me? I didn't have her number. Would I go as far as to stalk her just to set up a "chance" public encounter?

I wouldn't have to go that route. Someone texted me immediately after I arrived home and was unloading my gear. I didn't see it until after I was in bed. It was Tori thanking me for making this birthday the best one ever. Beginning a ritual of near-nightly texting that continues to this day. And as I write this. Although it's late now and I think she just fell asleep.

The running gag over the years among Tori's husband and their friends is referring to me as her boyfriend. She's certainly set a gold standard for me as to all the qualities I should seek in a woman. Someone ridiculously beautiful inside and out who recognizes and builds up my strengths. It's uncanny how we think alike. As I wrote this chapter, she brought up nearly every point I made without knowing I was making it. Even the subtlest of details I was already including.

CHAPTER 36

It was time to get serious about bringing in other entertainers. A prospect that filled me with both excitement and dread. Candidates came to me back in the day. That's how I acquired my angels of the past. Now chiefly relegated to that online cesspool of scumminess known as Craigslist. I hated placing a help wanted ad alongside those posted by questionable people with dubious intentions. And I shuddered to think about the quality of respondents. All the scary photos they would send me.

Although business was up, there weren't enough male stripper bookings justify having even one more guy. I still got responses from would-be male strippers. Most seeing this as a do-nothing joke of a profession. Or so I thought at the time. I see now they were lashing out at me over their low self-esteem, because that's my fault somehow. The only serious candidate was a young, skinny dude who applied multiple times with various shirtless images along with a snapshot of him ice skating. He also sent me a photo of his feet. At least he was wearing shoes. And at least it wasn't his dick.

I fared better with female applicants. The first girl who came on board with Hardbodies Reborn was Star. A petite twentysomething who became the first and only redhead I represented. For all the talk in the media of red hair being hot, this made her a tough sell to prospective clients. She was also high strung and had issues with promptness along with zero experience. As raw as raw potential gets. She did have stage acting experience and took seriously the idea of being an exotic entertainer. This impressed and intrigued me enough to make her the first of my new angels.

She was followed by Brandi. A beautiful blonde with an athletic body and adorable personality. More than worthy of new angel status. She had prior experience. Much of it coming from upscale gentlemen's clubs on the East Coast. We talked about how she excelled at making money from patrons simply by talking to them, which is not something you see in Arkansas. She did come with limitations in the form of a child and ex-husband along with living outside Central Arkansas. But she was too good to pass up. She was also into girls, which meant I could once again book parties with bi-curious women after passing on them for the past few years.

I took photos of Brandi in lingerie and a bikini. Not only did we click instantly but there was a mutual attraction between us. Internal conflict ensued. I was feeling overtly sexual again. A feeling emboldened by Tori's influence on me. But I wasn't sure about getting sexually involved with another female stripper. Did I again want to put that much stock into one girl? Could I even if I wanted to? There were already enough obstacles to work around with Brandi. I didn't see a need to complicate things any more.

With two new angels in the Hardbodies fold, I was gunning to complete the trifecta and return to full Charlie status. Other female applicants were deficient in one way or another. Many were of the big beautiful woman variety. At odds with the rhetorical symbolism of the Hardbodies moniker. The rest ranged from likely meth addicts to burlesque entertainers, which is pretty much the same thing. I have no respect for burlesque or its practitioners. Brag all they want about being higher class than real strippers, they're quick to seek bachelor parties on the down-low. Hoping to make money for a change. And I've never known a burlesque entertainer who wasn't a drug addict and/or a communist. Not sure which is worse. It's communist.

I received an email one evening from a hopeful angel. Judging by her photos, she had the body for it. Her face appeared average, but I chalked that up to a lack of cosmetic enhancement. That could easily be fixed. She had dark brown hair with reddish highlights. Her experience was limited but included bachelor parties. She said all the right things and came across as if she had her shit together. I decided she was worth a shot and set up a time for us to meet, take photos, and discuss ways to improve her appeal.

As with Brandi, I set up a shoot in the garage as I waited for her to arrive. The door was open. While watching an unfamiliar car park in front of my home, I noticed the passenger with her face pressed against the glass. She had grotesque features and neon blue hair. I'm not kidding. That shit looked radioactive. A fucking dumpster fire of a human being if I ever saw one. My new girl was bringing along a friend, but what the fuck was this thing? It looked like a living, breathing troll doll. I didn't recognize the driver when she got out. That's when I realized the troll was my new angel.

There was no way I could use her for anything. Not wanting to create a scene, I delivered an Oscar-worthy performance as we went through with our shoot. I'd considered getting some shots in the living room as well, but I didn't want her getting on the furniture. She needed to change clothes. I stepped outside and pulled down the door three quarters. Returning to find her in a hot pink lace top and black boy shorts that read "sparkle" on the rear. I hate boy shorts on women, but it made no difference this time. Not only was she ugly and had blue hair, but she was totally out of shape. Her ample gut oozing outward. What a lying, nasty fucking pig she was. Sparkle, my ass.

She wanted her stripper name to be Pandora. That was apropos given that my contacting her in the first place constituted the opening of a Pandora's box. It also seemed like a sick joke. Who the fuck would want to get in her box? She had a kid, so someone did at least once. There was no way Pandora would ever be an angel. At best, she'd have to be Bosley. And that's how she's known to this day by those privy to the story. Fucking Bosley. And that's being charitable.

This was not something easily fixed by cosmetics. Had I summoned the ghost of Coco Chanel, she would've taken one look at Bosley and been all like, "Fuck this. I can't help you." *Troll 2* wanted to do an outfit change. I told her to knock herself out and once again stepped outside. I returned to find her in light pink boy shorts and a black fishnet top sans bra. I snapped a few shots of her malt liquor belly and sad, frumpy tits before telling her to get dressed and sending her far away from me. When she texted a few days later, I informed her that her services would not be required after all. Then I blocked her number.

If anyone thinks I'm being unfairly harsh to Bosley... I found out shortly after our shoot that her parents sued for and won custody of her kid. Because she refused to break up with her meth addict boyfriend. Never mind the boyfriend being more than enough for me to pass on her. If she's not willing to do right by her child, then I couldn't have expected her to do right by my agency and clients. I don't care if she'd been drop-dead gorgeous. There's no way in hell I'd have kept her around in light of these piss poor life decisions. Everything about her was a fucking disgrace.

***

My own bookings kept coming throughout the spring and summer. I once again spent my nights traveling all over Arkansas. Music blaring and windows down on state and U.S. highways as I absorbed the clean, rural air. Along with making runs into Texas, I scored my first Louisiana booking. A bachelorette party in Shreveport. This was before the opening of I-49 from Texarkana to Ratchet City, so my route was a sightseeing tour of Southwest Arkansas in the early evening sunlight. The most notable town I passed through was Stamps. Where Maya Angelou spent part of her childhood. *I Know Why the Caged Bird Sings* is partly set there. And it has a Piggly Wiggly. This trip also allowed me to be in both Benton, Arkansas and Benton, Louisiana on the same day. That's some straight-up *Twilight Zone* shit right there.

A more exciting Saturday night saw me knock out two bachelorette parties in Little Rock. The first was an early affair at 6:30pm. They were slightly on the conservative side yet loads of fun. I entertained the bachelorette and other younger women while the older ladies watched from the kitchen. The latter faction couldn't bring themselves to actively participate despite my best efforts to convince them otherwise. My twentysomethings and thirtysomethings were quick to indulge my lap dances and Reddi-wip fetish. The bachelorette was wonderful. Eager to accept all the naughty attention I gave her.

Another girl who enjoyed the pleasure of my naked company was an attractive blonde named Samantha. Her friends expressed amazement at her antics with me. Lively as she was, there was an underlying shyness about her. She was charmingly awkward in her extroversion. It was sweet, endearing, and incredibly sexy. I instantly had the hots for her. The attraction seemed mutual, but I wasn't getting my hopes up. If I did that every time a girl and I clicked, my entire life would be one broken heart after another. The cruel joke being that I never would've met any of them if not for stripping.

I stayed as long as I could before my second party. Handing out business cards as I left and letting them know I had girls too. Samantha took a card, saying she knew of someone who might require my services. She asked if her friend could text me at that number if necessary. I don't like booking with first-time clients via text, but I wrote my cell number on her card and instructed her to let that person know to tell me she'd referred them. I also considered the possibility that Samantha may text me for personal reasons.

My second party was only seven miles away. I arrived twenty minutes early. As I sat in the truck and joked around with my friend the Trashman on Facebook, I received a text from an unfamiliar number:

"Hi. This is Samantha. We just met a little while ago. I hope you don't mind, but I wanted to wish you good luck at your next party."

My mind was totally fucking blown. Instantly filled with countless thoughts racing faster than the speed of night. I thanked her for the kind text. She responded by inviting me to text her anytime. I said I would and wished her a good night before dominating another group of party girls. My work was cut out for me, with one of them decked out in a leather teddy and sporting a cat o' nine tails. Challenged fucking accepted. I showed her and the rest who's boss. After rocking their world and drinking the abomination of a cocktail they fixed me, I was on my way home.

I spent the rest of my Saturday night alone as I drank Jack and Coke. Tori must've been up to something as she never texted that night. Instead, I read about the Original Night Stalker. Still at large in 2013. While I've always enjoyed reading about serial killers, this one grabbed my attention like no other. Not only would I develop my own psychological profile of the killer, but I'd later have my own person of interest. When Joseph DeAngelo was apprehended and charged five years later, both my profile and POI were nearly dead ringers. I've always had a knack for reading people and getting a solid handle on them. I'm not always right, but I am more often than not.

Imagine my surprise at midnight when Samantha texted me. Wanting to play it cool, I waited five minutes before responding. Once again, she was adorably considerate. Apologizing for texting so late and asking if she'd caught me at a bad time.

Our conversation quickly turned to sex as she opened up about her experiences and fantasies. She'd only been with one guy. Her high school sweetheart from whom she'd split a year prior. She'd spent her life eager to please others. Now she wanted to experience pleasures all her own. She shared precious fantasies including feeding each other chocolate-covered strawberries and being held against a wall. And she was curious about girls. That's not something I seek out in women or expect from them. It just finds me. I can meet a girl and within minutes she's telling me all about her fantasies and/or experiences involving girls. Along with bachelorette parties, I'm apparently the patron saint of hot girl on girl action. I guess life could be worse.

One thing led to another, and Samantha wound up taking my virginity that night. My sexting virginity, that is. I took hers as well. I always thought sexting sounded unsexy, but it was totally hot with my new sexual target. The tension kept building as we texted back and forth what we wanted to do to each other in the dirtiest language imaginable. It was a life-changing experience for me. I'd never wanted anyone as bad as I wanted her. My mission was clear. I was going to fuck this girl, and nothing would stand in my way. There would be no rest for the wicked until I came deep inside her.

But first, sleep.

CHAPTER 37

How groovy was the summer of 2013 for stripping? I had a client named Becky. And she was all right. It was a bachelorette party on Eden Isle. One of several I've had on this swanky island in Greers Ferry Lake. My party girls that night sought refuge from the humidity in a luxury condo. That didn't stop us from working up a sweat as we celebrated my bachelorette's last night of freedom. The lap dances and Reddi-wip led to a full-on dance party. Like many other places in Arkansas, Greers Ferry Lake is a gorgeous locale that's perfect for parties.

It was my second party on that Saturday in August. The first was a birthday surprise at an optometry office in Little Rock that afternoon. I arrived as a cop and pretended there was an arrest warrant out for my birthday girl. She wasn't buying it. But she was game for a sexy as all fuck lap dance. Cold air blasted from the ceiling vent above me. It felt refreshing on my bare skin as I thought about the sweltering Arkansas summer heat outside. This was a one-song performance for which the booking fee and gratuity had been paid days beforehand. It was fun to simply walk in, do my thing, and leave.

More pleasant than the muggy night in Little Rock when I arrived at what was supposed to be a birthday party. The client was a prominent local businessman in the watercraft industry and wanted to watch me fuck his wife. I was pissed as hell. So was she, as she had no idea what he had planned. He went inside after I made his dumb ass pay me in full since I was ready to hold up my end for a birthday party. I could hear her screaming at him as I left. However, this being Arkansas, she probably blames me.

There was no escaping the heat a few weeks later in early September at a bachelorette party in DeGray Lake State Park. Another spectacular Arkansas lake. This one located an hour southwest of Little Rock off I-30. Little Rock was hit with a combination of heat and rain that left me without electricity as I prepared for my gig. In a moment when most male strippers would've said, "Fuck this," and either canceled or no-showed, I thought nothing of showering and shaving by candlelight. I wasn't about to disappoint my bachelorette and her girlfriends over a dark bathroom.

I'd previously done parties at DeGray Lake. All had taken place in cabins. My party girls on this Friday night had opted for a yurt. I think that was how they afforded me, and God bless them for going that route. It had rained there too. Humid as all fuck. And hotter than hell. I was a firefighter, but nothing could've prepared me for this heat. No matter. If they were ready to sweat it out for my performance, you can bet your boots I was going to sweat it out with them. One thing I've learned from Arkansas summers is that it's futile to resist the effects of hot, sticky, soaking wet air. All I can do is embrace it in a savage fashion.

And that's what we did. We were sweatier than KeysDAN waiting in anticipation at a Taco Bell drive-thru. I entertained my bachelorette and moved from girl to girl. Multicolored party lights illuminated the yurt. Itself surrounded by the darkness of the forest at night. I had to lick my Reddi-wip fast before it slid from damp cleavage. My performance was raw and animalistic. The girls followed my lead every step of the way. Proving yet again that it doesn't take much to make your own fun wherever you are.

One girl was fascinated with my tear-away pants and wanted to wear them. I let her experience the joy of removing them to reveal her bikini bottoms. In return, I talked her and another girl into making out for my viewing pleasure. The others got a kick out of it too, so everyone was a winner. With no more ground left to cover, I made my exit. The electricity was back on when I returned home. I would've showered in total darkness if necessary because I fucking needed it.

The following Friday was rainy yet cooler as I drove to Fort Smith. It was another bachelorette party and I was once again a firefighter. The bachelorette and other girls were great, but the standouts were the client and her roommate. The client was a walking stereotype of both cute blonde and sexy librarian. As if she could quickly go from being sweet and innocent to removing her glasses and unleashing the naughty girl within. The roommate was a beautiful and quirky brunette. She wasn't my type per se, yet I found myself attracted to her. The intrigue was mutual as I clicked with her more than anyone else. Enjoying a flirtatious conversation about cars.

I hung out afterward. We played some homemade card game with a truth or dare element to it. I had my first mimosa and liked it. Please don't tell anyone. It was my turn to draw a card. This one instructed me to kiss the person to my right. I seized an opportunity by passing it to my two favorite girls and instructing them to kiss. They didn't hesitate as each girl slipped her tongue into the other's mouth. It wasn't the first time they'd done this. My imagination couldn't help but speculate how far they'd gone before.

The spell was broken when the roommate's boyfriend came home. This made me disappointed in her because he was soft and weak. I thought she could've done better than him, and I'm not talking about me. Perhaps he made her laugh, but no one is funny enough to bridge that aesthetic gap. He didn't come across as being funny. More like Droopy Dog mainlining soy lattes. Giving me food for thought on the long drive home.

***

It was a warm and sunny September afternoon when I met with a girl in downtown Little Rock. She'd applied with Hardbodies but was more interested in escorting than stripping. A naïve but not uncommon fantasy among women. She was a tall, attractive brunette of 25. Real pretty, as Becky and Charolette would say. There was a charming sweetness about her. She possessed a romanticized notion of being a call girl that was adorable yet dangerous. I liked the idea of her as a private party stripper and my elusive third angel. If nothing else, I wanted to talk her out of the escorting idea.

We sat near the entrance of a pool hall in the business district. Sunlight forcing its way past skyscrapers to illuminate everything around us. The streets were dead as they always are during this time of day. We were surrounded by thousands of people out of sight. Working deep inside steel and concrete towers. The only other person in the pool hall was our bartender and server. I kicked back Coronas with lime in a cavalier fashion as my companion nervously sipped ice water. She wasn't so much unsure about me as she was about herself. That made me like her even more.

She opened up about being a tomboy all her life only to recently outgrow that and begin embracing her femininity. Judging by her impeccable hair and makeup, she was a quick learner. She told me about her limited sexual experience and wanting to change that. And she was curious about girls, because of course she was. In her fiction inspired mind, escorting was an idyllic way to achieve all of this. I wished in that moment she was right. That she could have her cake and eat it too. Living out a real-life *Emmanuelle* film plot and getting paid for it. But sex work is scummy, and I didn't hesitate to write her that reality check.

I related to what she was experiencing and not only due to my conversations with Tori and Samantha. These three weren't the only ones experiencing a sexual awaking. I was too. Following the personal and professional doldrums of 2010 through 2012, I had my own carnal ax to grind. This wasn't about padding stats. I was pickier than before. No, I desired earth-shattering sexual encounters full of sensuality and multiorgasmic release with the right women. Some men may interpret this as weak and submissive. On the contrary, it makes me even more dominant and aggressive than I already was.

And let me tell you… Guys who think it's cool to make themselves as unsexy as possible, who treat sex as over-glorified masturbation, and who proudly say things like, "Let her worry about her orgasm," and other idiotic nonsense are setting themselves up to be cucked. So much for being a "real man."

Although I managed to give her pause on escorting, she wouldn't bite on stripping. She clung to de rigueur excuses about not being a good dancer and so forth. A motivation for some girls to pursue escorting over stripping is a belief that the former will provide a degree of slack when it comes to physical imperfections, real or perceived. Yes, shitty clients and audiences will nitpick a stripper's body. But I imagine the same hold true for escorting. Why wouldn't it? I admit that my knowledge of sex work – and no, stripping is not inherently sex work – is limited, but that must go without saying.

I didn't want her for bachelor parties. She wasn't cut out for them. However, she had the potential to succeed with coed audiences at birthday parties or teaming with me for bachelorette parties. This would allow her to explore and express her sexuality in a safe environment without having to fuck random dudes. She could entertain bi-curious women such as Tori, who would've been game for meeting her sexy ass. As a talent agent, I was infatuated with this girl. I genuinely liked and wanted to work with her. She had "it." But "it" wasn't meant to be. I wished her all the best as we parted ways forever.

***

Despite how much I enjoyed the idea of having that tomboy turned femme fatale as an entertainer, the girl I truly coveted as a stripper was Samantha. She totes had "it" with her all American blonde good looks combined with a sweet yet sassy disposition. That mix would've made for an amazing private party female stripper. A bad girl answer to Ann Jillian if you will. I would've utilized Samantha exclusively for coed and female audiences. Either solo or as my partner. We had excellent chemistry together. And yes, we were lovers by this point. But no matter my promises to keep it confidential, she flat out refused to strip. Not because she was opposed to the idea. She loved it. But the fear of being discovered by family and friends was too strong for her to let go and just do it.

That same fear prevented us from being a full-fledged couple. What would people say if they knew about Samantha and me? She didn't want to find out, and that relegated me to dirty little secret status. We enjoyed plenty of lovemaking sessions at her place and even went out on dates occasionally. But a true boyfriend-girlfriend scenario out there for the entire world to see? That was out of the question. This would be a constant source of frustration for me over the next few years. Still, she indulged me intellectually and sexually like no one before. And she wasn't bugging me for things like marriage or a baby without considering the life-changing implications of such an action. It was exactly the romance I needed at that stage of my life.

The day after I shattered a young woman's call girl fantasies had me rocking an early evening fiftieth birthday party in Sherwood. Following that wham bam thank you ma'am performance, I drove back to Little Rock and picked up Samantha. It was a Thursday night and we went to a bar where no one would recognize her. Karaoke was in full swing as husky-voiced women lived out Janis Joplin-esque fantasies before a largely indifferent audience. A fat girl sang that "Memory" song from *Cats*, because of course she did. I was too busy flirting with Samantha to notice much beyond that.

There is a trend I've noticed about karaoke nights. Some young guy will inevitably deliver a spoken word performance of a country song. Ostensibly as a joke, but one that only he finds funny. Not a song that was originally delivered in spoken word such as "Giddyup Go". A song that was originally sung like "The Gambler" or "Okie From Muskogee". It's just stupid. This night was no exception as a scrawny ass-clown dressed in grunge attire twenty years too late giggled like a dumb fuck as he walked on stage. That was bad enough, but this time really pissed me off when the music began. Oh, fuck me. He continued mugging it up while awaiting the first verse. At which point he pulled together a straight face and spoke in a listless monotone:

"Amarillo by morning."

As much as I hate to admit it, the George Strait version of this song had really grown on me by 2013. It achieves the haunting melancholy only aspired to by many country songs before and after. Both the lyrics and music perfectly convey the romance and harsh realities of pursuing an unconventional career path. I know he didn't write the song or record it first, but there's something about Strait's delivery that makes his version shine above all others. That something is soul. Also, passion. Whether or not Strait has ever sat upon a bull is irrelevant. He's living in that moment for everyone who has. To such magnificent effect that I find it hard to listen to sometimes. As if the song is too good for mortal ears. Eat your heart out, Patrick Bateman.

Samantha's front door had been closed for nanoseconds when I grabbed and pulled her body tight against mine. Our lips locked together. Her tongue teasing every part of my mouth and vice versa. She and I never tilted our heads to kiss. This allowed us to maintain eye contact during our oral embraces. Her jeans were tight, but not so tight that I couldn't slide my hand down the rear to discover she wasn't rocking any underwear. I squeezed each of her firm, round cheeks as she wrapped her arms tighter around my neck. Even fully clothed, the feeling of her sizeable breasts pressed against my muscular chest was ecstasy.

She lifted her arms as I removed her tank top. We resumed our insatiable kiss as I unclasped her bra with only my thumb and forefinger. This time, I got them all. I placed my hands on her tits. They were so big and round. I held them and rubbed her nipples with my thumbs as we kissed and licked each other's neck. She and I effusing our respective gender's version of Eternity. I leaned forward and swirled my tongue on her right nipple before covering it entirely with my mouth. Sucking while flicking it rapidly. I moved to her left nipple as she held my head with both hands and breathed heavily.

Samantha removed my black t-shirt and returned the favor. I tilted my head back and closed my eyes. It was when I opened them that I realized we were standing in total darkness. Save for the outside light creeping through the Venetian blinds in uniform lines. Enough illumination for me to see her looking at me with her naughty smile as she played with my chest. God, she was one sexy ass motherfucker.

She stopped to put on music as I flipped on the kitchen light. Improving visibility in the living room while maintaining ambiance. With top forty radio playing, we resumed our seductive game. I unbuttoned her jeans, then dropped to my knees and pulled them down. They came off easily once I got them past her ample booty, which I grabbed tightly as I licked her clit for a moment. She was already soaking wet. I couldn't wait to spend more time enjoying her sweet juices.

She removed my jeans and teased my hard cock with her silky soft mouth and tongue. I pulled her up and we embraced tightly. My face buried in her neck and hers in mine. We expressed affection for one another as friends. We were friends, after all. Friends who were passionate lovers. That may have been the hottest aspect of our relationship. Something about the idea of two friends knowing each other sexually and giving each other carnal pleasure. When I ponder the hypothetical Miss Right I hope to meet someday, I think of her as the best friend I've been waiting for my entire life.

I made a quick sojourn to the kitchen and retrieved the bottle of Korbel I'd brought with me earlier. Now chilled, I grabbed a tea towel and popped the cork. After finding a pair of champagne glasses, I returned to my hot, naked friend.

Before filling the glasses, I took a swig of sparkling wine straight from the bottle. Holding it in my mouth, I pulled Samantha to me and kissed her. I passed the champagne from my mouth to hers. She responded by passing it back. We did this dance several times before swallowing it all between us. Electricity rushed through my body. She experienced the same sensation. I filled our glasses and we drank like civilized people. Dancing naked as "We Can't Stop" by Miley Cyrus oozed from the speakers. We truly couldn't stop in that moment and many more like it.

My toxic masculinity was in full effect as I took her hand and dragged her to the bedroom. I could not get there fast enough, and neither could she. Once we made it, her own sexual aggression kicked in as she pushed me back against the wall and kissed me like there was no tomorrow. Dropping to her knees, she licked the shaft of my cock on either side and underneath before taking it entirely inside her mouth. She pulled back and continued sucking the head as she licked my frenulum. Her tongue was absolute magic as she teased thousands of nerve endings with expert precision. How I managed to stay standing is beyond me. I kept my bare butt pressed tight against the wall and held onto the back of her head.

Then she did something that no one else had ever done as she gently pressed the tip of her tongue into my urethral opening. Holy fucking hell. It was unbelievable. My juices were already flowing like crazy, but this opened the floodgates. I'd never heard of this being done before. Neither had she. As she stopped to ask me how it felt, I asked her where she learned it.

"It only occurred to me just now as something you might enjoy," she shrugged with faux modesty.

After barely handling the pleasure of her fellatio mastery for a few more minutes, I had to turn the tables and thoroughly explore Samantha's pussy. This wasn't our first time, but every time we were together was as exciting as a first encounter. The intense feeling of the chase was always present even though we planned to have sex nearly every time we got together. Maybe it was the Romeo and Juliet tabooness of our relationship. The nice girl having wild and crazy sex with the male stripper. She was supposed to be seeking a "good" man. Not sexy or exciting. A man who sought and received the approval of similar men. One who would give her children as they spent the rest of their days fighting over money. Someone, in all honesty, more likely to hurt her than I was. Not knowing what he was missing out on with other women. I did.

I laid Samantha upon her bed and got on top as we made out some more. Our kisses increasingly sloppy as the night went on. The combination of her saliva and champagne was intoxicating. I paid her tits some more attention as I kissed and licked my way down her torso. Her skin deliciously soft and smooth. Even the feel of kissing her naval sent volts of electricity through my body. I spread her legs and ran my tongue along the inside of each shapely thigh from knee to pelvis before teasing her pussy by licking around it. Having built so much anticipation within her, she moaned as I slowly, gently touched my tongue to her clit.

I loved the way we talked and joked as I ate her pussy. Alternating between laughter and moaning. Anecdotes and orgasms. And not just her orgasms. I experienced my own while going down on her. Every muscle fiber in my body tightened more and more until they could tighten no further and all relaxed at once as a tidal wave of endorphins washed over me. I licked and sucked her clit while massaging her g-spot as we reminisced about the fat girl singing "Memory" and the doofus who butchered "Amarillo by Morning".

"I think you like that song," Samantha opined with a sassy tone.

I changed the subject by removing my fingers from her soaking wet pussy. Having her suck them as I teased her delicate, pink lips with my tongue. I licked the entire length of her pussy. She shook and moaned uncontrollably. I attempted to consume every drop of her warm juices. Licking her velvety smooth sugar walls inside as they flowed forth, but they were too much for one person to consume. With my tongue in need of a break, I resumed the g-spot massage as I pulled myself up and kissed her like there was no tomorrow.

It wasn't enough as I rolled her over and laid on top. Kissing her neck and shoulders while rubbing my throbbing cock against her bubble butt. I slowly kissed and licked my way down her back to her ass. After kissing and licking her cheeks, I ran my tongue back and forth in her crack. She spread her legs as I opened her honey buns to gaze upon her tight, pink butthole. It was pretty. Really pretty, as Becky and Charlotte would say. As with her pussy, I teased my way around it before lubing the surface with my saliva and licking its subtle ridges. Like everything else about Samantha, it was unbelievably sweet. She moaned and sighed incessantly as her entire body went limp. This continued as I kissed and licked her sexy hole before pushing my tongue inside.

Rimming has been a kink of mine since the first time I saw two girls do it to each other in a porno. I suppose guys and girls do it too in porn, but that's a moot point since girl on girl is the only porn that exists in my world. My opportunities to explore this have been limited. I haven't wanted to eat the ass of every girl I've been with. And it wasn't until recently that I finally stopped being embarrassed about it. I think turning forty helped, because that's when I fully stopped worrying about what other people thought of me. I was game for eating Samantha's booty right after meeting her, and her booty didn't disappoint.

That one bachelorette party in 2004 aside, I'd been consensually rimmed a few times. But I derived more pleasure from giving. Samantha changed that as she rolled me over and did to me everything she just learned. She proved herself a star pupil as she evoked the same reactions from me as I had from her. Perhaps what made pleasure from such an act possible was the friendship and trust between us. I knew I could relax and be myself around her without fear of judgment or ridicule. The same was true for her in my company. She slid her body across mine and laid upon me. Her warm breasts pressed against my cool back as she kissed my neck and shoulders.

My big, hard cock couldn't wait any longer. Neither could her tight, wet pussy as I flipped her over and mounted her from on top. She was so tight that, even with all those juices gushing forth, it took a minute to penetrate her completely. Once inside, I wrapped my arms around her hot, naked body and fucked her deep and hard. She fucked back. Aggressively thrusting her pelvis against mine. All I could feel was her soft skin all around me. Her tits pressed tightly against my chest as I took in the fragrance of her perfume and sweet pheromones. Even the feel of her smooth cheek against mine made my cock grow even larger. With every thrust, I reached the end of her velvety tunnel. I couldn't have physically had her any more than I did in that moment. And yet I still couldn't get enough.

I planted kisses on her cheek then moved to her lips. Our tongues enjoyed their own intercourse during an oral embrace that seemed to last forever. There were tears in Samantha's eyes. Mainly of joy, but there was a hint of sadness as well. Of course, it wasn't the first time I'd seen that while making love to a beautiful woman. I knew what it meant but didn't want to deal with it now. Instead, I lightened the mood by giving her an Eskimo kiss. This made her laugh.

"Now we're really getting naughty!" she giggled.

That turned the page as we shifted into overdrive with bone-rattling fucking. Her soft and gentle voice turned deep and raspy. She alternated between moaning and ordering me to fuck her hard. As we grew closer and closer to climaxing, I felt like my whole body might ejaculate. My cock could not go deep enough inside her pussy even though I was touching the end of her tunnel of love.

"My cock loves your pussy, Samantha," I declared with an aggressive whisper in her ear.

"Oh, Stefan. My pussy loves your cock," she responded in her phone sex operator voice.

I continued squeezing her in my arms. Her arms and legs wrapped around me as we thrusted violently against each other. Our vicious aggression gave new meaning to the term "tough love" as we showered each other with as much affection as we could physically put forth. She was ready to cum. Her moans turned to screams as her back arched further and further.

"Cum with me, Samantha," I whispered in her ear as I kissed it.

She responded by squirting hot juices all over me while screaming like Siouxsie and the Banshees. It was too much for me as my cock exploded and filled her pussy with hot cum. I had no idea it was possible for anyone to cum that much, but we set a new world record that night. We held each other tight for comfort. Our bodies shaking uncontrollably. Chills covered our skin. We squeezed each other tighter. I know it sounds crazy coming from me, but I often feel shy and embarrassed after sex. As if I'd opened myself up too much to someone else. But I didn't feel that at all with Samantha. I felt safe with her for as long as she would allow me to.

CHAPTER 38

With autumn in full effect, I drove to Mountain View, Arkansas on a Friday night in early October 2013. This town of approximately 2,800 people two hours north of Little Rock rests on the southeast corner of the Ozarks. A popular tourist destination due to its status as a hotbed of folk art and music as well as its proximity to Blanchard Springs Caverns. The caverns are located near the community of Fifty-Six. Named for its school district number after the locals' choice of "Newcomb" was rejected by the federal government. Thirty minutes northeast of Fifty-Six is the similar community of Forty-Four. This one named for the 44 people who petitioned for a post office.

I can't emphasize enough how much I love Arkansas road trips on state and U.S. highways. This night was no exception. The cool, early autumn air possessed leftover hints of summer combined with the ever-growing feel of the new season. While the trees were still green, you could almost feel the leaves starting to change color. My journey took me through towns like Bee Branch, Dennard, and Timbo. Each with its own unique name origin story, I'm sure. Off the highways but nearby were curiously named places such as Flag, Onia, and Rumley. Each one nothing more than a smattering of private residences. But their existences intrigued me. They still do.

Darkness had fallen by the time I'd wound my way east on AR 66 into Mountain Home. I looked for a house on the edge of town and found it with surprising ease given the unusual layout of the streets I took. This was a bachelorette party for a twentysomething bride-to-be with both mom and grandma in attendance. I was a cowboy this time. "Amarillo by Morning", for all its greatness, wouldn't have set the right tone. I instead turned to Kid Rock as always. Cracking my bullwhip to shrieks of female hysteria before wrapping it around my bachelorette. Turning yet another Anytown, USA living room into a den of iniquity.

It was fun giving one on one attention to three generations of women. None of whom were shy in the slightest. After showering my bachelorette with oodles of rubbing, thrusting, and booty shaking, I gave the same treatment to mom for a song. Grandma was leaned back in a recliner when I got to her. Eagerly awaiting me. Slowly and gently, I climbed on top. Hovering above her with my knees on either armrest as we found ourselves face to face. She placed her hands on my thighs before planting them firmly on my ass as I rose and gyrated my cock in her face. The rest of my party girls got a huge kick out of this, especially the bachelorette.

"Grandma's getting excited!" she squealed with delight.

Much like me, grandma didn't hesitate to up the ante when it came to her response:

"Grandma's getting wet!"

This resulted in uncontrollable laughter from the other women and me. It was hilarious but touching as well. I'd already won over my audience, but something so simple as making someone's grandmother feel young again endeared me to them. And I was flattered. She may have been slightly out of my age range, but I took the compliment and ran with it. Along with earning a living, making women of all ages, shapes, and sizes have fun and feel alive is what stripping is all about to me. Those idiots who only use stripping as a sad attempt to get laid cheat themselves in this way. Their fucked-up priorities preventing them from experiencing these little moments of magic. Sex is indeed wonderful with the right girl at the right time. But I'd rather make the night of a bachelorette and her grandma than relegate myself to a lame fuck with some random chick for the sake of fucking. That's no accomplishment.

***

The nature of my relationship with Samantha made it an open one. She would go on dates with guys here and there. Mainly to appease her friends, who couldn't understand why she was single. It's not easy being a pretty boy, but I'm aware that pretty girls don't have it any easier. "Nice guys" are constantly trying to rack up sex points. Meanwhile, family and friends constantly push the "any man is better than no man" mantra in passive-aggressive fashion. There's pressure for these girls to settle down with someone even if it means settling.

While I had no interest in being the next Wilt Chamberlain, I occasionally dated other girls during this time. It was nice to go out on the town with someone here and there, given my limited access to Samantha. Feeling like I'd missed out on a lot during the previous few years. I quickly discovered I hadn't missed out on that much, but dating girls knocked the rust off my non-stripping social skills.

The most notable of the non-Samantha girls was a former *Penthouse* Pet living in Arkansas at the time. She found me on Facebook, sent me a friend request, and wasted no time trying to get my attention. She was in her forties. Blonde and athletic with large, fake tits. Not unlike Tori, but Tori is more attractive in my opinion. I had dinner with this girl. Not only did she like me, but she had a decent-sized nest egg from a successful business venture in marketing or something along those lines. She was also one of the most boring people I've ever met in my life with the personality of a tree stump. We had little in common. There was no motivation for me to become the kept man of a wealthy former centerfold. I still fucked her. Because, you know, *Penthouse* Pet.

A date that didn't end with the tube snake boogie occurred in Hot Springs on a Friday night in early November. I was in town for a bachelorette party at a nightclub. My party girls rented the venue's private room, complete with its own bar. I held sexy court with my audience as people drank and danced to live blues-rock on the other side of the wall. On my way out, I posted my location on Facebook to see if anyone I knew in Hot Springs was around. Wanting to hang for a while before I drove back to Little Rock. Visiting with Tori while in town was now a thing, but she wasn't home that night.

With no responses, I got in my truck and began the drive home. As I passed the city limits, I received a comment from a Facebook friend in Hot Springs. She was at the club I'd just left and asked if I'd like to hang out. I accepted, turned around at the next exit, and headed back. Upon entering for the second time that night, I found her seated alone at a table. She was a petite, attractive brunette three years older than me who worked in the medical field and fancied herself a part-time model. As I'd recently begun to experiment with photographing female subjects with mixed results, I was partly motivated to visit with her given the prospect of a shoot.

She'd already sent her friends, who were also her ride, on their way. Since live music isn't conducive to conversation, we left and headed downtown for a more appropriate spot. Settling on a small bar that was rather empty for a Friday night. It wasn't the most exciting place. A DJ spun tunes as people drank, talked, and played pool. She and I danced for a few songs. We were the only ones. Some nearby patrons looked on as we strutted our stuff to "Billie Jean" and Drake's "Hold On, We're Going Home".

We grabbed a table where we drank and talked. Sipping my Jack and Coke as she told me about her modeling career, which consisted entirely of posing nude for the private collections (read: spank banks) of male photography hobbyists. It took a lot from me to nod politely because that's not modeling. Technically, it's escorting. And I was already annoyed by all the prospective "models" I'd talked to who couldn't grasp what I was doing creatively. Whether clothed or nude, I was attempting to make an artistic statement for the world to see. My date was no exception. Acting smugly and indifferently towards my photographic objectives.

Things continued southward. She nearly got into a fight with a toothless woman over some retarded, white trash drama that I still don't understand. Once that dust settled, private model and I resumed our conversation as she pulled out her phone. I'd already decided against sleeping with her, but she doubled down on that decision for me with the next words out of her mouth.

"Want to see photos of my grandbabies?" she asked as if inquiring about the weather.

I know it's Arkansas, and most women start young, but for fuck's sake. She was 37. What the fuck was she doing having not only one grandchild but two at her age? My politeness was even harder to feign than it was while hearing about her bullshit modeling career. A taboo had been broken that night without even trying. I was on a date with someone's grandmother. Still not sure how to feel about that.

She knew I wasn't impressed and that her chances had vaporized. We called it a night. I offered her a ride home. Our conversation resumed pleasantly as she navigated me through the residential streets of downtown Hot Springs. There was no animosity. The spark wasn't there and we both knew it. Nevertheless, she asked for a goodnight kiss. It was harmless enough. Pressing our lips together for a few seconds as we embraced in the middle of her street. Bathed in the streetlight's dim, amber glow. Surrounded by the cool autumn air. This wasn't a particularly good date, but not the worst I'd been on.

***

Two significant lasts occurred in my life the following week. The first was that Hardbodies would never again book a bachelor party as Star called it quits. And by quit, I mean that I blocked her number because she wouldn't stop calling me. She turned out to be a drunk. While taking the idea of being a stripper seriously and being good at it when motivated, she wasn't reliable. She was also a hard sell due to her red hair. I tried talking her into going blonde, but she refused. That left me and Brandi, who didn't entertain male audiences. I didn't know it at the time, but we were now out of the bachelor party business.

The other notable last occurred seven days after nude grandma model failed to get me into her Craftmatic adjustable bed. This was the night I delivered my final male revue performance. I don't say that because I haven't done a male revue since. No, I will never again perform in a male revue. The combination of my exclusive focus on mastering the private party performance and the continued pasteurization of the male revue makes this an easy decision. A natural evolution. I didn't even want to do this one. Only relenting as a favor to Blake from Clear Channel.

Except he wasn't with them anymore. He was now working for a Little Rock modeling agency. In one of the dumbest moves ever, a nightclub manager in Hot Springs approached them about using their male models for a revue with only a week's notice. It wasn't as if she had a touring group booked that canceled and left her scrambling for a last-minute replacement. She honestly believed she could throw together some attractive men at the last minute and all would end well. This woman, an old bag named Georgia with a faced like a worn-out catcher's mitt, even called me with her stupid idea. After I aired her out for this hubris, she turned to this modeling agency that wasn't even good at getting work for models.

Panic set in over the following days. It quickly dawned on everyone involved that, yes, stripping is a skill for which talent and experience count big time. Blake contacted me three days before the show. Asking me not only to perform but also give their guys a crash course in stripping and lead them through this mess they'd created for themselves. Since I didn't have anything booked for that night, and because I like Blake, I agreed to do it. After I negotiated a suitable base pay, the right to openly promote Hardbodies, and full authority and creative control over the entire revue. It was understood that I answered to no one including the modeling agency or the venue. I immediately set about Gordon Ramsaying my way through this stripping nightmare.

I met with these "strippers" the following night. What a fucking mess. There were two highlights. The first was an aspiring stripper who would go on to work with some touring group. He was the antithesis of me in that he simply wanted to get laid and was eager to let others script his every move. Although nice and polite, he lacked the individuality and creativity to entertain a private party. But I couldn't complain. Good followers were what I needed in this situation. He also got points for bringing in the second highlight. A ringer with experience from Texas. After talking to that guy for all of thirty seconds, I could tell he knew his shit. He was the only one I left to his own devices.

The rest were… Fuck, I don't know. I can't even remember them all. There was some young guy with a swimmer's build. And an obvious juicer, even more obvious than me as I was on a cycle at the time, who ate dried salmon the entire meeting. As if he needed the extra protein with all that gear in his body. There was also a dude who was totally out of shape. He knew it, and I felt bad that he was being pushed to strip. It allegedly wasn't the only instance of this agency pressuring its models into adult entertainment, but I digress. We assembled a show itinerary and song list, went over the relevant liquor and municipal laws, and crossed our fingers.

I repeated this with the club staff on Friday night before the show. While Hot Springs is one of the least socially conservative places in Arkansas, I didn't want to take any chances. I put security at ease by telling them I'd handle talking to any vice cops or alcoholic beverage control agents who might drop in. As I walked around the club and went over everything with the staff, DJ, and Blake (who served as emcee), my would-be strippers hung out nervously by the pool tables and drank to calm their nerves.

One reason why I've permanently retired from male revues is that I will no longer use a men's room as a dressing room. That's bullshit. On this night, I entered the "dressing room" to find one of the modeling agency owners, an absolute cunt of a woman named Erin, nagging two of the guys over their hair or something pointless. Fuck that. This was my dressing room now. And these were my guys. I cranked up the intimidation and glared her sorry ass out of there for the rest of the night. I knew she hated me being there, but she needed me. Not only did she know it, she knew that I knew it. I immediately commandeered the entire counter space for myself. The ringer claimed a good chunk of the restroom. Pushing the wannabes into a small corner.

As a woman from the audience rubbed my naked body with baby oil after paying me twenty bucks for the privilege, I prepared mentally to open the show. I was going first. Everyone else was too chickenshit and not intoxicated enough to lead off. I was drunk on nothing more than my own histrionics. I dismissed my oil wench and put on my cop costume as I thought about the two hot cocktail waitresses seated in chairs facing each other on stage. Placed there at my request. I knew on some level this would be my swan song male revue performance. I was going out the only way I knew how. On top.

I strutted with a vengeance, head held high, out of the dressing room and onto the stage as Blake introduced me over the *COPS* theme. My girls, one blonde and one brunette, greeted me with nervous delight. I handcuffed one and made the other assume the position as I ran my hands up her legs. The music shifted to "Salt Shaker" as I began my striptease. Alternating lap dances between my girls as I tore away my shirt and pants. Down to my g-string, I was free to be even more flexible. Launching myself in the air and bridging my waitresses with my crotch in the lap of the brunette and my face between the blonde's legs. I miscalculated slightly and did a faceplant right in her crotch. The heat I felt informing me that she was enjoying the show.

The male revue went downhill from there. Save for the other experienced stripper turning in a top-notch set, it was mediocre. A few women went apeshit over the swimmer's build guy. Not so much sexually. More like they wanted to tuck him into bed that night. My guys gave it their all, but it wasn't enough. To be fair, this wasn't entirely their fault. The audience kind of sucked. Confirming to me that there's little overlap between private party audiences and male revue audiences. These women cheered for my set, but none were generous tippers. We also had poor turnout due to the short notice and virtually nonexistent marketing of the show. Georgia was yet another fool who assumed that the presence of male strippers would magically pack her club.

If not many women in the area knew we were here, plenty of guys did as they filled the club after our show. This brings me to another reason why I've retired from male revues. Venues only want to pay for a male revue based on the bar revenue generated during the show. Refusing to credit the entertainers for the revenue generated afterward by all the dudes who show up and buy drinks nonstop for both themselves and women. It's a huge amount of money for which the male revue is directly responsible. That's the reason nightclubs book male revues, and I fucking want my slice of that lucrative pie.

But nasty old Georgia was having none of that. Blake informed me that she was claiming a loss from the male revue. Even if that were true, it was all her fault for booking a group of mostly amateurs at the last minute. I told Blake to tell his bosses at the modeling agency, despite how much I loathed them personally, to not let her push them around with this bullshit. Even though I'd been paid and received everything I'd been promised, my conscience wouldn't allow me to let this slide.

I didn't care about the agency. Erin and her husband/partner immediately went to a nearby casino and blew their entire cut. Especially poor money management for a business that couldn't afford its downtown Little Rock office. Whoever fronted them money to later open their own bar should be ashamed. What I cared about was Georgia fucking everyone who bent over backward for her at the last minute. I stayed until last call. Watching the bartenders and servers ring up purchases nonstop on two registers. Georgia had the nerve to declare our show a financial failure as she raked in money hand over fist for hours that night. Fuck that dog. I hope she gets parvo.

But I didn't just sit and watch cash registers all night. I entertained myself with a group of young women celebrating their friend's 21st birthday. The birthday girl was a hot brunette. We bonded over conversation and dancing for an hour or so until her friends cockblocked me by claiming they were going to another bar. Cockblocking has always been my biggest adversary when it comes to romance. Since I always go for the shining star of the group inside and out, the lesser friends are quick to get jealous. Not only did they never leave the club, but I later saw the birthday girl with a scummy looking motherfucker all over her. Coming across like someone who was no stranger to meth. If he wasn't older than me, he sure as fuck looked otherwise. Her friends were totally cool with this piece of shit groping her right at the bar. They'd never be jealous of her for bonking that loser.

After that, I occupied myself by talking to a whiny voiced, fortysomething woman. She gave me a drink someone bought her that she didn't like. Something with vodka and lemon-lime flavor that wasn't great but not hideous. I downed it as she wasted no time telling me about her only sexual encounter with a woman, because of course she did. Then she told me all about her two failed marriages. I nodded along while glancing back to the registers as I continued my research. After learning all about her piss poor taste in men, she started talking about her friend Georgia. Yes, that Georgia. Because sure. Why the fuck not at this point?

With the end of last call, I couldn't get out of there fast enough. I was exhausted physically and mentally as I made the hour drive home. And yet I couldn't sleep once I arrived. I made something to eat while watching Jean-Luc Godard's *Breathless* for the umpteenth time. Something told me no one else at the club that night was doing the same thing. What was my greatest naked ambition in life anyway? Perhaps it was to become immortal, then die.

CHAPTER 39

A cold and rainy Saturday night in early December. I'd arrived home from a bachelorette party only minutes earlier when Tori texted me. Between she and Samantha, I often found myself constantly switching back and forth between conversations as I avoided texting the wrong thing. It was an amazing experience. One I enjoyed and more than made up for the loneliness of the previous several years. I had friends again. Sexy friends to boot.

Tori had big news for me this night after also returning home from a party. She went down on a woman for the first time. I was enthusiastically supportive. Encouraging her to share explicit details with me. Which she did, God bless her. This was a huge fucking deal for her. She'd been the shy and well-behaved girl for so many years.

Downplaying her sexually adventurous instincts. It took her a long time to realize that embracing her hedonistic inner child didn't stop her from still being a nice girl. Nor did it make her a slut. If the experience of eating another girl's pussy brought her joy, then so be it.

But the year of bi-curious women wasn't over yet. Although I was enthralled with her as an entertainer, Brandi and I hadn't yet worked together nor interacted much. Part of this was because of her limited availability. Had she lived closer and been childfree, she would've been my ideal collaborator on stripping, photography, and more. She probably would've made for an excellent girlfriend who wouldn't hide me from family and friends. Nor would she have allowed me to be cockblocked. But that's the sort of breaks even Kurtis Blow would appreciate.

I accompanied Brandi to a party for the first time in late December. It was not only a Saturday but the winter solstice. The client booked her for his bi-curious wife. She'd never had sexual contact with a woman. Her raciest request was to take a shower with Brandi. I thought that was adorable. And I enjoyed talking with the client. I knew Brandi would be game, so I didn't hesitate to book it. They lived in another part of the state but were making the trip to Little Rock solely for this purpose as a Christmas present to themselves.

Brandi met me downtown. We walked to one of several hotels on River Market Avenue. All at which I'd performed before and since. She was dressed casually in jeans and a green sweater. I knew this couple wouldn't want to jump right into things. They'd want to talk first and get comfortable with Brandi. And I knew Brandi would want that too as her own girl on girl experience to that point was less than Tori's. The room had a kitchenette with a dining table at which we sat. Conversing while drinking vodka mixed with various fruit drinks from a vending machine in the lobby.

I remained silent for the most part. Allowing Brandi and the couple to get to know one another. Interjecting to rejuvenate the conversation whenever things got shy and awkward. While ostensibly present as

Brandi's security escort, my true role was that of a consultant. I was clearly the elder statesman of girl on girl at this table. A ridiculous-sounding thing to say, but it's true. Consider all I've experienced over the years and compare that to two girls working up the courage to make out, play with each other's titties, and take a shower together. It's not like they were all getting ready to play a game of Who's Going Down on You? I had to give the husband credit. Not only was he about to get a hot show for his viewing pleasure but was building the groundwork for a possible threesome someday.

Things got underway once Brandi and the wife got a little too buzzed. Brandi ran to one of the bedrooms to change before returning in full stripper attire that left little to the imagination. She took two steps from the bedroom in her clear platform heels before falling on her ass. I told her not to worry about shoes as I put on music. Now barefoot, she gave the wife a lap dance on the sofa as her husband sat next to them. Meanwhile, I hung back at the table. Texting play by play to Tori. She got a kick out of it. Flattered that I included her in my devious nocturnal activities. I tossed Brandi a can of Reddi-wip so she and the wife could lick it off each other's nipples.

After an hour of this and more alcohol, Brandi and the wife moved to the shower. Which I skipped. They didn't need me crowding them. and I didn't care. I'm sure it was cute and sexy but whatever. The girls followed this by rolling around naked on the bed and giggling. I was more invested in my conversation with Tori as we discussed Hallmark movies she'd watched recently. I understand that all of this was extremely hot for both the couple and Brandi. But it made me realize how far I'd come. How much I'd experienced over the past decade. Hardbodies was a few months shy of its tenth anniversary. I was hell and gone from selling pools and spas while plotting and planning my very own business.

The combination of too much alcohol and early morning hours took their toll on the girls. Dude helped his wife to the other bedroom where she promptly passed out. I struggled to get a naked Brandi on her feet and dressed as she fought to stay conscious.

The husband returned and told me the magic words, "You two can stay in this room if you want."

I expressed my sincerest gratitude as I shoved still naked Brandi into bed. Pulling the covers over her as she immediately went to sleep. With the light turned out, I headed back into the living room with the husband. We got along well, which is rare for me when it comes to other dudes. Besides girl on girl, we had other interests such as photography. We also discussed music. Specifically, "Rise" by Herb Alpert & The Tijuana Brass along with its sampling by the Notorious B.I.G. for "Hypnotize". He was feeling celebratory and decided he wanted a cigar. We hit the streets of downtown Little Rock at 1:30am on a wild goose chase for cigars. There wasn't even a convenience store within walking distance where we could've scored some Swisher Sweets.

We walked and talked while on the lookout for cigars. Settling for two Marlboro Lights bummed off some dude outside a nightclub. Considering this a victory, we returned to the hotel and smoked our hard-earned cancer trophies by the pool. We talked about Brandi. I still didn't know her that well, but he and I were on the same page. While we understood and supported her maternal devotion, the small town she calls home holds her back. A place of few opportunities. Even for those with familial roots. Little Rock is no boom town but would provide her with personal and professional opportunities.

I thought about the future of Hardbodies as I laid next to Brandi for the next few hours. I already have a hard time falling asleep in hotels, and she snored a fucking fiend. Perhaps she wouldn't have been an ideal girlfriend. I reflected on 2013 and it left me feeling bittersweet. My agency had experienced a near return to form after several lean years. But I couldn't see how to take that success any further. It was the end of 2006 all over again. Only I was self-aware this time. There would be no downward spiral into darkness and despair like I'd experienced in 2007. But the looming threat of a return to Hardbodies Lite hung overhead like dark storm clouds. Threatening and ominous no matter how I looked at it.

Talent, or lack thereof, remained an issue. Brandi would end up being one of my favorite entertainers in the league of Kyra, Leah, and Chantelle. But her limitations, understandable as they were, would always present logistical hurdles. And she was the best I could do in 2013. Star was comparable to Amber. Serviceable at best. But I was tired of serviceable. And don't get me started on Bosley again. The rest of the rejects were all sorts of awful. The best one, so to speak, freely posing nude for my camera one afternoon. Those photos suck and so does she. At that moment, the entire Hardbodies roster fit comfortably upon a queen-size bed.

Yet another time when I should've retired the Hardbodies brand and gone solo with Brandi as an occasional collaborator. I could've booked two girl showers for her along with my bachelorette and birthday parties. But I still wasn't ready to let go and come out from behind that name. Even if I knew it was holding me back. Going solo presented its own set of challenges, but I could've worked through them then as opposed to now.

***

It was a gorgeous December afternoon late the following week. Still cold, but the sun shone brightly in the blue sky and chased off any trace of winter blahs. I was eating lunch at my computer, which is where I eat nearly all my meals. White light filled my office through the south-facing window before me as I gazed outside. I could've sworn it was spring if not for the bare trees and brown grass. It was a feeling the sun impressed upon me despite the season at hand. I experienced it again recently when a late spring day felt like early autumn. Please don't ask me to explain it. I can't.

While eating, I was messaged on Facebook by two girls at once. Attractive brunettes who lived in Little Rock and wanted to come on board with Hardbodies. So many girls wanted to because they coveted my upscale clients. Most applicants weren't up to par and couldn't grasp why. But these girls had the potential for sure. They were charming and said all the right things. I still wasn't getting my hopes up as they convinced me on that beautiful afternoon to give them a shot. And just like that, the Hardbodies roster doubled with the addition of Jade and Sophie. Once again, I was Charlie with my three angels in tow.

CHAPTER 40

It was just after 4:00am, two days into 2014, when I awoke suddenly. Heart racing. Breathing heavy. Body trembling from head to toe. Soaking in Samantha's presence next to me. I reached out to feel her warm, soft skin as she slept on her side. Facing away. Running my fingers along the curves of her drop-dead gorgeous figure. My cock was hard and throbbing as it ached insatiably for her pussy. I pushed it tight against her ass and rubbed. At the same time sliding my hand over her left breast while kissing her shoulder. I'd warned her this could happen one night. She said she'd be game for it. I was about to find out if she meant that.

She was barely awake as she moaned and started rubbing her booty against my cock. We held hands over her tits before I slid mine down between her legs. She spread them open and I inserted my finger inside her drenched pussy. I rubbed her clit with her juices. Her trembling and breathing matched mine. I was hell-bent on taking what I wanted yet felt a twinge of guilt for waking her.

"I'm sorry," I whispered in her ear.

She rolled onto her back and kissed me.

"Don't be," she whispered back in her raspy bedroom voice.

I moved down her body and ate her pussy. Her face barely visible from this view in the dark bedroom. She held my hand and stroked my face as my tongue danced on her clit and between her lips. I was ready to penetrate her, but she wasn't letting me without first returning the oral favor. Even half-asleep, she was a magician with her mouth and tongue. I couldn't wait another second.

"I have to fuck you," I forced past my lips in a near breathless whisper.

"I want you to fuck me," she responded in kind.

Samantha became my sexy cowgirl as she straddled my massive cock and lowered her tight, wet pussy onto it. She rode me slowly. My hands all over her delicious body. Playing with her big, luscious titties before squeezing her firm, round ass. I slipped my finger in her mouth and got it wet before pressing it gently inside her butthole. Sam moaned even louder. Throwing her head back from the sensation of this double penetration. She laid forward. Pressing her tits against my chest. We kissed for what seemed like an eternity. I continued thrusting my cock deep inside her and fingering her butt. Her pussy squirted more and more juices as we moved closer to exploding together in carnal bliss.

After yet another epic climax shared with my sexy friend, we cleaned off and promptly fell back asleep.

***

2014 began for Hardbodies where 2013 left off. I had two bookings the first weekend. The first a birthday party in Little Rock originally booked for December. It was rescheduled due to a snowstorm in Northern Arkansas, where my audience was coming from, which made the highways in the Ozarks undrivable. While initially consisting of five women, only two – the client and the birthday girl – made the trip in early January. We enjoyed our own threesome of stripping goodness. I give them much credit for moving ahead with their belated weekend trip after their friends dropped out. Both are Facebook friends of mine to this day. I'd love to do something with them again in the future.

I was in Hot Springs the following night for a party at Tori's. Jade came along. This would be her first Hardbodies gig. Sophie was initially booked as well, but she'd found a new boyfriend and quit before doing a single party. So much for the angel trifecta. While I was excited about Jade's potential, she was rough around the edges. Not knowing how to properly shave her legs or pussy. This was a thirty-year-old woman at the time. I instructed her on what items to purchase and how to use them.

In case anyone is wondering… My silky-smooth body is achieved using the Schick Hydro 5 and liberal amounts of Edge shaving gel (the one with the orange cap that comes in a two-pack) in a hot shower. Men's shaving products are superior to their female-targeted counterparts. Designed for removing facial hair, which is thicker and coarser than body hair. Making for an overkill approach that works beautifully.

At least that issue with Jade was easily rectified. The lingering problem was her dumbass friends. I would get her in the right attitude and mindset about stripping during our interactions only to have these assholes fill her head with ignorant nonsense later. The most horseshit of which being that she wasn't getting paid enough despite Hardbodies having always secured its entertainers a base pay among the highest in the nation. These friends were white trash losers without the first fucking clue regarding what spewed from their toothless mouths. Expertise based on nothing.

I made two major decisions at the beginning of the year. The first was eliminating the BodyRoxxx brand. It was clear that I would never do anything serious with it. Over the past few years, it had gone from barely paying for itself to being dead in the water. It needed to go. The second decision was that Hardbodies would no longer book bachelor parties. That may sound crazy, but we rarely got calls for them by this point. Nearly all female stripper bookings were for birthday parties and the like with coed audiences. I never fully excelled at booking bachelor parties as I had trouble connecting with those clients. Personally, I couldn't imagine throwing a party with male guests only.

Still, I had two female strippers coveted by prospective clients. I stayed busy with my own parties. In Samantha and Tori, I had two wonderful friends. And yet I was depressed in early 2014. Partly due to the end of another steroid cycle, but that wasn't all of it. As I began to realize at the end of 2013, Hardbodies couldn't possibly go any further than I'd taken it. This was the second time I'd taken it from nothing to its full potential relevant to our market and its economy at the time. As prolific a stripper I'd been all these years, I was still largely unknown in Arkansas. Exposure, or lack thereof, was always an issue. I continued to languish in Pierre Kirby-esque obscurity.

A return to Hardbodies Lite was an inevitability from all evidence before me. I was depressed, but I wasn't going to get angry. Or go crazy. I viewed this as an opportunity to expand my entrepreneurial interests beyond stripping. I had oodles of ideas for various projects worth pondering. There were also ideas presented to me by others. Such as the suggestion from various people that I use my skills to organize swingers' parties in Central Arkansas. Although not my thing, I was intrigued by the earning potential and explored the possibilities. I quickly hit an impasse. While I was cool with the idea of facilitating classy social gatherings where couples could meet, chat, and dance, no way in hell was I hosting the sex orgies that many interested people had in mind. I neither wanted nor needed to see that.

There was a film degree collecting dust as it hung on my office wall. I considered opportunities for video production as well as photography and writing. This resulted in some extra income during 2014. I directed and shot documentary-style footage for a proposed reality series set in Arkansas than was never greenlit, along with dabbling in real estate photography here and there. And I picked up bits of technical writing work. None of this brought in much money. That wouldn't have bothered me had it led to bigger and better things, but there were zero hints that it ever would. Unlike with stripping, I was one of many people in the world who could do these things competently enough to warrant getting paid for it. Much like when I used to apply for jobs, I once again found myself being passed over in favor of candidates who "needed" the money more than I did. Regardless of talent.

I was bored with and uninspired by the subjects about which I was contracted to shoot or write. I made every attempt to get fired up over each task at hand, but it wasn't happening. The work I produced was top-notch, and I went above and beyond as I did for my stripping clients. But it never excited me. Because none of it was sexually provocative. I am, if nothing else, a born agent provocateur. Several people in these circles spotted this as well. More than one even suggested that I consider producing and directing porn. I didn't want to go that route for any number of logistical, creative, and legal reasons, but their point was that I'm best suited for doing sexy stuff.

Apart from Samantha, I didn't date anyone during this time. I was too wrapped up in trying to decide where to go from here. Not that romantic opportunities didn't present themselves, so to speak. Like when I had some legal documents notarized in March. The notary public I always used was a middle-aged man on the autism spectrum. He may have talked my ear off every time I utilized his services, but his work was flawless. This time he mentioned that his girlfriend's daughter was single. He showed me a photo of some dumpy looking woman and explained that she lived in an apartment with her two kids and a male friend. Making nude grandma model look like the catch of a lifetime by comparison.

"Do you want to meet her?" he asked me in true autistic bluntness.

Instead of responding with an equally blunt, "Fuck no!" as I should've, I instinctively wrapped my rejection within a shamefully phony, "I'll think about it," before trailing off. I should've said I was seeing someone, which was true, but I was like a deer in the headlights for some reason.

I know he would've never caught the true meaning of my response, but either his girlfriend or her daughter should've taken the fucking hint when he told them later. That didn't happen. He blew up my phone with calls and texts about how they had my first date with her all planned out. Now I tried being blunt, but it was too late. They'd found a man for that loser, and no way in hell they were letting him get away. I decided it was time to take my business elsewhere and blocked his number. So, he began calling me from his other number. I blocked that one too.

Cut to two days later when I received a text from the girlfriend's daughter about our impending date. She, in her ignorance mistaken for confidence, assumed I was shy. That she needed to make the first move. Yeah, that was it. Not that she has kids. Not her questionable living arrangements. Not her god-awful semi mullet with bangs hairstyle straight out of 1988. Not that I didn't find her attractive in the slightest. And certainly not her annoying as all fuck mother and her boyfriend. No, it was a matter of me being shy. Because, as we all know, I am a shy person. Especially around girls. I blocked her too and they finally got the hint. I think. Maybe. Who the fuck knows?

In between all this madness, I did what I always did during Hardbodies Lite. I ran. I ran so far away from everything on my mind. There was no nearby park with a track this time, so I sprinted through the neighborhood. Dodging not only reckless drivers but also political canvassers as it was an election year. I did this every day for several months through heat and humidity. Rain or shine. I learned disturbing things about my neighbors. Like the parents who allowed their young children to play naked in the front yard. How the fuck does that seem like a sensible idea in any era. Much less this one? All I could do was adjust my route accordingly and keep an eye out for windowless vans.

I returned to Hot Springs in March for Tori's birthday party. This would become a near-annual tradition. For my first anniversary as Tori's "boyfriend," we had dinner before mostly recreating our first night together. She's always had the knack for making me forget all my troubles when in her company. For years a small part of me kind of wished she'd leave her prosperous husband for a male stripper just scraping by. After all, he'd accused her of chasing after me on one occasion. I can't help but think he slightly regrets the monster he created. Don't know what to tell you, dude.

Hot Springs beckoned again a few weeks later. This time for a bachelorette party at the Austin Hotel located downtown. I don't remember much about this party, and that's kind of the point. The client was a charming and attractive blonde whom I enjoyed entertaining. They were all tipsy off some mixed drink that they immediately began serving me. I can't recall what it was, but it was potent as fuck. Not only is it unusual for me to start drinking at a party that soon, but I normally have a respectable alcohol tolerance. This unholy concoction hit me almost instantly and resulted in a rare buzzed performance, the summer of 2007 notwithstanding. I want to say we spent a lot of time laughing over nothing.

When it was over, I was faced with the reality of driving back to Little Rock in this state. But this revelation alone helped me to sober up somewhat as I returned to my truck parked on the street. I popped some Tic-Tacs in my mouth and slapped myself across the face several times before hitting the road with windows down. The cool, early spring air was icy as it pounded my face on U.S. 70, but it kept me focused. For the drive home and everything else.

CHAPTER 41

While not quite as busy as the one previous, the summer of 2014 turned a respectable profit. There were shades of 2006 at times. Such as the Thursday night when I had two bachelorette parties. The first was in Conway. One of those odd instances in which the bachelorette was the client, paid the booking fee herself, and was the only girl who tipped. Accordingly, I devoted 100% of my attention to her. Her friends were boring and stuck up anyway. I admired her. She wanted a male stripper at her party. And since her friends weren't going to make that happen, then fuck it. She took matters into her own hands. Respect.

I made a mad dash to Sherwood for the next event. This party had a far more enthusiastic and generous audience prepared with party lights and the living room floor cleared for dancing. I have occasional bookings that quickly turn into one big dance orgy. That's cool if they just want to dance with me. I love running through my standard performance, but I'm not going to complain if I can simplify things and still get paid. Especially after all my running around that night.

Things didn't go so well the following evening when the unthinkable occurred. A bad party in Hot Springs. It started horribly when I arrived at the house to find no one there. I called the client, whom I thought was named Shelly, to find out where she was. She chuckled something about taking too long at dinner. I should've cut my losses and gone home without notice because she clearly wasn't taking this seriously. Instead, I waited. I sat and waited for twenty minutes until they finally arrived. No apology as Shelly took the opportunity to inform me that her name is Shelbi. I'm sorry I got it wrong, but couldn't she have corrected me the first time I called her Shelly during our initial phone conversation?

If everything so far hadn't motivated me to bail, what happened next most definitely should've. Shelbi insisted on only paying half my booking fee upfront. Giving me a sob story about her husband once getting stiffed by a female stripper. Either he was an idiot for not booking his stripper through Hardbodies or she was lying. I'm leaning towards the latter. Either way, she was attempting to renege on our agreement in true Becky fashion. I suppose I didn't leave then as to not prove her correct within the logic of her bullshit paranoia, but I wasn't accepting that offer. I tossed her my keys and demanded she pay me in full right there.

The party was fucking awful. They didn't tip and were standoffish the entire time. Why the fuck did they decide to book a male stripper in the first place? Some haggard old skank danced next to me the entire time in a blatant show of disrespect. As if jealous of my presence. She was fucking gross. Old and scrawny with saggy skin. She reminded me of this ugly pit bull mix that roamed my childhood neighborhood and chased after people until someone finally shot it. It would've been my pleasure to put this nasty woman out of her misery if not for all the witnesses.

After spending time with the bachelorette, I tried showing attention to the other girls. They mostly ignored me. I remember a morbidly obese girl who steadfastly refused to acknowledge my existence while double-fisting Jell-O shots like they were going out of style. Why couldn't Buffalo Bill have made it rub lotion on its skin? After fifteen minutes of this bullshit, I fled as my audience flocked outside en masse for cigarettes, because of course they did. Once on the road, I texted the client and instructed her to never again contact me before blocking her number. Welcome to my blacklist, Shelly. Or Shelbi. Whatever the fuck your name is.

2014 was by far my most prolific year for people adding themselves to the blacklist. Six women made the cut that year. Four were clients. The other two were would-be clients who couldn't even wait until after booking me to be rude. I suppose I can give them credit for saving me the headache. If 2009 was the year of the cancellation, then 2014 was the year of blacklisting. This would also be the last year anyone was added until two women dumped themselves on it in 2018. I'll bet $150 you can't guess who they are. And if you do, I'll offer you $120 instead.

The night following my encounter with Shelly and the dog woman took me to a bar in North Little Rock for a birthday party. A man celebrated his fiftieth birthday. His wife booked Jade for a lap dance. Without a party of my own, I ran security on this one. I also wanted to see if my time and effort invested in Jade had paid off despite her loser friends. I was floored. Over the course of "Girls" by Prodigy, she was everything one could want in a female stripper. Hot and sexy with a beautiful face and perky tits. In complete control of her audience from start to finish. She embodied the classic femme fatale archetype as she moved on and around her birthday boy with elegance and grace. Everyone present, male and female, loved her. Because who wouldn't have? She had come into her own as an exotic entertainer.

And that was the final booking Jade did for Hardbodies. After the show, I spoke to her about taking photos of her to share with current and prospective clients. Given where she was now as an entertainer, I knew I'd have no problem scoring her more bookings. She promised to get in touch early the following week to set up a shoot before heading off to party with friends.

I heard from her on Wednesday morning. She texted only to ask how much I was going to pay her for the photoshoot. Yes, the photoshoot designed to get her more bookings with upscale clients. I knew she was no longer the phenomenal stripper she'd been only a few nights prior. Just like that, her fucking friends had undone all my work. I could've gotten her back on track, but this vicious cycle would never end. Devastated, I cut my losses and moved on. She'd occasionally text and email me over the coming months asking for work, but I knew where her loyalties lay. Not only were they not with me, they weren't even with herself.

Hardbodies soldiered on with Brandi and me as the parties rolled in at a steady if unspectacular pace. There was no rest for the wicked in late July when I did a bachelorette party in Northwest Arkansas late on a Friday night. After making the three-hour drive back to Little Rock I immediately cleaned up and drove three hours to a funeral in Northeast Arkansas near the Missouri border. Following the service, I drove back to Little Rock and prepared for a bachelorette party that night. Then drove ninety minutes to Greers Ferry Lake. I'd been up for 36 hours when I arrived. As always, I knocked it out of the park. Sleep deprivation be damned.

The drive home was scary as I fought to stay awake on dark and twisting two-lane highways back to the Interstate. Not even having more Red Bull than blood flowing through my veins kept me from seeing the black dog that ruined Patrick Swayze's life in that film of the same title. What? You didn't like *Black Dog*? It's a fun film and it stars Patrick Swayze. He was fucking cool. I made it to bed at midnight and slept until noon. I never want to do that again but know I would in a heartbeat.

August brought much-needed fun starting with a bachelorette party in downtown Little Rock. I'd barely entered the room when the bachelorette ran to me and jumped in my arms. Fortunately for my joints, she was petite. And though alcohol was a factor I was extremely flattered by the gesture. That alone made up for Shelly and dog woman. My party the following night was in Fayetteville with a bachelorette named Yentl. Just like that film I never saw. Barbara Streisand is no Patrick Swayze.

I was back in Fayetteville a week later for a bachelorette party at the Chancellor Hotel. This was without a doubt one of the most aesthetically pleasing hotels I've ever been inside. The entire place is art deco. From the architecture and furniture to the fucking urinals in the men's room. I got off the elevator to be greeted by soft gray walls and room numbers in Century Gothic font. The party itself was a fucking blast. It was only six girls, but they tipped extremely well. I visited with them after my performance as we discussed our shared appreciation for David Lynch among other highbrow topics.

I began partnering with Brandi for coed performations. The sexual tension between us worked to our advantage in entertaining audiences. I would often undress her, and we'd linger on each other's nipples while licking Reddi-wip. My motivation to get us booked for a party at Tori's was sky-high because the experience would be legendary. Tori and Brandi getting it on was a realistic possibility if I facilitated the right mood and atmosphere. Brandi had become the stripping proxy for Samantha in a way. In that regard, I was now doing girlfriend by committee with Samantha, Tori, and Brandi. Three hot blondes demanding my attention. Why does everything bad happen to me?

A fourth hot blonde briefly entered the picture in early September. She was my client for a bachelorette party in downtown Little Rock. Once again at the DoubleTree. She was a preacher's wife. My curiosity piqued. I was greeted by a smoking hot blonde in a slinky, leopard print dress. That night I licked Reddi-wip off the bare ass of a preacher's wife. Not a rim job. Just off her firm, round cheeks as she laid face down on the bed. The bachelorette and other girls were fun too. But the highlight for me was dat God-given ass. Praise the Lord indeed.

I encountered a traffic accident on my way to a bachelorette party the following Saturday night in Cabot. Being the stickler for punctuality I am, I struggled to maintain my cool while waiting for traffic to get moving. I was only a mile or so from my destination. Oh, so close. But Tori came to my emotional rescue. Texting photos of she and a busty, attractive friend sucking each other's titties. This put me at ease and helped me to refocus on the party at hand. And, eventually, I got it done.

Drama once again reared its ugly head at a bachelorette party in late October. It occurred in Springdale just north of Fayetteville. There's not much to say about Springdale other than it has tuberculosis and leprosy epidemics no one wants to talk about. An even bigger local plague is the Duggar family. This party was a first, and to date only, for me as I took my booking fee and left without performing.

I had no choice. As soon as I entered some girl started bitching me out about fuck knows what as the others stared in silence. I didn't know what her problem was, and I wasn't about to find out. So, I grabbed my stuff and left. As for the booking fee, fuck them. I drove over three hours one way and was ready to hold up my end of the deal. No fucking way was I about to do them a favor. To this day I haven't the faintest clue what the problem was. Crazy as it sounds, I think their objective was to experience firsthand some *Bridezilla*-esque drama.

Adding insult to injury... I was booked for a 98th birthday party the following week only to have it canceled. This disappointed me not only for the lost income but because I'd been totes psyched about doing it. The assisted living facility where she resided said no. While obviously for insurance reasons, I like to joke that they didn't want her doing anything she might regret later in life.

This was made up for by a dentist in Conway who celebrated his fortieth birthday by booking me to entertain his staff. He took photos and cracked jokes as I had my way with his assistants and hygienists. I thought it was a cool gesture and something I'd probably do if I were him. I'm not mentioning this to garner sympathy, but no one has ever thrown a birthday party for me. At this point, I don't think I could handle it. I'd be more comfortable using the occasion as an excuse to do something memorable for those around me.

2014 was quickly coming to an end. But the best was saved for last. Brandi and I were booked for an adult Christmas party at Tori's.

CHAPTER 42

Brandi talked nonstop on the drive to Hot Springs. The result of being simultaneously excited and nervous. After eighteen months, she was still getting used to stripping at private parties. And still worried that others would misinterpret her sexually provocative brand of fun as being slutty. It was present in her ramblings about how she wasn't going to fuck anyone at the party that night. I knew this wasn't directed towards me. She trusted me. If not, she wouldn't be next to me as we cruised down I-30 and up U.S. 70. This was self-preservation as she attempted to calm her nerves before showtime. I assured her these concerns proved that she had more in common with Tori and me than she realized.

But she voiced equal amounts of enthusiasm as well. She knew what Tori wanted and was totally game for it. Each had viewed photos of and expressed physical attraction to the other. As much as she'd enjoyed giggling in the shower with that girl the previous December, the encounter had left Brandi hungry to experience more in-depth sapphic pleasure. Tori felt the same twelve months after her first pussy eating experience. Save for Tori and a couple of girlfriends sucking one another's tits occasionally, neither she nor Brandi had explored their shared interest in other girls over the past year. Each was shy about expressing these desires as well as protective of them. Not wanting this kink to be mistaken for lesbianism. Each an example of how fluid female sexuality can be.

I see parallels between girl on girl action and my interactions with women. On more than one occasion, I've witnessed two women have sex purely for the physical pleasure and taboo rush of it, then go right back to talking about typical girl stuff as if nothing had happened. There was zero romance. Just two girls showing an extreme amount of affection towards each other as they had fun together. Comparable to all the times I've bumped and grinded on women, spanked their butts, played with their tits, and occasionally let them suck my cock. Afterward returning to strictly platonic chitchat.

Tori's house was an ideal refuge from the bitter cold of that late autumn night. Like a Thomas Kinkade wet dream, it immediately embraced Brandi and me with its holiday warmth. Not only by the fire burning in the living room and the Christmas tree in the corner, but also the friendly faces that greeted us. Tori stole the show dressed in a Santa teddy that left nothing to the imagination. Diane frolicked about in a black lace thong bodysuit while looking especially bootylicious. Also present was a friend of Tori's I was meeting for the first time. I know this is kind of a spoiler, but let's call her Becky. She's a perfect Becky. When setting up this party with Tori's husband, he'd asked me if I'd be alright with having Becky and her husband present. I said sure, as I had no reason for concern.

Becky wasted no time making her jealousy of my friendship with Tori known. As she and I got caught up in the flesh for a change, Becky made a performance of walking up and aggressively embracing her while bluntly declaring their longtime friendship to me. After that awkward display, Tori excused herself to attend to something else. Becky doubled down on her gesture by telling me all about Tori's kids. As if that trumped my bond with her. This was extremely uncomfortable for me because it wasn't Becky's place to tell me any of this. If I want to hear about Tori's family, I'll let Tori enlighten me on the subject as she sees fit.

With Brandi's assistance, I got out of that exchange by getting things started. I did the cowboy thing that night. Bullwhip in one hand, Reddi-wip in the other as Kid Rock blasted from the living room stereo. Oohs and aahs filled the living room as I gave Tori a lap dance. Not holding back any show of affection to my special friend whom I rarely get to see, I spanked her butt before grinding my crotch against hers while treating her neck to light kisses. I pulled down the front of her outfit to unleash her beautiful girls to everyone's delight. Licking and sucking each nipple long after the Reddi-wip had been consumed. We shared a kiss before Brandi took over with her as I moved onto Diane.

Unlike Tori, Diane is a bit shy. That's not to say she isn't fun to be around. She totally is, as she's also quick to get naked and occasionally indulges Tori in mutual titty sucking. Not only have I sucked Diane's tits as well, but Tori and I once took turns making out with her. Still, I adjusted my performance to Diane's comfort level. Sweet and timid Diane. She succeeds in making everyone laugh at her antics and banter with her husband, who doesn't at all mind my interactions with his wife. It's sort of his thing, I guess. He's a great guy and I genuinely like him. After Tori, he's the person at these parties with whom I converse the most. Always with something interesting to tell me.

While I indulged myself with Diane, Tori wasted no time pulling Brandi's towards her for a kiss. Their tongues getting to know each other. Tori cupped her hands over Brandi's tits before licking and sucking her nipples. After which Brandi returned the favor. Besides the fact that it was two drop-dead sexy women being naughty with each other, I especially enjoyed watching my kind and gentle friend sexually dominate another woman. It was a side of Tori I'd never seen, and it made me love her even more.

The night would've been perfect if not for fucking Becky. Since the show began, she'd loudly screech Tori's name at every instance of my friend getting wild with Brandi or me. Becky's shrill and obnoxious voice packing all the sensuality and grace of a human resources manager. I did not like this woman at all. Nevertheless, I took one for the team and gave her a lap dance in the hopes it would make her shut the fuck up for a few minutes. Her tits were out, but I wasn't about to put my mouth on them. I gave her nipples a quick squeeze between my thumb and forefinger that was the breast play equivalent of a grandma kiss. I followed this with the sort of basic, no-frills lap dance reserved for women like the bachelorette friend of Shelly and the dog woman. It's the most Becky was worth.

Tori and Diane were antsy to get up and move, so the performance shifted into our very own Dance Party USA. With "Uptown Funk" thrusting its musical pelvis, I danced simultaneously with Brandi, Tori, Diane, and (ugh) Becky. Tori was down to her g-string, but that wasn't good enough. Slowly and seductively, she pulled it down while dropping to the floor before stepping her platform heels out of it. Becky shrieked out another hideous "Tori!" catchphrase. Acting like Tori's mom or some bullshit. I half expected her to ask to speak with a manager. And for all her bragging about how many decades she's known Tori, she sure seemed surprised by these antics.

My biggest concern was that the sexual progression between Brandi and Tori might stall no thanks to Becky. Brandi, so sweet and considerate of others, already worried that she'd done something to upset Becky. I assured her that wasn't the case and to focus on Tori while I handled Becky. So, as Brandi and Diane got butt ass naked too and danced with Tori, I ran interference by devoting my attention to Becky. She became increasingly intoxicated as the night wore on. And more obnoxious, because of course she did. I danced with her as she slurred on about God knows what while trying to draw my attention to her bare breasts in true horny old broad fashion.

"I could give you one hell of a blow job," she whispered creepily in my ear.

I know all too well that hell hath no fury as a woman scorned. Especially one who is drunk. I was now standing on a tightrope one thousand feet above a pit of spikes. There was no easy way out of this. Only a way that was least painful. Sad to say, I probably would've let her blow me in my younger days as to not hurt her feelings. But now, only days shy of my 36th birthday, I knew better. I was aware of my individual right to tell any woman no without explanation. Everyone, male and female, owes it to themselves to be their own sexual gatekeeper. I won't be guilted or shamed into anything. Any so-called man who thinks I'm crazy is an insecure loser who can go fuck himself.

Although refusing her offer, I still couldn't bring myself to firmly say, "No." Instead, I played aloof. Pretending to be ignorant of what she'd proposed. This was a lame copout. I'm a terrible liar, and Becky wasn't buying it for a second. It would've been more polite for me to give her a literal no as opposed to a figurative one. Then again, my unintentional insult served her right for the way she'd acted. And yet I couldn't help but feel bad about hurting her feelings. The further I get writing this book, the more I realize just how nice a person I am. I've failed in that regard here and there, but I'm not the asshole some make me out to be. If anything, I've been too nice overall.

After that painful exchange, Becky retreated to the comfort of her equally creepy husband. Everyone else had taken a break. Brandi chatted with Diane, her husband, and Tori's husband. Tori and I once again earned our hardcore partier stripes by engaging in mutual lap dances. She loves attempting my move of facing away, kicking my legs back, and landing on my hands with my crotch in the recipient's lap. Not once has she fully nailed it. Still, I enjoyed the sight of Tori's naked ass wiggling in my lap. Her pussy too. So pink and delicate. I was sure it tasted sweet like candy. It made me jealous of Brandi being on the verge of eating it while I hadn't.

I couldn't let that happen. It was Tori's turn to sit as I gave her another lap dance. Butterflies filled my stomach. I tried my damnedest not to tremble. My g-string could barely contain my now-massive cock as I treated my friend to the most sensual lap dance I could deliver. She smiled at me the entire time as she always did. Was she aware of what I was about to do? Oh my God. Was I really going to eat Tori's pussy?

Yes, once I worked up the courage. I had to. After all the nights we'd been there for each other. All the morale and support she'd given me through thick and thin, and vice versa. After all the secrets we'd entrusted with each other. I had to know what it was like to eat my friend's pussy. To lick and suck her clit. Know how her juices tasted. I wanted to. I needed to. I had to. If only this one time.

After bypassing the whipped cream and sucking her tits like foreplay between lovers, I grabbed my can of Reddi-wip and applied a line of cream to the inside of each of her thighs. My heart pounded as I dropped to my knees and slowly licked the length of each silky-smooth thigh from knee to pelvis. Inching my way up the second time, I knew it was the moment of truth. I could barely contain my anticipation as I dragged my tongue closer and closer towards her pussy. The room may have been dimly lit with the fire directly behind her, but her pussy shined liked a star. Beckoning me forth. Would she accept my tongue on her pussy, or would she throw me out and never again speak to me? With the last bit of Reddi-wip devoured, I continued licking forth until my tongue finally touched my friend's clit for the ultimate moment of truth.

A massive electrical shock of an orgasm shot through my body as I drew circles on Tori's clit with my tongue. She instantly responded by spreading her legs wider and grabbing the back of my head while her body trembled in delight. I knew eating her pussy would be amazing, but nothing could've prepared me for how out of this world it was. Her juices gushed forth like crazy and were sweeter than I'd imagined. I consumed all I could as I licked and sucked her clit, teased her delicate lips, and thrust my tongue deep insider her warm, velvety pussy.

There was a strong emotional component as well. Tori was not only one of my closest friends but a confidant and mentor. To this day, she lifts me up with encouragement and wisdom. Instinctively understanding me better than most people. I knew she had a crush on me, and I had one on her. Not only did I satisfy a sexual curiosity about her in that moment, but I thanked her for everything in the best way I knew how.

The camera flashes going off as I ate Tori's pussy let me know her husband was cool with it. After pleasuring my friend, she lifted me up and we kissed. She had me stand and pulled down my g-string to return the favor. I stood there in shock and amazement as Tori took my cock deep in her mouth. Having been so focused on the drama of eating her pussy I hadn't considered her responding in this manner. But I wasn't complaining. I loved every second of my friend, so beautiful in every way, licking and sucking my hard, throbbing cock as more camera flashes went off. "Mmmm," she enthusiastically expressed as my juices flowed like crazy inside her mouth. This exchange of oral pleasure and consumption of each other's sweetness was our sexy version of a blood pact. We can always end our friendship, but we can never undo giving each other head. That's kind of hot. I think everyone else thought so too.

Except for Becky, who blasted forth several more "Tori!" exclamations during that magical moment. Fucking bitch. While clearly jealous of me being so close to Tori, I began to see that she was also jealous of Tori for having me as a friend. That I allowed Tori to blow me right after I'd rejected Becky's offer didn't help. So be it. I didn't want Becky's mouth anywhere near me. And I'd rather die a slow, painful death than go down on that piece of trash. Fuck her. She could go to hell for all I cared.

Tori and I took a break as Diane began feeling ill. This is a common occurrence as Diane doesn't stomach her liquor well. Efforts have been made by many to ensure she eats plenty beforehand and is kept strictly on beer or wine. She always feels bad about it. Like she's wrecking everyone's fun as they dote on her. That's not true at all. Everyone is concerned about her wellbeing. And you have no idea how much it means to me that she and everyone else appreciates the concern I show her every time. This wonderful group of people, excluding Becky and her husband, is the antithesis of those horrible bitches at that shithole, white trash beauty salon in DeWitt. The one owned by a woman really named Becky.

With Diane and her husband bowing out and the night not getting any younger, it was time to get seriously naughty. After putting on my stripping mix, I had a still naked Brandi sit in the official lap dance chair. "Salt Shaker" cut through the air as I led a still naked Tori to Brandi. Becky complained about the song, because of course she did. Tori immediately took control via one of the sexiest lap dances I've ever witnessed. Grinding her wet pussy on Brandi's thigh and stroking her face as they kissed. Tori then kissed and licked Brandi's neck before slowly making her way down to lick and suck her tits. They giggled adorably and incessantly as Tori dropped to her knees and spread open Brandi's legs.

"Tori!" shouted Becky yet again. Not wanting her to fuck this up I shot her a look that said, "I'll kill you if you say one more word." She was silent after that.

As her husband snapped photo after photo, I watched in awe as Tori ate Brandi's pussy with the exact technique I'd used on her moments earlier. She proved herself an excellent student. Dabbing saliva on Brandi's clit and licking circles on it. Tori switched to sucking it as

Brandi threw her head back in ecstasy. Stretching one hand in the air while the other held onto Tori's head. Brandi embodied true decadence. Reveling in the hedonism of being pleasured by a beautiful woman who'd just been taught by the best. Tori wasn't shy about exploring every part of Brandi's pussy. Sucking her lips and licking deep inside her until finally making her cum.

After tasting her own juices on Tori's lips, Brandi was ready to channel her own sexual dominance as they switched places. She'd never gone down on a woman before and was much quicker than Tori in getting to the main course. The taste of Tori's sweet pussy still fresh on my lips made me even more excited for Brandi as she replicated what Tori had done to her. Tori expressed her sapphic indulgence by watching Brandi eat her pussy from start to finish. With Tori's hand on her head, Brandi teased her clit and lips before licking deep inside her pussy and then from bottom to top. Tori moaned and sighed in a sassy tone that made Brandi and I laugh until she finally came on Brandi's face.

I was feeling high and mighty after facilitating sex between two rocking hot girls. The three of us danced together as Becky continued bitching about the music. "I don't like this music!" she kept screeching. Like fingernails on a chalkboard. My girls and I tried to ignore her as we moved in a naked huddle pressed against one another. Once again, I felt like Malcolm McDowell's portrayal of Caligula. It's not every night I get to have oral sex with a friend before watching her fuck another girl. The energy between the three of us was out of control. My emotional bond with Tori further strengthened as the sexual tension between Brandi and I was now at its breaking point.

Becky complained about not liking this "nigger music" yet again, and that was the final straw for me.

"Yeah, I heard you the first hundred fucking times you said it!" I shouted at her.

Tori's husband immediately led me to the master bedroom, where he apologized for Becky's behavior. I refused his apology, as it wasn't his fault, and apologized to him for losing my cool. An apology that he in turn rejected. Explaining to me that Becky could be a bitch sometimes, but that he'd never seen her act like this before. This was followed by some backstory about she and her husband on the verge of closing their longtime family business due to competition from an international chain. Which did happen eventually. I sort of understood why they acted as they did. Remembering when I went crazy several years prior when Hardbodies experienced its first major setbacks. But there was no excuse for their behavior that night. Just as there wasn't for mine in 2007.

It was 2:00am and everyone was getting tired. I still had to drive back to Little Rock. Brandi and I went into the spare bedroom where our clothes were stashed and got dressed. I was on my knees as I checked my duffle bag to make sure I hadn't forgotten anything.

"Hey, Stefan," I heard her say directly above my head.

I looked up only for her to plant her lips on mine with an aggressive and sloppy kiss that was pure heaven. We stayed that way for what seemed like an eternity as our tongues danced in ecstasy. It was a kiss eighteen months in the making. The tension building tighter and tighter over time as we slowly and steadily emboldened each other sexually through our shared love of exotic entertainment. Watching each other play naughty games with Tori that night proved to be the final straw. Intense sexual desire flowed from us equally with the force of a tsunami. We had coveted each other physically for too long. There was no way we could make it through the rest of this night without finally knowing each other intimately.

We endured the horniest 45-minute drive in history. Brandi was beside herself with excitement about her first full-on sexual encounter with a woman. She gushed incessantly about how incredible Tori was at eating her pussy and making her cum. This only served to make my cock ache even worse for Brandi's pussy as I recounted my own sexual exchange with Tori. We agreed that, whether sucking cock or eating pussy, Tori is an oral sex ninja. And we bonded over our shared enjoyment of eating Tori's pussy and how incredible it tastes. I couldn't get Brandi back to my place fast enough.

   This wasn't the first time Brandi spent the night after a party. I had a guest bedroom she was always welcome to use. We'd barely made it through the front door upon grabbing onto each other and kissing insatiably. I slid my hand inside her yoga pants. Her pussy was drenched. I had no problem slipping a finger inside her. She was so tight. We'd already done our foreplay with Tori. Brandi was ready to fuck and so was I.

   I dragged her to my bedroom and immediately tore off her clothes. She did the same to me. Still kissing like mad all the while. I laid her upon my bed and climbed on top. My cock couldn't get deep inside her pussy fast enough. Despite her tightness and my massive endowment at that point, she was so fucking wet that I effortlessly slid all the way inside her. I may not be as close to her as I am with Tori, but Brandi and I were friends and remain so to this day. There was no romantic future for us given numerous circumstances, but there existed a burning mutual desire to know what it would be like if we made love. And we found out that night.

   We couldn't stop kissing as we thrusted hard against each other. My cock filled her pussy completely as it reached the end with every stroke. She gushed and squirted as we both moved closer and closer to climaxing. Everything we had experienced that night, and on every night leading up to it, exploded all at once. As with Tori, I've wondered what became of us in parallel universes. Are we together in one? Does this book begin with a prologue titled "Brandi Stripped Bare" in another? I suppose the possibilities are endless if infinite universes are indeed a thing.

   We fucked harder and harder while moaning uncontrollably. When we could no longer hold back the visions of that night, we completed the consummation of our once unrequited mutual lust. Holding each other tight and still kissing with reckless abandon as we simultaneously ejaculated hard in ecstasy followed by the sweet surrender of release. We maintained our embrace. Now for mutual comfort as we struggled to catch our breath. A sense of satisfaction fell upon us, as did one of melancholy. There were no regrets, but there was no future either. The story of my life by this point. She chose to sleep in the guest room. I tucked her into bed and kissed her goodnight before returning to my room for what remained of the night.

Happy birthday, Stefan.

CHAPTER 43

I find February to be the most inherently depressing month of the year. Cold, gloomy, and foreboding. Its gray skies invading every nook and cranny of my being. Wake up in the morning? Everything is gray. Go outside? Nothing by gray. Gray, gray, fucking gray. Even the rain, unlike the refreshing showers of spring and summer I find romantic, is gray. I've had enough of gray by this stage of winter, yet every day of February taunts me that spring isn't close to being here. A month so cruel it sometimes throws in an extra day to harass me further with its incessant grayness. Fuck you, February. Fuck you right in the ass.

But February has nights too, and the night forgives all. Or, at least, it forgives me. Its favorite native son. Not even stupid February with its bullshit grayness can come between me and the night. Nor could Searcy on the first Saturday of February 2015. If Arkansas cities were months, Searcy would be February. An odd, depressing, and overly conservative place with poorly marked streets that are a bitch to navigate at night. It's the seat of White County, and residents prefer to say White County rather than Searcy. So, where is your bachelorette party? White County, you say? You'll have to be more specific.

But my party girls that night were rebels. The SLC punks of Searcy, err... White County. They had no problem allowing the name Searcy to escape past their lips. They were bad girls. So bad, in fact, that they honestly thought they were doing something illegal by booking me to perform at their party. And somewhat disappointed to learn they'd broken no laws. They took delight in watching, touching, and dancing with a nearly naked man in a county defined by its stupid, hair-splitting rivalry between the Baptist locals and Church of Christ affiliated Harding University. My girls were true counterculture radicals within the confines of their cultural geography. God blessed us all that night in bringing us together.

***

2015 picked up where its predecessor left. Hardbodies rolled along with Brandi and me. We kicked off the year with a January bash at Tori's that was largely a repeat of the previous chapter sans Becky and her husband. After their piss poor display in December, they were never invited back to the lake. This made everyone more chill as Tori and Brandi totally got it on again. And that's the important thing.

I launched an exhaustive search for additional female strippers. It became clear that the Arkansas talent well had run dry. There was no shortage of applicants. But none came close to making the cut by my rigid standards. And they had to be rigid. Tori and her husband were the textbook Hardbodies clients for female strippers. This demographic wanted girls who were not only attractive but classy, upscale, and charming. Not the ink-covered, green-haired skanks with bitchy dispositions who flooded my inbox with underwear selfies taken in messy bedrooms.

Thinking back to that girl I met in 2013 who wanted to be an escort, I ran an anonymous Craigslist ad under the guise of hiring girls for an escort agency. While nearly all those Hardbodies applicants applied for this position as well, I also received inquires from several women who certainly looked like and came across as what Hardbodies needed. I spoke with a few. The consensus being that escorting would land them a sugar daddy or rich husband, so they could laze around all day and not do shit. That's just fucking sad. There's nothing wrong with seeking financial security in a man, but that doesn't mean a woman shouldn't still do something productive with her life.

Despite that, I began 2015 in excellent spirits that lasted throughout the year. That was a blessing as 2015 would be the final good year for Hardbodies. The brand may have hung around until 2018, but this was truly my agency's swan song year as a fully-realized business. The void of suitable talent combined with an angry and untrusting cultural climate would take a permanently damaging toll upon all I had built. I would begin considering other possibilities beyond stripping. This was nothing new, but I was becoming more serious about it. Slowly but surely.

Early 2015 was a fun and exciting time. This was helped partially by my latest steroid cycle. All that synthetic testosterone in my body had me chill as fuck. But it was more than that. I was feeling confident and creative about everything. For the first time in years, I made significant updates to my stripping costumes. Police officer got a new shirt and longer Maglite while firefighter received a new jacket and helmet. The only change to cowboy was that I finally replaced the old hat. I picked up the new one at a western wear boutique. Sitting on a table next to a life-size cutout of George Strait. Surely this hat would help me reach Amarillo by morning.

I'd settled into a groove around this time. Working with Brandi, texting with Tori, and sleeping with Samantha. It was the first time in my life that I felt okay with allowing myself to relax at times. There were nights with Sam when I'd lie in bed while holding her and not have a care in the world. I could accept things for what they were. Not that I was complacent in any fashion. I was still focused on achieving bigger and better things as always. Hardbodies remained a priority, but I also thought about writing, photography, filmmaking, and music. I began to consider working towards my bachelor's degree, although I couldn't decide on a major.

For the moment, however, there were plenty of bachelorettes and birthday girls to keep me busy through the final glory days for Hardbodies Entertainment of Arkansas.

***

Stripping has taken me to many of the state and national parks in Arkansas, but the spring of 2015 marked my first trip to Mount Magazine State Park. The mountain itself is the highest point in Arkansas at 2,753 feet above sea level. Located in an area of Western Arkansas, on the southern edge of the River Valley region, that I've rarely visited over the years. Economically depressed since I've been here, it's not a hotbed for strippers. But, like most of the state, it is gorgeous. A thick, endless tidal wave of trees exploding with green lushness throughout the spring and summer. It's no wonder my party girls had chosen this magical place as ground zero for a bachelorette party on a warm and cozy June night.

I made excellent time getting to the park, at which point I had no idea where to go. Not only was GPS not anywhere close to accurate for my destination, but I kept losing cell service. And that was Verizon, which is a must for me as I drive late at night through the backwoods of Arkansas. With GPS dropping the ball and no way to contact the client, I drove around the park for 45 minutes until I finally found their cabin on my own. Embarrassed by my lack of punctuality, I was apologetic to my party girls. Fortunately, they didn't mind. I got things started as a cowboy while rocking my George Strait-approved hat.

Everyone had a blast, but no one enjoyed my presence more than the one lesbian in the audience. I'm not joking. She was absolutely fascinated with me and everything I did. It wasn't the first time I'd encountered this, and I think it has to do with me not being the average guy. I inspire audiences to follow my lead with a no-pressure approach. They do things with me because they genuinely want to. Even this girl. And she was so sweet. As I packed up to leave while her friends began talking about sleep, she argued for me to stay longer. When it became clear that wasn't happening, she told me goodbye by running at me and jumping into my arms. At that point, I didn't want to leave her either. I'm sure we could've danced and talked all night.

I closed out spring with a bachelorette party in Hot Springs. The weather was heating up, but this Friday night was perfect. I arrived as the sun began to set. The location was a small bar on the lake that had been rented for this event. I'd spoken with my bachelorette before arriving, as she was directly involved in booking me. A former stripper herself, she was adamant about having a male stripper entertain her that night. Arriving early, I sat for a few minutes and took in the evening as I drank a Red Bull. It was around this time that a wistfulness stirred within me before and after each party. I was a long way from hanging up my g-string, but it truly hit me for the first time that I couldn't strip forever. I began treating each performance as if it were my last.

Having looked her up on Facebook, I knew my bachelorette was a real pretty girl. But nothing could've prepared me for meeting this cute and bubbly blonde in Daisy Dukes, who was so full of life. Her name was Dixie. How perfect was that? She ensured I was treated right by everyone and tipped extremely well. We instantly clicked and played well off each other. Out of the countless women I've arrested over the years, she may have been the most fun of all. Playing along perfectly each step of the way with zero resistance.

Like me, she took exotic entertainment seriously and held a certain reverence for it. Not all strippers past or present do that, and rarely do guys. Spending time with her once again reminded me how much more I have in common with female strippers than other male strippers. It's in that reverence, along with our business-like approach. We're here to entertain and get paid. Our objective isn't to get laid. Should a quality hookup occur on occasion, that's a bonus. I think of all the guys who use stripping to get laid. And by that, I mean they use it to beg for pussy. Missing out not only on making real money but on experiencing the memorable and special moments I've enjoyed over the years. Becky should've told those losers, "It's your loss," instead of me. But she's about as smart as them.

Dixie and her friends were lights out fun. Proving she still had some stripper left in her, she insisted on giving me a lap dance. She was amazing. Everything about her was. She would've been perfect for Hardbodies. And she kind of broke my heart in that regard. I found myself not wanting to leave, but the party began wrapping up immediately after my performance. I took my bow and drove back to Little Rock. Soaking in the fresh memories of another successful booking as if it were my last.

It wasn't, but an equally devastating last occurred days later when Brandi called it quits after two years with Hardbodies. She'd recently obtained a new boyfriend, so I was expecting it. Perhaps that's why I began romanticizing my parties in the moment. Hardbodies Entertainment of Arkansas, in essence, ended when she left. I would never represent another entertainer. From that point forward, it was only me. Once again, and this time forever, I was the last stripper standing.

CHAPTER 44

As I write this chapter in the summer of 2019, the "dad bod vs. fit bod" debate among women has heated up once again. But I first became aware of it four years earlier. At face value, it's a stupid argument for which there is no right or wrong answer. Individuals like what they like. If the differing taste of someone else bothers you, that's your problem. This is yet another social media shitstorm of a deathmatch that shouldn't exist in the first place.

And that's what I loathe about this debate. How participants, male and female, attempt in vain to define a universally accepted physique standard for all men. Why is this even a thing? It shouldn't be. If you're a woman attracted to fit guys, then so be it. What if you're a woman attracted to flabby guys? Same fucking answer. And if you're a self-aware woman who gravitates towards dad bods because they're physically in your league, then kudos to you for that. Because I can't stand fat men or women who reject others for being fat. But why must so many people demand that everyone likes what they like?

I do get why some women may assume dad bods to make better mates. I'll quickly concede that there are plenty of aesthetically pleasing douchebags in the world. God knows I've encountered more than my share. But outer and inner beauty are by no means mutually exclusive. There are plenty of men and women with both and just as many with neither. And there's no shortage of dad bods droning on about their alleged inner beauty while chasing hot girls solely on looks. The same goes for certain women regarding them chasing after hot guys.

This is where I get upset personally about the debate. Yes, I'm a vain and self-absorbed pretty boy who constantly ogles himself in the mirror. I've also devoted my life to treating others as I want to be treated. My self-confidence is generated entirely from within as I constantly invest in myself. It is not achieved by tearing down others. If anything, I want to spread this wealth with others in the hope they'll feel better about themselves. You can think of me as the anti-Narcissus as every compliment I receive from any woman never fails to melt my heart. And I make sure they know it. The value of mutual flattery and its positive effects is priceless.

This isn't one of those simple Ginger vs. Mary Ann discussions indulged in casual conversation. I'm not sure what the commonplace female equivalent is to this, but I've heard women debate Vin Diesel vs. Paul Walker. In either debate, despite one's personal preference, it is universally agreed that each is physically attractive in their own way. No disrespect is paid to anyone. The dad bod vs. fit bod argument runs deeper and darker than that by attempting to define a man's character and worth based solely on his façade. And that is morally wrong.

To men and women both... Like what you like and be true to yourselves. But don't let personal feelings of inadequacy instigate unprovoked attacks on others. There is no inner beauty in that. If you're truly happy and confident in who you are, I raise my glass to you no matter what you look like. If you're not, then it's on you – and you alone – to fix it. We all must do that at times. Even a shallow, vapid fit bod like me.

***

It was slightly past 7:00am on a magnificent Sunday morning in mid-August when I awoke on the shore of Lake Hamilton. The fresh smell of the trees outside filtered through the screen door. From the backyard to my nose as I laid on Tori's sofa. The temperature was refreshingly cool. A respite from the searing heat that would soon dominate the day. It was in that moment when I fully, truly understood why my friend was so in love with living here. The calming magic in the air that morning was undeniable. Elevating my senses into a state of relaxed euphoria. Complete submission was my only option and I gratefully embraced it.

After a few intoxicating minutes of this, I arose to join Tori on the deck. We discussed the beauty of the lake and surrounding landscape while drinking coffee and watching her dogs enjoy this dream place just as we did. She wore only a long bathrobe out of which her breasts continually fell. No matter. Save for the cool breeze upon us through the trees. We were secluded from neighbors on either side. Other than our voices and the dogs barking, there was only the sound of water and rustling leaves. I was still dressed in a t-shirt and swim trunks from the night before. Following my first time on a boat. That's right. I was 36 when I finally earned my sea legs. Another example of how I've experienced so much yet so little.

Tori went inside as I walked down to the lake along a narrow dirt trail. It wasn't treacherous but I did have to mind my step as it declined unevenly while twisting ever so slightly. Trees towered over me. Their collective fragrance filled my nostrils. A variety of birds sang their respective anthems. The sun had risen higher from the east. Its glowing amber rays of the morning illuminated every vibrant shade of green along my stroll. I reached the shore and stood in awe at the majestic, deep blue sight before me. In a rare instance, I allowed myself the luxury of visualizing myself living in such a place. Perhaps if my naked ambition were to ever pay off and I finally caught what I've been chasing. Or maybe I've been chasing the wrong thing all this time.

But that internal discussion would have to wait. Despite my desire to stay here forever, I had to get home. There was so much I had to do that day. And I had to be at work on Monday morning.

Work?!

***

Along with a steady supply of parties, August 2015 also provided me with gainful, full-time employment for the first time since before I launched Hardbodies. I was a senior editor for a travel website startup based in Little Rock. Although I want to say that my ever-growing talent for writing landed me this gig, I scored it in true Arkansas fashion via straight cronyism. I guess it was finally my turn. It paid well and allowed me to further replenish the coffers after bleeding them dry during the Hardbodies Dead era. It didn't impede my ability to keep booking parties for myself. And only myself. Hardbodies was now and forever an agency only in name. Not that I didn't keep searching for female talent. But I'd never again come across an applicant I'd want to represent.

I dove headfirst into my new professional opportunity. Although free to telecommute, I often went to work in the hoity-toity Little Rock neighborhood of the Heights. I loved the novelty of getting out of the house every day for a change. Part of my agreement to come on board included my own office. Located upstairs away from everyone else, it was spacious with a large window and small fridge. Upstairs also had its own thermostat I could set to my comfort and mine alone. Life was good.

I instantly settled into a routine of waking up at 5:00am, arriving to work at 7:45am, and grabbing coffee from the breakroom while my computer booted. The breakroom was more of a nook. Sometimes this weird deaf girl who was a staff writer would do a stretch routine in there. I would've asked her why, but… You know. I'd begin working at 8:00am sharp. Spending my days editing brief descriptions of museums, amusement parks, and other tourist attractions throughout the country. On sunny days I'd work with the overhead lights off while listening to the smooth and exotic sounds of David Sylvian at low volume. Little things that helped me achieve the right mindset for assisting every writer in looking his or her best. Some requiring more assistance than others.

Along with the eclectic mix of restaurants within walking distance was a Kroger across the street. This made grocery shopping a breeze as well as any time I needed to make a run for Reddi-wip or Red Bull before a party. Having my own office allowed me to take calls and book parties without anyone overhearing. I didn't feel bad about doing this on someone else's time. My productivity was exceptional and other employees left often for personal matters. While I didn't care for the constant staff meetings, because staff meetings are costly bullshit, that was a minor complaint. All things considered, it was the closest I ever came to the perfect job. I was doing something I enjoyed, my talents were being appropriately utilized, and there was zero micromanagement.

And the parties kept coming. Including my final performance at Clarion Resort on the Lake in Hot Springs before it closed. I don't know why this place stands out to me after all these years. Like I almost want to pour a forty out on the curb in its memory. There wasn't anything special about it in a tangible sense compared to other hotels. I don't know. It just had a vibe that always caught my imagination. This was a bachelorette party in early October. Only four or five girls, but they tipped generously. I devoted most of my attention to the bachelorette as she sat upon an ottoman next to the window. Feeling a bit daring, I said it was fine to leave the drapes open. Life was great.

I saw Mötley Crüe perform live for the sixth and final time in my life. It was the band's farewell tour. On which I saw them twice. The first time a year earlier in Southaven, Mississippi. They were in Little Rock now, and that afforded me one final taste of hearing "Home Sweet Home" in concert:

"My heart's like an open book

For the whole world to read

Sometimes nothing

Keep me together at the seams"

Is that not this book – and my life – in a nutshell?

Also, in Hot Springs during October, I attended a wedding for only the second time in my life. A favor to my longtime social media friend Shannon. Although never meeting in person until that evening, she and I had conversed online for years. Starting on Myspace and carrying over to Facebook. It was her daughter's wedding. Since her ex-husband would be there with his new wife, Shannon didn't want to attend without a date. So, I helped her out. We went to a hotel bar afterward and chatted over drinks before I headed back to Little Rock.

I'm including this story as a shout out to my friend. She's never hesitated to show her support for me, and I've never taken that for granted. We haven't talked much over the past few years due to circumstances in her life, but we still acknowledge each other when we can. If she reads this, I know it will mean the world to her. Love you, Shannon.

***

As quickly as my senior editor position had come into my life, it was gone. The company partnered with a web development firm out of Tennessee shortly before I came on board. Over those months, these assholes gained more and more influence over our operations. Taking over completely in mid-October and immediately changing everything for the worse. Once talk began of making everyone work in the same room under constant micromanagement, I took my bow. I couldn't have functioned under those circumstances before Hardbodies. Much less after years of being my own boss. I was right to resign when I did because the new management literally made everyone else beg to keep their job. Can you imagine what would've happened if they'd done that to me? Do you really want to?

The website went live days before I left but only lasted a few months before the entire project was run into the ground. Lawsuits ensued. And all that content, that massive amount of time and effort, was lost forever. If there is a silver lining here for me, it's that I singlehandedly operated a profitable business for over a decade on a shoestring budget. But this venture – for all its capital, manpower, and collective talent – resulted in a short-lived website that went unnoticed and never earned a cent. Hardbodies Entertainment of Arkansas was the more successful business in every way and it's not even close. Sometimes we must take our victories where we can.

With forty extra hours per week suddenly on my hands, I threw myself into other projects for the remainder of the year. Mainly photography as I experimented with shooting products and food as well as architecture in downtown Little Rock. I continued staying busy with parties. But for the first time, I didn't bother making plans for Hardbodies in 2016. I continued keeping an eye out for potential female talent. But as long as it was just me, there was no agency to manage. Much less one for which to make plans in the coming year. Life was adequate.

CHAPTER 45

"How can I help you, sir?" asked the gate attendant in a faux chipper tone.

I replied nonchalantly, "I'm here for the bachelorette party," as if I'd done this before. Probably because I had.

He gave me a suspicious, "Of course," as he opened the gate. Fuck him.

I followed GPS as it led me through an endless maze of McMansions. All that money and zero individuality. Each one a suitable answer to the question, "If Patrick Bateman were a house, what kind would he be?" Seven days before Christmas and my final booking of the year. A bachelorette party in Fayetteville. The second Friday night in a row this happened. Tonight, it was cold but not intolerable. Brisk like those annoying and creepy iced tea ads. It was even refreshing as I stepped out of the truck and got ready while awaiting my client.

She was sexy. Petite and blonde. Having traveled all the way from California for the bachelorette party and wedding, she'd decided that a male stripper was a must. Although determined to party down in style, she projected a shyness as we talked. A sense of intimidation being in my presence. But also a sense of excitement. She wanted to do something dangerous. And she wanted her friends to get dangerous with her. My role was that of danger incarnate. Their dirty little secret for approximately one hour. The role I was apparently born to play.

Upon entering McMansion #287580427524, I was greeted by a bachelorette party divided over my presence. This wasn't some typical case of some girls being more reserved than others. Half the girls, including my bachelorette, were beside themselves with enthusiasm. The other half wanted nothing to do with me. The client had not anticipated that my reception would be polarizing to this extreme. But she and the party girls weren't going to let the uptight contingent stop their fun. We moved to an upstairs den while the others kept the living room nice and frigid.

I made the most of the cozy confines I shared with a half dozen tipsy, twentysomething girls. I gave them lap dances before we all danced together. No one enjoyed me more than the client. I liked her too. She exuded understated confidence that made her especially attractive. Her shyness gradually gave way as she opened herself up to me.

"I love how, like, you don't put any pressure on us. We can just totally be ourselves with you," she confided in me at one point.

I was beyond flattered by this as I searched for a worthy response. Finally pushing forth an, "I'm just here to show you all an amazing time," or something similarly generic. It certainly wasn't worthy of that compliment. A compliment that succinctly defined my approach to entertaining every audience. This – this right here – was and forever is what being an exotic entertainer is all about to me. And, truth be known, this no-pressure approach is what gets me laid.

Under more ideal circumstances, I could've gotten laid by my client. She followed that statement by bending over and rubbing her foxy butt on my cock. She did this repeatedly as I attempted to remain within the tight quarters of my g-string. After an hour, as the incessant whining of the squares downstairs grew louder, I made my departure and the long drive back to Little Rock.

I didn't know it at the time, but this would be my final performance in the Fayetteville area to date. While there has been an active male stripper in that area for some years, he's black and therefore not direct competition to me. I know nothing about him as an entertainer, nor can I speak to his abilities. And while he's been ostensibly running his own agency of guys in the area, I can't see that he's had any more success with finding male strippers than I ever did. I think the real issue is prospective clients either assuming I wouldn't travel that far (something I've been told over the past few years) or forgetting altogether that booking a male stripper for a private party is indeed an option in Arkansas. Times were changing.

***

Baby, it was cold outside on Christmas Eve Eve (not a typo) night. But hotter than hell in Samantha's house. And I didn't need a key to unlock the door as she strutted around in a short, tight, black dress sans underwear. It barely contained her breasts and consistently failed at covering her ass with nearly every move. I was totally cool with all of this, because of course I was. As ready as we were for the main course that night, we needed to carb load first. So, in the holiday tradition of not giving a fuck about healthy habits, we ordered a pizza. Now I had thirty minutes to kill.

I grabbed Samantha and we danced as "Good for You" by Selena Gomez played on the radio. Sam's dress immediately rode up over her butt. She went to pull it back down, but I stopped her. We kept dancing as I squeezed her bare cheeks. They needed warming and I was more than happy to oblige. She wrapped her arms around my neck. We kissed. I was so close to her. Yet after two and a half years, she was still at an arms-length distance from me. She didn't want to introduce me to her family, but I didn't want to meet them either. How would I have explained myself to people who had no idea someone like me could even exist? I wanted her to run away with me, but that would never happen.

So, I did the next best thing in that moment. With her skirt still in its hiked position, I maneuvered her to the sofa and made her sit. Her legs spread, I dropped to my knees and enjoyed dessert before our dinner in transit. We never broke eye contact as I devoured her delicious pussy. Her juices flowed like crazy as I held her lips open and danced my tongue on her clit. The combination of spit and juices making it increasingly slippery. The same went for the rest of her pussy. Samantha moaned and sighed as she grabbed my head and pushed my tongue deep inside her. I could barely breathe through my nose, but I was determined to taste every inch of her sugar walls. I experienced my own intense orgasm as she came all over my face.

Following a fancy dinner of Domino's and Korbel, we continued our naughty brand of holiday cheer with champagne kisses and more dancing. I'd had enough of that dress and pulled it off her before reaching the bedroom. I dragged her hot, naked body by the hand and directed her onto the bed. She got on her knees and undressed me. I joined her on the bed, where we kissed uncontrollably. She was eager to suck my cock, but I still wanted to taste more of her sweet pussy. A compromise was reached as I lied down and she got on top.

This position with Samantha required little effort on my part to please her. With a pillow under my head as she sat on my face, my tongue slipped perfectly inside her pussy. And just having my tongue inside her drove her wild. I consumed an endless tidal wave of juices as she licked and sucked my cock. Her big tits pressed against my stomach. An incredible view of her gorgeous ass right in my face. We joked and laughed about all sorts of things as always. Something about being irreverent during sex made our naughtiness even naughtier.

With her sexy butthole right above my eyes, I got to work. Wetting my middle finger in my mouth and slowly, gently pressing it inside her ass. She responded with a long, relaxed sigh of relief. As if this small yet kinky gesture immediately lifted the weight of the world from her shoulders. I continued licking her pussy as she sucked my cock with even more ferocity. After a few moments, I removed my finger from her butt and replaced it with my tongue. She moaned and giggled as I explored her most taboo area in the most intimate fashion possible. Not wanting to be outdone, she guided my pelvis forward and returned the favor simultaneously.

We couldn't wait a second longer. She lifted herself off me. Remaining on all fours as I got behind her on my knees and slid my painfully throbbing cock deep inside her aching, soaking wet pussy. I held tight onto her hips as we thrusted violently against each other. I filled her with every stroke, but neither of us could get my cock deep enough inside her. The sensation of her firm, round ass caused intense tingling on my pelvis as it bounced off with each viciously passionate thrust. Her moans turned to screams. Demanding me by name to fuck her harder and harder. I didn't know how much longer I could hold back. The instant she unleashed an explosion of hot juices all over me was too much as I came deep and hard inside her for what seemed like an eternity.

After needing about ten minutes to recover from the lovemaking equivalent of a neutron bomb, we went back to dancing, eating, and drinking for an hour. Before doing it all again as we often did.

This wasn't the last night I spent with Samantha, but we began to drift apart in the coming year. It was increasingly difficult for me to accept the nature of our relationship. I was growing tired of being the dirty little secret. Of us not being free to commit the simple act of walking hand in hand among people she knew. I'd had enough. Not only with her, but with every other woman for whom I'd felt something and wanted more only for them to allow the fear of disapproving opinions of others to color their decisions. Why did those opinions matter? These people weren't paying the bills, so fuck 'em. Why was it so important for Samantha and the other girls to make the same life choices as everyone else? To settle for mediocrity? Each of these questions is its own answer because misery loves company.

***

I spent Christmas night experimenting with product photography in my garage while drinking Jack and Coke. This session centered around creating sexy settings including items like handcuffs, lingerie, wine glasses, and bedsheets. Attempting to tell an erotic story through still images using only inanimate objects. This was sexier than photographing some wannabe female model naked in the woods. The results were better than anticipated. Providing me with three fine art photography pieces that I would later sell online in a variety of print options.

As I enjoyed this alone time, the phone rang. I should've let it go to voicemail as anyone with the nerve to call me on Christmas night must be trouble. Muscle memory got the best of me and I answered. Only to encounter a shrill and intoxicated female voice.

"Yeah, we need you to send a male stripper to our party we're having right now," she abrasively slurred with all the charm and grace of a drunken Hillary Clinton.

There was a time when I would've tried to book that party. Disgusting as that woman was. Even knowing that, if I did, it would be a disaster. But not tonight. Not only because I was a little buzzed myself, but because I was too good for this nasty woman and her surely god-awful friends. It didn't matter how much money they had. My time that night playing with photography and being creative was worth more than anything they had to offer me. So, I politely declined and hung up.

For better or worse, life was evolving. For better or worse, I was evolving.

My naked ambition was evolving……

CHAPTER 46

2016 kicked off like gangbusters as I performed nonstop during the first quarter. Mostly around Little Rock and Hot Springs. My first booking was a 21st birthday party in Maumelle. The equally young client was hell-bent on showing her friend a great time despite a limited budget. Although she ended up cutting much of the extravagancy originally planned, my performance was never on the chopping block. Gathered within a small, plain apartment with no decorations, we made our birthday girl's night special. While tipping was somewhat light, they were fully satisfied after twenty minutes. I probably shouldn't say this, but I was happy to do it based on how enthusiastic and respectful they were.

Most of my parties during this time went well, but there were two exceptions. The first was a late January bachelorette party in Little Rock. It was weird. The kind where I wondered why I was even there but not because they were rude or standoffish. They just kind of didn't give a shit. The bachelorette was a good sport, but the other girls acted too good for me. Like the sort of people obsessed with appearances. Saying and doing all the right things to blend seamlessly within the world around them. A room full of female Patrick Batemans. Patricia Batemans? Even the swanky apartment looked like someplace he would live. At least I wasn't murdered. Or lectured on Phil Collins.

The other and more conventionally bad party was an early April birthday surprise in Hot Springs. My second – and, to date, final – party from hell in Spa City. This one took place at a shithole restaurant and bar named Fat Jacks. The client and other women involved in putting it together were nothing but rude to me from the moment I arrived. And they got pissed because I couldn't give the birthday girl a proper lap dance as she was seated upon a high barstool. I was a lousy stripper for not being seven-feet tall. That's not hyperbole. They told me as much.

But the biggest problem was that a male stripper, any male stripper, should never have been a consideration. I took one look at the birthday girl and knew she was too shy to receive a lap dance. Especially before a large crowd. There was no excuse for any of her friends to not have recognized this as well. In a testament to how un-fucking-believably out of this world I am as an entertainer, I managed to salvage this party into something passable and make some decent tips to boot. I did this by ignoring the client, an odious cunt of a woman named Meredith, and ordering the show moved to another section of the restaurant with only close friends present.

I never did give my birthday girl a lap dance, but I chatted with her at the bar for several minutes. Beyond that, I spent 45 minutes giving lap dances to and dancing with the other girls. Any other male stripper would've bailed after the disastrous start and I wouldn't have blamed him. Yet I managed to take that dumpster fire and turn it into a serviceable performance. I did this solely for my personal satisfaction. The only morally correct reason for me to do it. Many of the previously rude girls changed their tune by the time I finished. A couple of them even hugged me on my way out. Except for Meredith, who refused to acknowledge my existence. After I had the nerve to save her ass despite being nothing but awful towards me. Whatever. Fuck that piece of shit.

***

A funny thing happened early in the year as I prepared for another steroid cycle. I'd done my homework, chosen my stack, and determined my dosages as always. At the last minute, however, I decided to hold off purchasing my gear. And I never would purchase it. Part of me was wary of enduring another twelve weeks of sticking long needles in my butt cheeks. My ass had been a pin cushion for so long that it was now filled with scar tissue. Making injections tougher as time went on. Although I knew how to shoot steroids into my shoulders, hips, and thighs, I was never comfortable self-injecting in any of those spots. While thigh injections are technically easier than butt injections for self-administration, they always made me queasy for some reason.

There was also a part of me curious to see what I could accomplish without steroids. Could I build muscle and burn fat naturally? It was a daunting proposition. I'd been led to believe that none of this was possible without performance-enhancing drugs. Sure, all the fitness articles online claimed any fitness objective could be achieved naturally. But I knew enough to recognize the wink and a nudge integrated into these pieces. I knew that the entire fitness industry was predicated on lies upon lies. Cashing in on the ignorant hopes of poor saps screaming, "Shut up and take my money!" to anyone promising overnight results. Regardless of any evidence to the contrary.

A decade of consistent steroid use had rendered my body a hormonal dumpster fire. Testosterone levels seemed fine, but my insulin, cortisol, and thyroid hormones were all out of whack. I showed symptoms of prediabetes. At times finding myself shaking, sweating, and faint for no apparent reason. I increased my overall physical activity only to watch my bodyfat rise when it had no logical reason to. I had entered a long period of detoxification that would take a couple of years to complete.

While spring blossomed around me, business withered. Parties still rolled in, but at the slowest pace I'd experienced since 2012. At the same time, there was a noticeable increase in women calling me with a disrespectful attitude right out of the gate. It was no coincidence that divisive rhetoric now permeated throughout society. A rhetoric causing decent folks to shy away from engaging new people and simultaneously empowering the rudest of self-loathing garbage to act towards others any way they please.

I pushed forward with more experimentation in other areas of interest. Photography was still a pursuit. I played around with video production. Writing became a major focus for me. I still wasn't passionate about it, but I had an undeniable gift. My biggest obstacle was deciding what to write about, how to package it, and how to market it. I'd launched blogs centering on a specific area in the past, only to give up on them after a few entries due to lack of inspiration. The summer of 2016 was no exception as I repeated the same mistake while expecting different results. It wouldn't be the last time.

Across these mediums, I possessed the means and talent. All I lacked was inspiration. The most important ingredient of all. It wasn't until I began writing this book that I recognized my ideal subject matter. My go-to muse when all else is lost forever stares me in the face every time I look in a mirror.

I considered earning my bachelor's degree. I'd been taking core classes two at a time for the past few semesters but couldn't decide on a major. The idea of earning another film degree didn't get my academic motor running. Having long joked that I should've been a lawyer, it suddenly dawned on me one day. Why couldn't I be a lawyer? It was a crazy proposition but provided the impetus for me to choose a four-year major. I enrolled in an online interdisciplinary studies degree program that allowed me to study three different subjects. I chose writing, legal studies, and political science.

The idea of attending law school was eventually dismissed. But pursuing this bachelor's degree and major has been one of the best decisions I've ever made. The study of writing has been especially rewarding. Although I'd intended to focus on technical writing, the creative nonfiction writing courses I took have alone been worth the cost of tuition. Not only have they made me a better communicator, but I couldn't have written this book without them. "Emily Stripped Bare" originated as a semester-long project in a personal essay writing course. My grade on this book's prologue? 100%, sexy butt.

***

I want to share more stripping stories from 2016, but there isn't anything else interesting. Nothing unlike what you've already read. There was a party at Tori's one night, but even that was tame compared to parties of the past. Along with she and her husband, another couple was present. They were strange. Although never having married, they'd been together for many years. Well, sort of. They were one of those couples that constantly break up only to get back together. Following their inevitable breakup shortly after this party, the girlfriend would text Tori and tell her awful things about her soon to be former ex. Tori would then fill me in. Although I'm not one for gossip, this was kind of fun.

Tori had risen to the role of guardian angel by this time. Our near-nightly texting sessions often the highlight of my day. She's a huge fan of Hallmark movies and live texts them to me while watching. Although not a fan myself, I do get a kick out of her love for these films. I love her unwavering belief in the existence of true love and romance in the face of so much negativity in the world.

***

I wrapped up 2016 with a birthday party in Benton. The client was my birthday girl's husband. It was a quick performance typical of a party with couples present. But they loved it. Gobs of money were thrown at me as I did well financially for such a short performance. Earning more than enough that night to stop off for a bottle of Jack Daniels on my way home.

With a huge wad of cash and the first semester of my declared major under my belt, I kicked back at my desk with a Jack and Coke while pondering the coming year. Unlike this time last year, when I'd forgone making plans for Hardbodies simply due to lack of talent, I knew the issues ran deeper than that. There really was no talent left aside from me. I wanted to pull the plug. Even posting a blog entry declaring Hardbodies dead and buried only to unpublish it after a few weeks. I had every reason to walk away with my head held high. Hardbodies Entertainment of Arkansas was a business that was never supposed to work. Yet I'd built it from nothing into a profitable enterprise. Not once, but twice. No one else could've done it once. Many tried, believe me. And still, I felt like a complete failure.

CHAPTER 47

2017 brought more of the same. A steady if unspectacular supply of parties as I threw myself back into higher education while also experimenting with other pursuits. Once again, I launched a new blog focused on arts, entertainment, and culture. And, once again, I lost interest after several weeks. While I published a ton of entries that were thoughtful and well structured, they collectively lacked any real punch. There was nothing to seduce readers and bring us all together. I was still holding back when it came to rhetorical expression. Simple to fix yet difficult to execute.

So, I shifted back to photography. Taking more product and architectural shots that, like my writing, were technically proficient yet uninspired. I was still holding back. Why was I so shy about expressing myself through these mediums? I was a stripper. A born agent provocateur of hedonistic escapades. I was afraid of offending someone through non-stripping channels. When not corrupting bachelorettes and birthday girls much to their delight, I was behaving like every person I'd ever criticized for kowtowing to the insecurities of others. This attitude is indeed a plague, and even I wasn't immune to it.

I struggled at learning how to achieve the physique I wanted by natural means. Although I hadn't abandoned the idea of ever doing steroids again, I at least wanted to form a better foundation before attempting another cycle. After all those years and drugs pumped into my body, I'd never once been completely satisfied with my results. Not one time had I looked in the mirror and said, "Damn. That's it right there." While managing to bring my fat down over the past several months, I was also losing lean mass. Without steroids, all that bro-science was rendered useless. In fact, all the general fitness information in the world is garbage. If I was to achieve the physique I coveted via natural means, I would have to carve my own path through the jungle.

As with the previous year, there's not much to say about parties in 2017. Most were a smashing success. A few were mediocre. One was fucking awful, but more on that later. I didn't even have a party at Tori's that year as life got in the way for she and her husband. We still enjoyed our texting sessions. They kept me going day after day. I'd once again retreated from social situations. Maybe it wasn't healthy, but I had to do it. I had entered a long process of reinvention. One that culminated with the completion of this book.

***

With the summer of 2017 in full swing, I made two major decisions. First, I would seek an opportunity like my editor position with that startup two years earlier. Second, I would start over from scratch and devise a fitness regimen to suit my needs through trial and error that would take however long it required.

I scoured the internet for remote writing and editing opportunities. Not only did I not expect to find anything locally, but I was reluctant to work around others. I've always been wary of getting too close to coworkers. It seems to invite drama. Sadly, many companies offering remote positions weren't much better. Preferring need and experience over talent and ambition. Many insisted on frequent group video chats and other interactivity between writers. That's ridiculous. You have a workplace that, by design, is inherently devoid of workplace drama. And yet these companies are all like, "Fuck that." It reminded me why I started Hardbodies in the first place.

After much searching, I landed a contract writing gig with a web startup based in Seattle. The pay wasn't exceptional but higher than what many other companies were offering for similar work. And there would be no video conferences or interaction of any kind with my fellow writers. The company would tell me what they needed, I'd write it, and they'd pay me. Why can't everything be that fucking simple? There's no good reason it can't.

The work was tedious and monotonous at times, but I wasn't complaining. There was much worse out there. I wrote tons of short pieces on a variety of industries. Faking my way through them to start but learning a little about each over time. I wrote about chiropractic before moving onto pest control. That was followed by dentistry before, of all things, law. I also wrote about a variety of other industries including landscaping, property management, and garage door repair. The one I hated was life coaching. Largely mystical, new age, Marianne Williamson-esque stuff I couldn't get behind.

Overall, I enjoyed my time writing for this startup. Spending my days typing away while listening to synthwave. And the additional cashflow was appreciated. It wasn't something I wanted to do long term as a writer, but neither were any of my attempts at blogging. Authoring those short pieces even improved my writing skills. I embraced the opportunity for what it was. And it was exactly what I needed at the time.

***

I got back to basics with fitness and nutrition. Reembracing the basic framework I followed in my pre-steroid days. This entailed high volume weight training combined with a diet built largely around complex carbs and devoid of processed foods. I was sick to death of hearing about caloric deficits and how carbs were my enemy. There was a time when I listened to my body and gave it what it wanted. And my body once again craved brown rice, oatmeal, and pasta before lifting heavy weight for long stretches of time. I was like a born-again Christian upon returning to that approach. It took effort and self-discipline but required no pain or suffering. No illegal drugs either.

That's what I finally got through my thick skull after all those years of jabbing my ass with needles. Being fit isn't about punishment and abuse. It's about being healthy and happy. Steroids or not, the idea of one's body responding positively to negative treatment is an oxymoron. Not to mention stupid as all fuck. Starvation diets sans drugs result in a significant loss of lean mass that can be equal to or greater than the amount of fat lost. In exchange for all that suffering, one is left with a body that is smaller but not better. It may even be worse in terms of both aesthetics and health.

And it's not sustainable. You can't starve yourself while beating your brains out with cardio for very long. Inevitably you're going to hit a wall. And what happens after that? You get fat again. Probably fatter than you were to start. That's what happens when you rapidly force fat off your body as opposed to slowly coaxing your body to carry less over a long period of time. How is this slower approach achieved? By embracing a permanent lifestyle change and allowing your body to become a result of this healthy and active lifestyle over time. Want to know an easy way to boost low testosterone or a slow thyroid? Embrace a healthy and active lifestyle. Seriously.

We seek the quick-fix solution to our aesthetic issues not only for instant gratification but also because we've been conditioned to believe that any fitness regimen is unpleasant. But there's nothing unpleasant about taking the long road to victory. Quite the opposite, in fact. I never go hungry. If I'm hungry, I eat. I only perform fitness activities that I enjoy. I lift weights because I enjoy it. The combination of heavy weight and proper form delivers a cathartic experience that rejuvenates both body and mind, not unlike what practitioners of yoga experience. I also dance every night, because I enjoy dancing at night. Since I never enjoyed running, I no longer run.

Our collective view of what constitutes healthy and fit is more skewed than ever. While morbidly obese women are claiming to be healthy at any size, juiced up douchebags are accusing anyone not shredded to fuck of being fat and lazy. First off, there is no such thing as being inherently healthy at any size. Science says otherwise. Second, there is nothing inherently healthy about a man or woman being shredded. Quite the opposite in fact. Some guys can obtain single-digit body fat percentages with relative ease and without drugs by virtue of genetics, but they are few and far between. On the other hand, it's all but guaranteed that any woman with chiseled abs is on anabolic steroids and/or human growth hormone. It's simply not possible genetically or by any natural means.

Just as crash dieting isn't sustainable, neither is being shredded. The body hates being in that state because it isn't healthy. As with having too much fat, having too little also results in the depletion of hormones. A man who manages to shred without drugs is most likely impotent due to the low testosterone that comes with ultra-low body fat. Even some juicers experience impotence at these levels as the massive amounts of drugs they inject are busy fighting against the body to maintain lean mass. This is a crash diet of its own that leads practitioners to also hit a wall and wind up fatter than when they started. It's why more and more juicers are eschewing cycling as to remain shredded permanently. They're also destroying their internal organs and dying young. I sure hope those YouTube ad revenues and protein powder endorsements are worth the eventual hassle of begging someone for a kidney.

Many juicers today don't do shit in the weight room. At my last gym, obvious juicer guy was obvious because his workouts were as half-assed and fundamentally unsound as those of every dad bod in the place. His maximum bench press was 165 lbs. Given how he constantly strutted around like an absolute dumb fuck, he totally would've benched more if he could for the sake of showing off. While I'm not proud of my own juicer past, at least my max bench in those days was more than double that. And naturally, it's still over 100 lbs. heavier.

It sucks that the term "body positivity" is merely an excuse for women to live unhealthy lifestyles. Body positivity should be a rallying cry for every man and woman to focus on embracing their individual long-term aesthetic results of healthy and active living. It should be about pursuing athletic activities through which pleasure and enjoyment are derived. About eating healthy (and delicious) meals with indulgences kept in check. Losing one's taste for refined sugars and cornstarch fillers over time because they don't contribute to this amazing new lifestyle. As for looks… It wouldn't matter whether a man looks like a swimmer or a powerlifter, or whether a woman is petite or Amazonian. If you're healthy, fit, and happy within your genetic parameters, it's all good. That, my friends, is what body positivity should be.

***

The shit booking of 2017 was a birthday party on Black Friday. My first ever gig on a Thanksgiving weekend. It was only three girls and they were odd. I think they thought that I thought I was better than them. And since everyone else's insecurities are my fault, they each copped an attitude with me around the twenty-minute mark. As I dressed and packed my gear, one of the girls asked me if I had any kids. When I said no, she responded, "Well, then you need to give us back our money." I didn't say a word, but my expression must've made me come across like a stone-cold killer. The other girls immediately made her go into the next room. I continued packing in silence before leaving without saying goodnight.

My writing gig ended abruptly a few weeks later as the startup ran out of investor money. What a shock. I spent the remainder of my year focusing on fitness and the coming semester. Also, I began giving thought to Hardbodies. What if I could bring it back a third time? This time reaching far beyond Arkansas. Not as one of those bait and switch nationwide agencies polluting Google search results. But something else. A cooperative of the best in male and female exotic entertainment from coast to coast. Likewise catering to only the best audiences. Perhaps it was time for a rebranding. I'd have to give it a new name. Nothing was set in stone, but the wheels in my head were turning…

CHAPTER 48

I couldn't believe it had been that long, but here I was with Tori on her birthday. Five years to the weekend since we first met in that same living room. Diane and her husband were present as well. Along with three other couples I was meeting for the first time. By this point, the whole "Tori's boyfriend" thing was so set in stone that people were taking it literally. While not avoidant in any way, the other women seemed to make a conscious effort not to intrude upon us. And though I didn't ignore them and made sure each received a lap dance, I did appreciate the consideration as I made the most of my time with Tori in the flesh. Truly in the flesh as she was butt ass naked nearly the entire time.

We were joined at the hip as always. Trading lap dances and licking Reddi-wip from each other's nipples before relaxing in the hot tub with a few other guests. Chatting about a wide array of subjects. Other parties notwithstanding, it was the first social situation in which I'd been for some time. I was still in my reclusive state and it wouldn't end anytime soon. For now, however, I was totally in my element as I maneuvered from conversation to conversation. Topic to topic. Never missing a beat. No matter how hard I try otherwise sometimes, I'm hopelessly a people person. The only thing to ever keep me from soaring high within this realm was aversion from others. And there was no aversion here. Not now. Not ever. Tori would never allow it.

It was late when I left. As always, Tori and I were the last two standing. When it comes to partying, no one holds a candle to either of us. While everyone else began leaving or dozing off in front of the TV, we continued our ever-lively conversations in the kitchen as we ate and drank. Eventually, I looked at the time and was shocked by how late it was. This happens every time I visit her. Still naked, she walked me to the front door and gave me a kiss goodnight before I headed into the cool March night.

And that, ladies and gentlemen, was the final Hardbodies Entertainment of Arkansas booking to be completed.

***

2018 started slow. Real slow. Hardbodies Dead slow. My nest egg was once again dwindling as I waited for the phone to ring. But it rarely did. My Google business listing was live and on point. All I could do was wait.

I won an award that spring. No, not for stripping. For writing. I won the award for best creative nonfiction work from a writing contest at my university. My entry was an essay on exploring the history and architecture of downtown Benton, Arkansas. Along with words, it incorporated numerous photos I'd shot in the area over the prior months. Like "Emily Stripped Bare", this was an upper level writing course project for which I received a grade of 100%. And now it had also earned me a certificate along with a check for $100. It may not seem like much, but this was a huge deal to me. Maybe there was a chance I could be acknowledged for my talents beyond stripping after all.

I also worked on plans for a bigger, better, and rebranded Hardbodies. For the name, I had chosen Hedonism Male & Female Strippers. This tied in with my languishing film project titled *Hedonism* for which I'd written a screenplay. In hindsight, that name kind of sucks. Even more so now as that semiautobiographical screenplay about stripping has been rendered obsolete by this book. I suppose the Hedonism moniker was inspired by my continued embrace of ethical hedonism as a philosophy for life. It was time I began truly living for myself, and I had a long road ahead of me on that journey.

And that conflicted with the very notion of the new Hardbodies. Which is why my efforts in assembling it were half-hearted. I was wary of once again representing other strippers of either gender after all I'd experienced over the past fourteen years. No matter how good they looked. No matter if they said all the right things. I couldn't bring myself to trust another stripper. Regardless, I soldiered on. Figuring that I'd get over this anxiety at some point and make it all happen.

I was still on top of my game as an entertainer. I'd made excellent progress over the past several months on my new personalized fitness and dietary regimen. I was still learning new things while unlearning old bullshit. But feeling better about myself than I had since I'd stopped juicing. Business was slow, but I hadn't given up. Maybe I could still pull everything together and turn this industry on its head. For fucks sake, someone needed to. I was now truly an elder statesman of stripping. This could totally work.

And then… Becky.

Followed by… Charolette.

Nope. I was wrong. So motherfucking wrong. I'd built a vast and impressive body of work as a male stripper over the years, and that's where I fucked up in a sense. By overachieving in an industry overrun by underachievers as well as con artists and other dubious folks. I was too big a fish in too small a pond. Not just in Arkansas, but anywhere I could've gone in the free world. All too often, true revolution is overwhelmed by the vast mediocrity that surrounds it. In the end, I was also a casualty of mediocrity. So much mediocrity. While there remains no excuse for the despicable actions of Becky and Charolette, I can see their mindset of a male stripper is a male stripper is a male stripper. Because that's what my industry has taught them and so many others.

A few days after Emily's birthday party, as I struggled to comprehend my various dilemmas, I received a stripping application from a 23-year-old man in Fayetteville. Looking at his photos, it was clear that he was on a ton of steroids and HGH. Despite his age, he had the "filled out" look that typically comes a few years later in a man's life. While ostensibly attractive by contemporary standards, he looked fucking weird to me. Throw in his stupid beard and he looked like 23 going on 43. And if he stays on all that junk, he probably won't make it to 43. Also, despite having zero experience, it was clear that he felt entitled to strip because of all his drug use. The juicer elitism vibe was in full effect with this clown. The belief that anyone who doesn't juice isn't serious about fitness. I recognized it in him instantly because I use to have it. And that, more than anything else, is the most embarrassing thing I've admitted about myself in this book.

I could see why so many women attractive inside and out would be repulsed by him. Aside from the painfully unnatural physique, everything about him smacked of desperate need. A need for affirmation and approval that bred a defensive entitlement regarding women. Believing he was giving women exactly what they wanted but had never bothered to stop and watch them occasionally. I may be the apex of male vanity, but that comes entirely from within me. This goofball is merely trying in vain to compensate for some internal void in an obtuse manner. My audiences love me not only because I'm hot but because I see them as individuals, indulge their whims, and make them laugh. Hopefully with me and not at me. They never cared how much, if any, gear I did. Many will probably be disappointed by my revelations of steroid use.

Viewing this loser's application had a profound effect on me in two notable ways. First, I decided then and there that I would never use steroids again. Nor would I keep my mouth shut about this widespread problem. I finally had to ask myself if steroids had improved my life in any way. The answer was a resounding no. They didn't make me a better entertainer. Nor did they further endear me to women. They'd never made me happy. If anything, steroid use made my life worse via depression, paranoia, and inconsistency. My life made less fun by their presence. And my health suffered.

Second, I realized that I never again wanted to professionally represent another stripper. And just like that, I realized that I didn't have to. That realization lifted a huge weight from my shoulders, and I was officially retired as a talent agent. No more excuses. No more cancellations. No more female strippers taking their brothers to parties. No more male strippers showing up with their dicks out. No more new hires showing up for photos with blue fucking hair. No more ever. Fuck 'em all. I was finally free.

With that goofy Hedonism rebranding suddenly not a thing, what was to happen with Hardbodies? The business I had created fourteen years earlier with only a specific skill, $400, and naked ambition. That I had singlehandedly captained through good times and bad. Through hell and back more than once. That had brought me ecstasy and agony. Pleasure and pain. The business that kept me afloat financially for so many years. It had been my baby. After fourteen years, and now with zero prospects, it was still my baby. The thought of letting go tore me up inside. It scared me.

And that's exactly what I did. In the spring of 2018, I created a stripping page on my personal website, took down the Hardbodies site, and pointed the domain towards the new page. My Google business listing was updated appropriately. It was as simple as that. Hardbodies Entertainment of Arkansas was gone forever. I didn't plan it this way, but the final booking for my longtime labor of love was Emily's birthday party. Thanks a lot, Becky.

***

For the first time in my long and impressive stripping career, I was an independent entertainer. Even though that's pretty much what I'd been the past few years, there was a sense of security that came from having that agency brand represent me on paper and online. And that's why it was time to retire Hardbodies for good if for no other reason. I was too dependent upon it. More than that, it tied me to Arkansas. And it's getting time for me to consider whether I should stay or go. I feel like I've exhausted all its possibilities for my ends. Since I first arrived in 2003, my audiences all over the state have constantly asked me the same question, "What are you doing here?" As if I should be somewhere bigger and better. Giving me more credit than I was giving myself.

Business was at a standstill as I made the switch from Hardbodies to simply Magnum and awaited my first booking as an independent. There was so much going through my mind. This included the mourning of Hardbodies and my uncertainties for the future. There was also the matter of Becky, Charolette, and whoever else was behind the odd calls and texts beginning to appear. The whole thing was so many shades of Vanessa, and I couldn't go through that again. And then there was Emily. A living, breathing cruel joke. Why does she have to be friends with them? Why is she friends with them? What was my father doing with a man in a cape?

After a couple of weeks with too much time on my hands, I was finally on my way to Hot Springs for a bachelorette party. Something I'd done a time or two before. Cruising west on I-30 before taking U.S. 70 northbound. The sun setting all the way until darkness arrived with me at my destination. As the sexy cop persona walked towards the house, I could hear the girls laughing and having fun. A soothing calm enveloped my body. Regardless of all I had experienced and endured all these years, I was still an amazing entertainer. And this new group of party girls made damn sure I knew it before I once again drove off alone into the night.

AMARILLO BY MORNING

Emily's birthday party was the proverbial straw that finally broke the camel's back. Becky and Charolette making themselves my whipping girls for all the bullshit I've endured over these years. While I've exploited them for comic relief and hope everyone enjoys a laugh at their expense, I'm not laughing. I probably never will. Between trying to entice me with Emily's beauty to do the party, implying that I only do parties if the bachelorette or birthday girl is hot, trying to renege on our deal, insulting my intelligence by attempting to trick me into doing it after I'd canceled, and the continuing harassment of me as recently as April 2019, I have not a single reason to laugh at Becky or Charolette. What they did, and continue to do, is genuinely fucking hurtful. And they couldn't care less.

My motivation for writing "Emily Stripped Bare" and bringing it to Emily's attention was to inform Becky, Charolette, and anyone else that I am in control. Not them. Me. I own every booking I take. And this one is no exception. Becky's swimming pool? Not while I was there. My performance would not have been compromised by the whims of horny old broads inhabiting a suburban Malebolge. I would never have allowed it.

I just levied perhaps the harshest criticisms ever towards male strippers in general. Criticisms based on stereotypes that are well earned. But this does not excuse Becky or Charolette from not paying me the benefit of the doubt. Thousands of women have set aside potential biases to see me as an individual and treat me with respect. As I've done with them. Would it be fair for me to treat every woman who contacts me as a potential Becky or Charolette? Or a Vanessa for that matter? Of course not. If a woman's expectations for any male stripper she can book are less than sky-high, then why is she trying to book one? Why throw away her money like that?

What disgusts me the most about Emily's birthday party is how fucking close I came to doing it. I have zero doubt this would've been the worst party of my long and extensive career. Becky, Charolette, and God knows who else were primed to treat me like absolute shit from start to finish. Because they felt entitled to. It makes me sick to think of how close I came to giving Becky and Charolette lap dances. And I'm one of the few male strippers in the world who would've given either of them the time of day. Because I don't allow my personal tastes in women to impede my performances. I'm sorry. Whose loss was this again?

This matters even more for the fact that Becky booked me less for Emily and more for Becky. She's so proud of that goddamn pool that she wanted me to arrive dressed like someone who was there to service it. Just that sentence describing her brilliant idea looks fucking ridiculous. This was all for Becky. If it had been at all for Emily, Becky would've gone with my cowboy costume. There are things about Emily that Becky withheld from me. Things any normal client would've told me. Fun and innocent tidbits that would've helped me further personalize my performance for Emily. But horny ol' Becky was too busy playing queen of summertime.

The harassment mentioned in "Emily Stripper Bare" has continued. Picking up steam in April 2019 as Becky once again attempted to book a male stripper for Emily's birthday. She obviously didn't contact me about it, but I was still aware. Because this is my industry and market. Nearly every time someone looks for a male stripper, I hear about it one way or another. Becky did try contacting me one Saturday night in early April. After noticing that my stripping page was first visited by someone in Sherwood followed by people in cities around the country that are home to so-called nationwide agencies, I knew what was up. Someone called me from a blocked number that night. People only do this to give me grief about something. I didn't answer. But I knew who was calling to bitch me out anonymously for being the only legitimate male stripper in Arkansas.

In late April, three days before Emily's birthday, I received a call from a Conway number. Greeted by a woman desperately searching for a male stripper. The specifics of her party were suspect. Something no one ever contacts me about doing and something I would never do. Being in the moment, however, I took the request at face value and politely declined. The prospective client proceeded to gush about my stripping webpage before saying, "I especially enjoyed your articles on stripping," with a tone that offered forth a wink and a nudge. What a fucking idiot. I knew then what was up.

Someone in Conway visited "Emily Stripped Bare" on my website three times the previous night. The only stripping related blog post that anyone in Arkansas had visited in over a week. Combine this web traffic with the phone call and timing, and I have zero doubt Becky was behind it. A sad and pathetic attempt to "get him" in retaliation for the events of one year prior. And probably for "Emily Stripped Bare" as well. Except Becky obviously didn't fucking read it. Or she wouldn't have wasted her time attempting to trick me. I was unable to connect the phone number to anyone online, but I wouldn't make this claim if I weren't 100% certain. Call it stripper's intuition. I fucking know Becky was the "mastermind" behind this birthday party equivalent of the Bayou of Pigs. She needs to stop trying to mastermind things. Because she totally sucks at it.

Becky is playing fast and loose with the notion of scoring a male stripper for Emily's birthday. There would be no shortage of male strippers in Arkansas willing to get all over Emily if they existed. A guy who wouldn't give Becky, Charolette, or the rest of the chunky dunk brigade a shred of attention if his life depended on it. All the while expecting nothing less than a blowjob from Emily lest he pitches a screaming fit. None of this is hyperbole. This shit happens all the time to women who don't do their homework before booking a male stripper. I've heard more than my share of horror stories from women over the years.

And before anyone says, "But, Stefan. Weren't you going to hit on Emily?" of fucking course I was. Hitting on a girl is not the same thing as trying to ram my cock down her throat before a gaggle of horny old broads. I would've been extra flirty and seductive with her. Further piquing her curiosity in me. Inspiring her to seek me out via phone or social media afterward. Then we'd talk in private and see where things go. That works. Sometimes even when I'm not trying to do it.

As for Charolette… It's possible all this post-cancellation drama could've been avoided if she'd treated me with respect. Instead of assuming I'm a fucking dolt and attempting to trick me into doing the party after all. She could've easily left the following message:

"Hi. My name is Charolette. I'm calling you regarding Emily's birthday party. I understand you and Becky had a disagreement that caused you to cancel. I'm trying to see if there's any way we can smooth things out so maybe you'll still come tomorrow. We were really looking forward to your coming. Can you please give me five minutes to see if we can work something out? Thank you."

No muss, no fuss. Had she left a voicemail along this theme, I would've totally called her back. I still wasn't doing the party but would've politely explained why I couldn't. It would've been so easy. But fuck that. Charolette had to act all creepy and weird and shit. Gleefully choosing to spit in my face. I barely slept that night because I was so upset by how she treated me. It made me sick to my stomach.

Unless the drama once again rears its bitchy head, I'm done with Becky, Charolette, and fuck knows who else. As it stands, I've said all I have to say on this matter.

Fuck, I need a drink.

***

The Emily drama is two separate issues. One is the Becky and Charolette conflict that stands on its own sans Emily. The birthday girl could've been anyone, and things would've played out identically. I'd cancel, followed by things getting irritating.

The other standalone issue is Emily herself. Or, more specifically, my crush on her. It was true when I wrote this had never happened before with a bachelorette or birthday girl. Fuck, I can't remember the last time I even had a crush on a girl. No later than junior high. When I was but a homely adolescent boy. No, really. I was a homely teen. Nothing could've prepared me for a crush on a guest of honor. It was a hard and bitter pill to swallow. Sticking to the back of my throat. Leaving it there for as long as I could.

Yes, Emily has read "Emily Stripped Bare". Upon completing the final draft in late November 2018, I posted it to my website as a blog entry. I shared the link publicly to my Facebook profile, added the phrase, "Hey, Emily. Check out my top post," to my bio, and sent her a friend request. Someone in her town visited it via Facebook within thirty minutes. Her response? No response at all. Which is what I'd anticipated. As pickup lines go, "Your friends suck, but I'd do you," is iffy at best.

And yes, I have a bit of inside info on Emily. I've made a strong impression on many women over the years. Including women north of

Little Rock from Sherwood to Cabot. It's not improbable that one such woman was to be present for my performance at Emily's birthday. One who may be sympathetic to my cause. Not openly admitting her familiarity with me, this being Arkansas and all, but inclined to slip me information anonymously. Information validated under scrutiny.

I won't reveal this information here. I did in the original draft of this epilogue. Though complimentary about finding it endearing, I feel that including it here is meanspirited. I'm not withholding for Emily's sake. I owe her nothing. I'm withholding for my sake. Affording myself one shred of dignity over Becky and Charolette.

I'm still not sure why I lost my head over Emily. Yes, she's fucking gorgeous. But it's not like me to find myself attracted to someone without having met her first. Looks alone aren't enough for me to find any woman attractive. I must know there are a genuine heart and depth behind a face no matter how "really pretty" it is. Despite what I wrote in "Emily Stripped Bare", it was never a sure thing with me. I gushed about her physical beauty. Not only because it captivated me, but because it was all I had to work with. Maybe I couldn't stand to be around her. Perhaps her kisses would taste like acetone to me as once happened with another girl. I can't stand her friends. That's a bad sign. Would she be willing to ditch them and run away with me? I'm not holding my breath.

Ultimately, I had to accept that it was okay for me to have a crush on Emily. That it was okay to be irrational on occasion. This also allowed me to reminisce about being 25 and having forty-year-old women hit on me. No matter how attractive, youthful, and confident they were, I now recognize in their tone and body language that they felt at least slightly foolish putting themselves out there. While polite at the time, I totally feel for them now as my own romantic interests at forty have shifted towards younger women.

There will never be anything between Emily and me. We will never meet. That's the way it is. She does have that smile though. Like, she should consider taking out a million-dollar insurance policy with Lloyds of London on that thing. I'm just saying.

The cruel joke of being a male stripper is that I've come across multiple women I would've dated. A few I did. And there was at least a mutual attraction with others. If not for stripping, I never would've met them. But stripping has also prevented me from achieving anything more than dirty little secret status with any of them. And no, I wouldn't settle for being Emily's dirty little secret if the opportunity presented itself.

That's still more pleasure than I would've experienced had I never stripped. Overworked and underpaid at best. No time or money to have fun. Pressured to marry the first available woman who was into me even if I could never love her. Fathering children I never wanted solely for professional advancement. A life built around cronyism and social status. Stripping may come with heartache, but what I just described is downright suicidal.

To any potential love interests reading this… I'm not carrying a flame for Emily. When the right girl comes along, I'll gladly forget all about… um, who was I talking about?

***

Remember in 2011, when I emailed that agency named Hunks & Babes? In July 2019, as I wrapped up the manuscript for this book, they finally replied. Asking if I was still available for parties. Eight years later. As if no big deal. The best part? They wanted me to cover a booking for which a black entertainer was requested. I know this because I'd already spoken to the prospective client as she scoured the internet for what she wanted. The agency was ready and willing to lie to both entertainer and client just to score a quick buck. And how bad is business if they're sifting through eight-year-old emails on a Saturday night? I had no idea they were still in business. Not sure they truly are.

This right here is nationwide exotic entertainment agencies in a nutshell. Just say no.

***

It was 93 degrees outside today when I laid out for a nude sunbathing session. 60% humidity made it feel like 105 degrees. I do this most days, twenty minutes per side, to maintain my bronze. Money is tight, and I can't afford a tanning package. I subject myself to these brutal conditions while hiding from my nosy neighbors to look my best for every audience.

So yeah, I have a serious fucking problem with women who wait until a party is underway to call and book me as if ordering a pizza. This bad timing implies that there is zero planning or effort into what I do. That I simply show up looking all fine ass and take off my clothes. Even Becky had the decency to call me over a week in advance and during the day. If Becky is showing you up, there's no hope for you. As a professional entertainer who takes what he does seriously, I need time. Time to prepare. Time to play out my performance in my head beforehand with variations. And time to look up my birthday girl on Facebook to see if she's indeed real pretty.

This was historically a problem with guys and bachelor parties. One of many reasons why I finally slashed bachelor parties from Hardbodies. But women have slowly devolved to the same level of inconsiderate numbskullery. Not only waiting to the last minute but calling drunk, calling while driving, and calling me while simultaneously having a conversation with someone else. Any of these are reasons for me to hang up on a prospective client, and I do so regularly now. Don't believe me? Try it. I hung up recently on one girl for talking to her friend. When she called back and left a voicemail, demanding to know why I hung up, she was still gabbing with her friend.

If I wasn't at a crossroads with stripping when I put Hardbodies Entertainment of Arkansas to rest, I sure as fuck am now. I still enjoy entertaining the right audiences. But the right audiences are becoming fewer and fewer. It's like more and more women are getting their phone etiquette from those atrocious *Real Housewives* shows. And I'm getting more of that "tee hee" cutesy manipulative bullshit which has never worked on me. If it did, I wouldn't have earned a dime from stripping because those women don't tip.

Perhaps no one will learn more about me from this book than I have. My self-awareness grew exponentially throughout the writing and revision process. I knew I went above and beyond for others but never realized how much and how often until now. I'm a better person than I've given myself credit for. Despite the scores of party girls who told me how sweet and kind I am, my harsh inner critic preferred the less flattering opinions of people who I now realize don't know shit. I think pulling off a successful party overall meant more to me than my clients because I honestly care that fucking much. I may be an angel after all, albeit one with a damaged halo.

This book quantifies my vast and impressive body of work as a live entertainer into a tangible form. An extensive boxed set anthology with bonus features of my nearly two-decade career in exotic entertainment. You won't find this with just any male stripper. Most of them don't give a fuck about anything other than begging hot girls for sex. Not only have I devoted nearly two decades to working circles around my so-called contemporaries, but I've outdone scores of "good people" with "real" jobs. Like the Saturday night in August 2018, when I drove two hours, performed at a bachelorette party for one hour, and drove two hours home with a poison ivy outbreak on my left foot. Wearing cowboy boots the entire time. I also had pneumonia.

This occurred just days following a phone conversation with a young woman who snottily asked, "Um… Have you ever done a bachelorette party before?" Fuck you.

I'm no longer taking shit from anyone. Anyone who doesn't take me seriously doesn't deserve me as her entertainer. It's not like she'd appreciate me and everything I'd do for her. If she tells me I suck, this book instantly colors her a fucking retard. Not only can she not do better than me in Arkansas, she couldn't do better than me anywhere else. If I won't hesitate to cancel Emily's birthday party, what the fuck makes her think I won't tell her drunk ass and her "real cute" fiftysomething birthday girl to go to hell?

As for age, I'm proving that it's truly but a number. The winding down of my stripping career has nothing to do with my appearance. At forty, I'm rocking my best physique yet. Neither the most jacked nor cut it's ever been, but a physique that is balanced, athletic, and natural. One that is easy to maintain and will be for decades to come. And, most importantly, one that is healthy. I'm as youthful and vibrant as ever, along with being a goddamn sexual tyrannosaurus. My gravitation towards twentysomething women is about compatibility and not status. Even my face is truly coming into its own as I'm apparently one of those guys who gets better looking with age. Why does everything bad happen to me?

I don't know, foxy buns. Times are changing. I don't necessarily see myself as a writer. But authoring this book has me entertaining the idea of swapping out stripping for writing as my fallback profession. I'm excellent at it, and I can do it by myself from anywhere in the world. I'll have to do it on my own and build my own brand. That's the only way to ensure long term financial security. Maybe this book will help…

***

But enough bitching about bitches and lamenting over birthday girls who got away. I'm ending this book on a high note. A poignant note. I'm ending it on you. The women to whom this book is dedicated. All you sweet and naughty bachelorettes, birthday girls, clients, and their girlfriends who welcomed me with open arms. And, sometimes, open legs. Accepting me as one of your own if for only a moment in time. We made the most of our short time together. Enjoying wild and amazing nights that none of us will ever forget. I did everything I could to make it money well spent, and it was always about more than money for me.

I'd planned for Hardbodies Entertainment of Arkansas to be a steady and successful moneymaker. That happened, but not to the degree I anticipated. Regardless, I loved owning and operating such a unique business for all those years. It afforded me constant opportunities to explore different parts of Arkansas in all its awe-inspiring natural beauty. But most of all it bestowed upon me the privilege of meeting and entertaining amazing women from all walks of life. I'm dead serious when I say that our parties rank among my most cherished memories.

I feel like I'm saying goodbye here. Finally saying goodbye to Hardbodies after laying it to rest. Perhaps saying a preemptive goodbye to the inevitable end of this stage of my career as an entertainer. Likely saying goodbye to Arkansas as I now contemplate leaving forever. I'm also saying goodbye to the end of my journey writing this book as I complete this final paragraph. Although I have no shortage of adventures awaiting me for decades to come, this one has finally reached its conclusion.

I ain't rich. But, Lord, I'm free.

MAGNUM STRIPPED BARE

It was so inconspicuous. Fun too. And profitable. Like any other successful bachelorette party by numbers. Its most notable attribute being the proximity to my home. A ten-minute drive on a refreshingly cool January night. The first Friday of 2020. An encouraging start to a year I entered with high hopes. We all know how that turned out, but I digress. An intimate performance with an audience of four women. We formed a sum greater than its parts within our cozy confines of a one-story home in west Little Rock. Totes on my game. Delivering perhaps the best performance of my stripping career in pure dancing terms. My party girls wore themselves out watching my relentless moves. Executed with seductive authority. The latest hour of flamboyant masculine power in my nearly two decades as a career male stripper. It would also be my last.

Afterward, I donned black leather pants and a leopard-print cardigan sans shirt, bid my party girls farewell, and disappeared into the night. Strutting to my truck. Massive cock in both hands. My client, the sweetest woman I'd encountered in a while, texted her gratitude moments later. Instilling me with motivation at that moment. Confirmation I was correct to continue pursuing bachelorette and birthday parties throughout Arkansas and the surrounding area. And not because I could use the money. I still loved performing for appreciative audiences. As I do right now. More than ever. That will never end. What does need to change is the execution. Aspects of the performance itself and how I target audiences. This reality has always lingered in the back of my mind. But I never knew where to go with it.

I'd been treating every performance like it may have been my last for years. But there was never a moment at any of these shows when I thought this was it. That night was no exception. As I write this second epilogue 600 days after the fact, I can now look back at that night and see how worn out I was too. Despite the outrageous energy and enthusiasm put forth in lockstep with my wonderful audience, exhaustion lingered beneath my exterior. As did boredom. And frustration with the limitations of stripping that I could stretch no further than I already had long ago. In hindsight, these issues had been lingering for perhaps a decade. They show in the back end of this book. Ever so faintly while obscured by my undying ardor for delivering private party erotic entertainment. And while that devotion remains intact, my patience for the method by which it was delivered is long gone.

Oh… And the name of the final bachelorette? Emily, because sure.

***

I'm rockin' out with my cock out more than ever these days. Black leather, studs, snakeskin, and animal print. Eyeliner and mascara. My hair once again shoulder-length as it was circa 2015 before I stupidly had it cut short. Short spiky hair worked with the platinum blonde edge. Short and dark? Meh. On me, it should be long and painted black. Besides, I'm now in my forties and still have a full head of hair. I'd be a fool not to go full force with it. Many other dudes would too in a heartbeat if they could. Not only do I not look my age, but I don't feel it either. I'll admit that my joints and lower back have wear and tear from two decades of stripping. And I have tennis elbows which is why I often wear wristbands high on my forearms. But my energy level is through the roof. More now than at any other point in my life. As for men hitting their sexual peak at nineteen… I'm most definitely an exception to that rule.

I've always been the rock and roll bad boy of male strippers. Yes, I've heard of corporate male strippers calling themselves (or being called) rock stars, but those dudes are boy band imitators. Something I already addressed, particularly in Chapter 33 if you need a refresher, so I won't repeat myself. But calling myself a rock star among male strippers is apt as all fuck. I became possibly the greatest private party male stripper who ever lived not because I asked permission or did as I was told. It happened because I went out and fucking did it on my own. I scored my first bachelorette party in December 2001 because a woman in attendance at a male revue I performed in bypassed the agency and approached me directly. And I accepted her offer because that agency was never going to do me any favors. Had she gone to them and requested me, they would've tried to push one of their favorites on her. She knew that too. And I never would've stayed in this business if not for private parties.

The rock star quality was always present throughout my stripping career. No surprise given my glam rock musician roots. But that quality became more pronounced throughout my final stripping performances. Letting my hair grow out again as I banged my head. Booty shaking, hip swiveling, and pelvis thrusting more aggressively than ever before. More than I've ever seen another male stripper dare to attempt. It truly feels like I'm entering my life's peak in every way. As if those many years of stripping were me passing time as I ascended to the top. Learning much about many things over the past two decades because of stripping. Knowledge I'm applying in earnest across my new artistic and entrepreneurial pursuits moving forward.

That final bachelorette party wasn't my final stripping opportunity. I booked a birthday party shortly afterward that was postponed due to a pandemic or something. But I decided against rescheduling when contacted later by the client. I tested her to see how enthusiastic she was about my performance, because I had my doubts. She texted to ask if I was back to work, as if I'd let a virus with an over-99% survival rate stop me but whatever. I told her that I'd decided to retire from stripping. She replied, "Okay. Thanks." And I left it there. Had she responded with something like, "But you're still going to do my party, right?" I would've done it. I was considering what I wrote in Chapter 29 regarding my need to be pickier about bookings. My online research of these women told me that they weren't an ideal fit for my performance, so I was as sold on them as the client was on me. As if the two of us were going through the motions and nothing more. And the birthday girl's name was Becky, because of course it was. Having a Becky as my final guest of honor is worse than having an Emily.

And I wasn't lying about my decision to retire. Having stopped accepting parties in May 2020. Still getting inquiries, pandemic be damned, but none of these prospective clients (and I use that term loosely) were worth a bucket of spit. The pool of strong prospects had dried up to the point where I was screening all incoming calls. Resulting in voicemails ranging from passive-aggressive insults to incoherent screaming. I needed a break, so I took it. Living off my investment portfolio (Bitcoin and GameStop, baby) while writing my second book and first novel. A sexually explicit collection of hardcore erotica inspired by my stripping experiences. Beginning as a series of short stories posted on my website in late 2019, this was my first attempt at writing literary fiction. A fun project that gelled quickly. Allowing me to publish my second book in less than a year following this one. Rockin' like Dokken, foxy buns.

Unfortunately, *Wild Nights of Arkansas Strippers: Based on a True Story* was a bigger commercial flop than this book, but more on that shortly. I debated what to do next creatively and professionally as I invested heavily in myself. Especially where health and fitness are concerned. Having abandoned the gym in May 2019 to construct a new regimen encompassing dancing, conditioning, and resistance training through calisthenics. That placed me ahead of the curve everyone was trying to flatten (or fatten, from what I've seen) when gyms were shuttered. Ultimately leading me to eschew nearly all conventional fitness "wisdom" in favor of a routine akin to that of Herschel Walker. A routine I can maintain with ease once the apocalypse is upon us. Take that, gym bros.

July 2020 brought a minor Facebook altercation with Becky. Yes, that Becky. I spotted her comment on an article about COVID-19 vaccines in the works. Because she's either that stupid or blinded by her anger at life, she remarked that everyone who believes COVID-19 is a hoax should be first to get vaccinated. This wasn't the first time I'd encountered a questionable musing she'd opined on an article, but people were piling on her for this one. I was so excited that I joined in the fun. She responded by calling me "that nasty stalker stripper guy." After I pointed out the sheer hypocrisy of that statement, she claimed to have informed every law enforcement agency in the state about my business. It's a thoughtless attack smacking of desperation that I've heard before. Would that include all the law enforcement agencies that Hardbodies Entertainment of Arkansas did business with over the years?

It was immediately following this exchange that I visited a local business and contracted COVID-19 from a sofa. Through my eye. Yes, I'm 100% confident in specifying when, where, and how I became infected. Ultimately, the 'rona didn't match its hype. I had sickness akin to a mild flu for a few days before recovering with no lingering issues. That aside, the pandemic didn't affect me much. I rarely dined out as it was, and I'd already become partial to having goods delivered to my doorstep. And I haven't worn a mask once during this bullshit. The mandate in Arkansas was never enforced, but that's not the point. It's a dehumanizing act of submission to an establishment that sees us as expendable pawns. Fuck them.

I gave stripping a final shot in April 2021. Building a website titled *Magnum Stripped Bare* with a blog I regularly updated. Shooting photos constantly. Producing short videos of me dancing and opining on various topics. It turned out that nothing had changed in eleven months. Picking up where I left off with calls from prospective clients ranging from so-so to fucking worthless. I could've snagged those so-so bookings, but even they weren't worth the hassle. Most didn't bother to visit my site or watch my videos. They saw my number in Google search results and made demands with no fucking clue what I offered. Or what they wanted. It took a dance video I shot in early August for me to finally see how wasted my talents are on these bitches. A fifteen-second YouTube short of me rocking out to "Everybody Up" by Saxon. And that's all it took. The fierce and authoritative sexuality oozing from my athletic physique, framed by long hair and black leather pants, delivered in one fluid motion from head to toe. I could no longer deny that I was too good for stripping. Or, at least, marketing myself as a stripper.

As I progressed in recent years, my client pool regressed. The women for whom my performances are tailor-made no longer contact me. All that's left are basic bitches lacking generosity and common decency. The women with low expectations for male strippers set forth by Hollywood and Las Vegas. And, aside from me, that's what being a male stripper has become. It's why the party girls I covet are MIA. They don't like that shit and sure as fuck don't want it in their living rooms. *Magnum Stripped Bare* was a final attempt to reach them, although I admit that much of my marketing had little to do with stripping. It was mostly me doing my rock star thing while shooting off-topic videos albeit intended to showcase my conversational skills at parties. Most blog entries consisted of enthusiasm waxed about favorite kinks like girl on girl, butt stuff, and girl on girl butt stuff. While I'm convinced this approach would've been successful back in the day, I can't change the fact that my ideal party girls are no longer seeking exotic male entertainment. Now convinced that every male stripper is Carol Channing. Contrary to the legacy media narrative, lots of women think he's fucking gross. And it's easy to see why.

I'll be honest… For the longest time, I was certain I'd cry when my stripping career wrapped. But my reaction wound up being, "Good fucking riddance," as I'm too enthralled with other projects to care. It ended as a nuisance. I don't want to embellish on the matter. Because I don't fucking care. The aspects of stripping I still love carried over to these new projects. And that's it. I've finally retired for good from marketing my performance talents within an arena where I'm overwhelmed by the sheer volume of mediocrity surrounding me. While this is a harsh reality of any artistic or business pursuit, most other industries have a window to rise above the masses and be heard. No such window exists anymore in exotic male entertainment. It is a bland and homogenized medium with zero opportunity to express individuality. A one-and-done business model existing solely to sell ridiculously overpriced merchandise and alcoholic beverages. While ridicule has always existed, being a male stripper used to be cool in a way. Now, every male stripper is a fucking joke right out of the box. The medium is dead, especially where private parties are concerned, and I don't see it ever making a comeback.

***

This memoir was universally unpopular right out of the gate when published in October 2019. As in no one in the literary world or media wanted to touch it with a ten-foot pole. The rock-bottom expectations for contemporary male strippers carried over to this book. Moving eight copies before I pulled it from online retailers and began giving it away on my website. I'm not giving retailers a 30% cut if they're going to hide it in search results due to adult content. Especially since the likes of E.L. James get away with it, and I write circles around her fat ass.

People simultaneously praising my writing skills and hating my message (and me) has been a recurring theme for years. Shifting into overdrive after I became an award-winning writer of creative nonfiction in May 2018. I responded to this critical acclaim by exploring my flamboyant heterosexual male drama beginning with "Emily Stripped Bare" which led to this book. Throw in a few personal essays from this period that delve into my stripping career and/or mercilessly air grievances towards specific women, and any goodwill I'd accumulated in literary circles was shot all to hell. The response was always the same. My storytelling prowess showered with glowing adjectives like "excellent" and "captivating" while also being told that my subject matter was somehow wrong. How is my individual experience adapted to a personal essay wrong? That's a rhetorical question. The problem is that I'm not woke. I'm failing to "check my privilege," "admit my guilt," "recognize my unconscious bias," blah, blah, blah… Fuck these people. Let 'em dance a mile in my cowboy boots. It's not all fun and games.

Regardless, I couldn't be prouder of what I accomplished with this book. Speaking as my own harshest critic… I was happy with it on completion, and my enthusiasm has grown over the two years since. It'll never break even financially but will forever be the "prestige" work of my bibliography. Checking all the boxes of hoity-toity creative nonfiction literature. A gritty, visceral, and uncomfortable dive into unlikely subject matter. It's original. No one wants to touch this book because no one can comprehend the idea of a male stripper-penned memoir that embodies literary excellence. A narrative that shifts effortlessly between the exploration of female sexual behavior, pastoral depictions of rural Arkansas, and moments of unrelenting bleakness. The stark black-and-white nude self-portrait showing off my large cock on this edition is what the cover always should've been. The joke is that no one will ever see it because no one is interested in this book. And this second epilogue is entirely for my satisfaction. This memoir is the magnum opus of what I've coined my "Naked Ambition Era" of writings that also comprises the personal essays of the time and a move towards fiction with my first novel. It was me breaking loose and expressing all that I wanted to without hesitation. Becoming a rock star among storytellers.

Once again… I ain't rich. But, Lord, I'm free.

And as for Emily… She's not taking proper care of herself and is aging horribly. Meaning that I came out on the winning side of being careful what I wish for lest I get it. Regarding her, this confession has meant nothing.

www.ingramcontent.com/pod-product-compliance
Lightning Source LLC
Chambersburg PA
CBHW072146070526
44585CB00015B/1010